PENGUIN BOOKS

PRESSURE
COOKER

PRESSURE COOKER

fast. easy. delicious.

Rachael Lane

PENGUIN BOOKS

CONTENTS

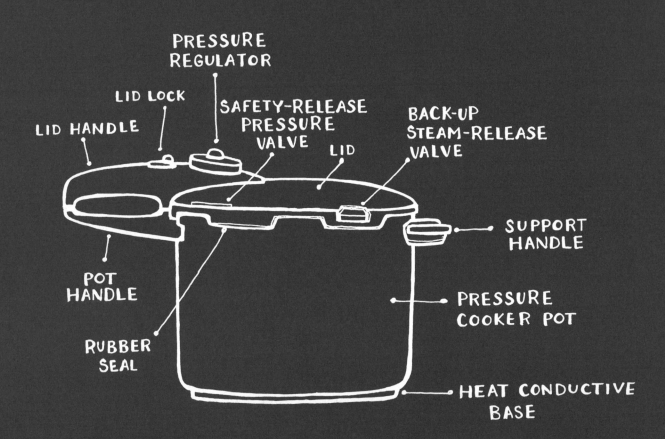

PRESSURE
REGULATOR

LID LOCK

LID HANDLE

SAFETY-RELEASE
PRESSURE
VALVE

BACK-UP
STEAM-RELEASE
VALVE

LID

SUPPORT
HANDLE

POT
HANDLE

PRESSURE
COOKER POT

RUBBER
SEAL

HEAT CONDUCTIVE
BASE

INTRODUCTION

Many of us have memories of pressure cookers hissing and wobbling away on the stove tops of our mothers and grandmothers, filling their kitchens with steam and wonderful cooking smells. Many will also remember stories of, or perhaps even have witnessed, explosions as a result of a blocked steam-release valve. I'm sure many a kitchen was redecorated in a lovely shade of pea-and-ham green as a result of a pressurised pea blocking the valve.

Such stories and hazards are now a distant memory. Pressure cookers have had a make-over! For those hankering for the pressure-cooked meals of yesteryear, and for those yet to discover the joys of pressure cooking – the time is here. Never has it been safer and easier to prepare nutritious home-cooked meals in a fraction of the normal cooking time.

Modern pressure cookers vary between manufacturers in style and design, but all second-generation cookers are fitted with safety features that their jiggle-top predecessors lacked. Featuring an advanced pressure-regulating system with enclosed spring valve, back-up steam-release valve, quick-release valve, and locking lid, they are now completely safe to use.

In a fast-paced life, busy with work, family and social commitments, it can be challenging to find the time to cook nutritious and tasty meals every day. Fast food, takeaway and pre-prepared packaged meals can seem like an easier alternative at the end of a long day. However, not only are these options often high in fat and full of nasty preservatives and additives, they're often expensive too – stretching both our budgets and our waistlines.

With a pressure cooker, healthy and delicious home-cooked meals are achievable in a matter of minutes. There is no longer a need to spend hours slaving over a hot stove or waiting for an oven-cooked meal to *finally* be ready. Slow-cooked favourites can now be prepared in next to no time. A bit of simple preparation is all that is required for most of the recipes in this book. Add the ingredients to the cooker, lock the lid in place, bring up to pressure and cook for the required amount of time. It's that simple! You can enjoy a creamy risotto in 5 minutes – less time than it would take to get to your local takeaway shop. Or make a tasty curry or stew in a mere 10–15 minutes, then whip up a rice pilaf for accompaniment in just 3 minutes!

With an extensive range of recipes to choose from, this book caters for everyone from the novice to the more experienced operator. Many of the recipes use everyday ingredients to create classic dishes, while others are more adventurous, exploring exotic flavours of lands near and far. With more than 200 recipes, everybody's taste is catered for.

BENEFITS OF PRESSURE COOKING

SAVE TIME

The pressure cooker's lid is fitted with an expandable rubber ring that creates a perfect seal. The pressure builds up inside the pot and the temperature of liquids rises to about 120°C (250°F) – around 20°C (70°F) above normal boiling temperature. Cooking at such high temperatures enables food to be ready in roughly one-third of the usual time.

Tough cuts of meat, which usually take hours of slow simmering to break down, are tenderised in the pressure cooker in as little as 10–15 minutes. A whole chicken can be cooked in 20 minutes, compared to an hour or more when using conventional cooking methods. Nutritious beans and pulses, wholesome rice and grains, nourishing soups and even comforting puddings can all be prepared in a fraction of the time.

Using a pressure cooker makes it just as fast to prepare a meal at home as it would be to heat a packaged meal or pick up takeaway. With a pressure cooker you can reduce cooking time by up to 70 per cent – and spend that extra time on doing the things you love.

SAVE MONEY

Pre-packaged, takeaway and fast foods are expensive, not to mention often quite unhealthy. With the substantially reduced cooking times that a pressure cooker affords, there's no longer any need to buy pre-prepared and packaged foods. With a pressure cooker, preparing delicious food using affordable seasonal produce, cheaper cuts of meat and inexpensive dried beans and pulses is fast and simple. You can save money, and potentially lose centimetres off your waistline too.

Cooking in a shorter amount of time can also save you money in another way. As cooking times are reduced, so is the amount of energy required. This reduces your energy bills and means more of your hard-earned money is in your pocket at the end of the month.

SAVE ENERGY

Using a pressure cooker is more energy efficient than conventional stove-top or oven cooking. Reduced cooking times means less energy is required to get a home-cooked meal on the table, helping to save some of our planet's precious resources.

With such short cooking times, you no longer need to keep your cupboards stocked with tins of cooked beans and bottles of sauces, nor your freezer with ready-made meals. Producing, packaging and transporting convenience foods requires energy and creates waste; minimising our dependence on them saves energy and reduces waste.

As pressure cookers are sealed vessels, they release minimal steam and heat. As a result, your kitchen remains cool in the summer months. This reduces the need to use air-conditioning or fans, and thus saves both energy and money.

A HEALTHY COOKING OPTION

The pressure cooker's ability to steam foods in a fraction of the time makes it a healthy cooking choice. Steaming requires no extra fat, making it easy to prepare completely fat-free meals.

The pressure cooker's sealed lid and quick cooking helps vegetables retain their vitamins and minerals, as well as their vibrant colours. In comparison, vegetables that are boiled for too long lose a great deal of their nutrition when the cooking water is drained, and can often end up a dull and unappetising colour.

Cooking under high pressure means cheaper and tougher cuts of meat – which are often leaner than more expensive cuts – will become tender in a third of the usual time, making them not only a cheaper but a healthier option.

Braises and stews cooked in a pressure cooker retain more of the natural flavours of the ingredients, and vitamins and minerals are locked in by the sealed lid. The nutritious cooking liquid becomes a tasty sauce or gravy, and fewer additives, such as salt, are required to enhance the dishes, making them a healthy option for those on a salt-reduced diet.

The efficiency of cooking with a pressure cooker makes it easier to prepare nutritious home-cooked meals from fresh produce, reducing the need to buy pre-prepared foods. With home-cooked meals, you can feel confident that you know exactly what ingredients have been used – which means no more reading the small print on cans and packages, trying to decipher the 'good' numbers from the bad. This is great news for people with sensitivities or allergies, or in fact anyone who wants to make more informed choices about what they eat.

REDUCE THE NEED FOR OTHER POTS & PANS

The pressure cooker is a multifunctional pot. You can braise, stew, steam, boil and even bake in it. The heavy-based pan can even be used for deep-frying – though *never* under pressure (hot oil is highly combustible and very dangerous when under pressure)!

The pressure cooker does away with the need for all your other casserole dishes, double-pot steamers and cumbersome deep-fryers, freeing up space in your kitchen cupboards. You can also use your pressure cooker just as you would a regular saucepan – just don't lock the lid in place.

Stainless steel pressure cookers can be used on a variety of heat sources. The thick three-ply base is suitable for gas and electric stove tops, and it magnetises to work on induction stove tops, saving you the need to buy specialised cookware. Pressure cookers can even be used on wood and coal fires, camping stoves and barbecues, so they are perfect for travelling or camping. The pressure cooker is a pot with endless possibilities.

KEEP YOUR KITCHEN CLEAN

With their locking lids, pressure cookers keep all cooking juices inside the pot, so there's no bubbling and spitting of hot cooking liquids over your stove top. This prevents mess and saves on cleaning time after dinner.

COOKING TECHNIQUES

Most conventional cooking methods requiring liquid are suitable for the pressure cooker.

BRAISING

When braising, the meat, poultry or vegetables are browned in oil first, then half-covered with liquid and cooked until very tender. The liquid – usually wine, beer, juice or stock (or a combination of these) – becomes the sauce or gravy. Conventionally, braises are cooked at low temperatures for a long period of time.

STEWING

Stewing is very similar to braising, the main difference being that more liquid is used. Ingredients are completely covered with liquid and the end result can resemble a thick, chunky soup. When making a stew in the conventional manner, meat is often coated in flour and browned in fat at the beginning of cooking, to help thicken the sauce. However, when stewing in the pressure cooker, a thickener such as a roux or slurry must be added at the end of cooking to prevent the pot from scorching.

STEAMING

Steaming is a method of cooking where the food is placed above boiling water in a sealed vessel. With the pressure cooker, food is placed on the steamer stand and the steam produced from the boiling water cooks the food above. This is one of the healthiest forms of cooking, as no added fat is required, and any fat in the food itself is able to drain away. Steaming is particularly good for cooking poultry and fish, as well as cakes and puddings.

BOILING

Boiling requires that the ingredients are completely immersed in liquid. The liquid used for boiling can vary but is often either water or stock (though additional liquids, such as wine or sauce, can be added). Dense foods such as meat, poultry, root vegetables, pulses and grains are best suited to this method of cooking.

COOKING IN A WATER BATH

Cooking in a water bath (or bain-marie) is a technique used when an even, gentle heat is required. Conventionally, ingredients are placed in a heatproof dish and this is then placed in a cooking vessel such as a saucepan or tray. Boiling water is poured into the cooking vessel to come about halfway up the sides of the dish, then the vessel is placed into the oven. With the pressure cooker, the heatproof dish is placed on the trivet in the cooker, then the water poured in around it. Water baths are perfect for cooking delicate foods such as custards and cheesecakes, ensuring they cook evenly and don't crack. Curds and sauces, which require a controlled heat to emulsify, also work well with this cooking method.

BAKING

Baking traditionally refers to food cooked in an oven. In the pressure cooker, 'baking' is done using the water-bath technique above. Using this method, some of the foods that conventionally are baked, such as cakes and breads, are able to be prepared in the pressure cooker. However, they will not develop the crisp exterior and golden colour that baking in an oven achieves.

A BUYER'S GUIDE

When looking to buy a pressure cooker, it is important to do your research. There are many reputable manufacturers offering an assortment of modern pressure cookers. Models come in a range of sizes and with a variety of features. What you choose to buy is predominantly dependent on two things:

Your Budget

How much you have to spend will influence the brand and size of cooker you are able to purchase. Once you have an idea of your budget, you can narrow down the search. Buy the best-quality pressure cooker in the largest size in your price range. In doing so, you will have a longer-lasting, better-performing and more versatile piece of kitchen equipment.

Pressure cookers are a big investment, but hopefully one that you only need to make once. It is worth buying the best you can afford.

Your Needs

If you know how you intend to use your pressure cooker, you'll know what features to look for when you begin your research.

- On average how many people do I intend to cook for?
- Do I want to make large batches of stock or soup?
- Do I intend to cook desserts such as puddings and cakes?
- Do I have limited storage?

Once you've answered these questions, read through the following information to determine what sort of cooker will best suit your needs.

COST

The average cost of a medium-sized good-quality pressure cooker is about AU$200. However, depending on the brand and size, prices can vary from AU$50 to AU$500. Generally speaking, the more you pay, the better quality you get.

SIZE

Pressure cookers come in a variety of shapes and sizes, and range from 2.5 L (5 pt 4 fl oz) to 12 L (3 gal) in capacity.

Larger pressure cookers are more versatile than smaller ones. They are ideal for making stocks or large batches of soup, and can easily fit large pieces of meat. They are also able to accommodate a variety of different-sized dishes for making desserts and terrines. Due to their higher maximum-fill level, larger pressure cookers are great for cooking big quantities of beans and pulses, which require that the cooker only be half filled.

Smaller pressure cookers save room on storage and are more portable – they are perfect for taking away on holiday or camping – but their small size means their use is limited. Small frying-pan-style pressure cookers are great for browning meats and cooking risottos – and they're the perfect size for singles or couples. Keep in mind that due to the lower maximum-fill level of these smaller models, you will not be able to cook beans in them.

A good-sized pressure cooker for a family of 4–6 people would be one with a capacity of between 6 L (13 pt) and 8 L (2 gal). If you're looking to purchase a second cooker, the 2.5 L (5 pt 4 fl oz) size is great for preparing side dishes, while a frying-pan-style cooker is good for browning meats and making stews. For most of the recipes in this book, a 6-L (13-pt) cooker will suffice. However, some recipes require a cooker with a capacity of at least 8 L (2 gal). These include: stocks, some soups, puddings and cakes, terrines, and recipes that require large pieces of meat.

PRESSURE LEVELS

Many modern pressure cookers have two pressure settings: high and low. Whether you require a cooker with the low-pressure option will depend on what you intend to cook.

High setting – All modern pressure cookers have a high-pressure setting. It is important to check what level of pressure, in psi (pounds per square inch), a pressure cooker's highest setting is. Most recipe books (including this one) are designed assuming a high-pressure setting of 15 psi. However, some manufacturers make models with a high-pressure setting of only 10 or 12 psi. If your pressure cooker does not reach 15 psi on high pressure, you will need to add 3–5 minutes cooking time to most of the recipes in this book – some experimentation will be necessary until you get a feel for your model's cooking power.

Low setting – Some pressure cookers come with the addition of a low-pressure setting of 8–10 psi. With the low setting you can cook cakes and puddings, as well as delicate foods such as fish and vegetables, which can quickly become overcooked if cooked at high pressure.

SAFETY

All second-generation pressure cookers come with a variety of safety features that older models didn't have.

Lockable lids, with expandable rubber seals, make it impossible to open the cooker while it is under pressure. Additionally, the cooker will not come up to pressure unless the lid is locked properly in place.

Reliable pressure regulators use a spring or weighted-valve system to safely regulate the cooker's internal pressure.

Safety-release pressure valves release steam out of the top of the cooker when pressure is too high – this makes a loud hissing sound to alert you that the cooker needs to be taken off the heat and the temperature reduced.

Back-up steam-release valves release steam in the event that pressure continues to build up (for example, if the safety-release pressure valve becomes blocked). The lid's rubber seal will be pushed out of slots on the rim of the lid, allowing excess pressure to be released safely.

Usually higher-end pressure cookers are fitted with more safety features than the cheaper models. Ask the advice of a reputable dealer and compare manufacturer guides to learn the safety features of particular models. Again, it is worth paying a little extra if you can.

STAINLESS STEEL OR ALUMINIUM

Pressure cookers may be made out of stainless steel or aluminium, or a combination of both. Stainless steel makes a better-quality, longer-lasting product. It is easy to clean and, unlike aluminium, does not react to acidic foods and become discoloured. Stainless steel also holds heat well, enabling the cooker to maintain pressure over a very low heat. Both aluminium and stainless steel cookers can be cleaned in the dishwasher. (Note: Do not place the lid of your pressure cooker in the dishwasher unless you have a removable pressure regulator valve. Refer to the manufacturer's guidelines.)

Whichever type of cooker you choose, make sure it has a 3-ply base, which conducts heat rapidly and evenly, preventing hot spots and potential scorching.

FEATURES & ACCESSORIES

Modern pressure cookers come with many components that their predecessors didn't have.

Quick-release pressure valves allow steam to be released quickly – to stop or interrupt the cooking process – simply by pressing the rod, button or lever. They are found in all modern cookers.

Pressure-indicator rods or levers are found in all modern cookers. They accurately indicate the pressure level, enabling you to know:

- when to start your cooking timer (i.e. as soon as desired pressure is reached)
- when to adjust the heat so as to maintain the desired pressure
- when your cooker has depressurised and it is safe to open the lid.

Timers are handy considering timing is pivotal when pressure cooking. Some cookers come fitted with a timer, or you can purchase one separately. Timers are readily available and inexpensive if you decide to buy a cooker without one included.

Handle type is worth considering when choosing your cooker. The options are: two short handles, one long handle, or one long handle accompanied by a smaller 'helper' handle on the opposite side. All should be heat resistant. It is important that you feel confident that you can easily and safely carry your cooker from the stove top to the sink, as is required when using the cold-water release method. Remember that the pot will be heavy and full of hot food. If choosing a larger pot, select one with two handles for safety. Some manufacturers also make cookers with fold-away handles; ideal for cooks with limited storage space.

Lockable lids are a feature of all modern pressure cookers. However, some are easier to fit into place than others – test this before you decide which model to purchase.

A trivet is a stand or rack used when steaming to raise foods or dishes above the water level in the cooker. They are included with some pressure cookers, or can be purchased separately from the manufacturer. A small round wire cake rack can serve the same purpose.

A steamer stand is essential for steaming vegetables. They are included with some pressure cookers, or can be purchased separately from the manufacturer. As an alternative, use a small collapsible steamer basket.

ELECTRIC PRESSURE COOKERS

An electric pressure cooker is an excellent option for people with limited space on their stove top. Although electric cookers work just as effectively as stove-top models, one limitation is that you can't use the cold-water release method with them – this slightly limits the range of recipes they can be used to prepare. Most models, however, have the quick release option, which can be used as an alternative to the cold-water release method when cooking delicate foods.

Consider all the other factors discussed in this section when choosing between an electric or stove-top model. Electric cookers tend to come in a limited range of sizes, and are generally more expensive and have a shorter warranty than stove-top models. Weigh up your options and decide which type is best suited to your needs. If you decide to buy an electric model, make sure that it reaches 15 psi at its highest pressure setting, so that you can easily prepare standard recipes.

REPLACEMENT PARTS

Check with the seller regarding availability and cost of replacement parts for the cooker you are considering buying. Pressure cookers are designed to last; however, their rubber seals need to be replaced every year or two. How often they need replacing will depend on the frequency of use and the level of care you give the cooker. A modern pressure cooker will not work if the seal is faulty, so it's a good idea to keep one in storage for when you need it. In the event that you need to replace a handle or steam-release valve, it is much more cost effective to buy parts than to buy a new cooker.

WARRANTY

A good-quality pressure cooker should come with a warranty of at least ten years. The length of the warranty is a good indication of the quality of the product.

SAFETY

READ THE MANUFACTURER'S MANUAL AND SAFETY INSTRUCTIONS CAREFULLY BEFORE USING YOUR PRESSURE COOKER.

Before using your cooker, ensure you know how to:

- lock the lid in place
- bring the cooker up to pressure
- regulate the pressure
- release the pressure safely.

Inspect your cooker before each use to make sure it is in good working order: ensure the valves are clean and move freely, and check that the rubber seal is flexible and has no tears.

Do not leave your pressure cooker unattended, and always use a timer.

Know the minimum-fill level. There is a minimum amount of liquid needed to bring a cooker up to pressure – always follow the manufacturer's recommendation for minimum-fill level. Never fill the cooker past the halfway mark when cooking beans and pulses. Never exceed the manufacturer's maximum-fill level at all other times.

Reduce the heat once the desired pressure has been reached to prevent pressure build-up and control the heat throughout cooking. If using gas, ensure the flame covers only the base of the cooker and doesn't come up the sides – the sides are not made of the thick metal that the base is, and can discolour.

When opening the pressure cooker, ensure all the pressure has been released before attempting to unlock the lid. (All modern pressure cookers have safety lids that will remain locked in place until all the pressure has been released.) When opening the cooker, always tilt the lid away from yourself to allow the steam to escape safely.

When releasing pressure, always use one of the three recommended pressure-releasing techniques to do so safely. If using the quick-release method, ensure the steam vent is pointed away from you, and that your hand is covered with an oven mitt or a tea towel to protect yourself from the steam.

Do not deep-fry under pressure: hot oil is highly combustible and can be extremely dangerous.

WHAT TO DO IF . . .

The Steam-release Valve is Clogged
In the event of a clogged valve, remove the cooker from the heat and release the pressure using the natural-release method. Remove the lid and clean the valve (referring to the manufacturer's manual), removing any stuck particles of food. Lock the lid back in place, bring back up to pressure, and cook for the remaining amount of time.

The Lid is Stuck
If the lid won't come off after releasing the pressure, bring the cooker back up to pressure, then release the pressure again using the natural-release method. If you still can't open the lid, contact the manufacturer.

CARING FOR YOUR PRESSURE COOKER

It is important that you take good care of your cooker to ensure it has a long life.

CLEANING

Read and follow the manufacturer's care instructions.

Stainless steel pressure cookers are relatively easy to clean. Generally, they just need a rinse out with warm water and a mild kitchen detergent, or a wipe with a damp cloth. If stained, soak in warm water with a little vinegar or lemon juice added. Do not use abrasive cleaners or metal scourers. For more difficult stains, refer to the manufacturer's guidelines.

The lid of some pressure cookers can be damaged if submerged in water. Many modern pressure cookers have the pressure regulator valves on the top of the lid and should never be immersed in water. To clean these, simply remove the rubber seal and wipe the lid with a clean damp cloth. Some lids, however, have a removable pressure regulator system, which makes them safe to immerse in water or wash in the dishwasher. Refer to the manufacturer's instruction manual to determine whether this is possible for your model.

The rubber seal around the lid is an essential part of your pressure cooker. It will need to be replaced every year or so, depending on the amount of use your cooker gets and the level of care you take. To help extend the life of your rubber seal:

- remove the rubber seal from the lid and wash it separately after each use
- wash the seal under warm water, rather than hot; this will make the rubber contract and help it to last longer
- thoroughly dry the seal before putting it away.

The pressure regulator valve should be removed if possible and cleaned as per the manufacturer's instructions.

STORAGE

Never store your pressure cooker with the lid locked in place, as this can damage the rubber seal or, if the seal is wet, cause it to become stuck and make the lid difficult to open. It is best to store the lid upside down on top of the cooker, to prevent the pressure regulator valve from being damaged.

PRESSURE RELEASING TECHNIQUES

NATURAL-RELEASE METHOD

To naturally release the pressure from your cooker, simply remove the cooker from the heat source when the allocated cooking time has been reached, and set aside. As the pressure slowly drops, the indicator rods will gradually lower – when they are flush with the lid, all the pressure has been released. This process can take anywhere from 3 minutes to 20 minutes, depending on how full the cooker is. Once the pressure has reduced sufficiently, the lid-locking mechanism will be released and you can safely open the cooker.

The natural-release method is the most frequently used release method in pressure cooking. It is used when cooking beans and pulses, and for most meat dishes – particularly beef, which will become tough and chewy if either of the quicker release methods is used. It also provides a gentle way for food to finish cooking as the pressure slowly releases.

When cooking beans and pulses, the natural-release method *must* be used. There are two reasons for this. Firstly, beans and pulses expand when cooking and have a tendency to foam and sputter – releasing the pressure too quickly can cause the foam to rise, potentially blocking the steam release valve. Secondly, if the pressure is released quickly, beans tend to burst and split, again potentially blocking the steam release valve, but also resulting in a mushy bean mess.

QUICK-RELEASE METHOD

Second-generation pressure cookers have an added quick-release feature that older systems lacked. Pressure can now be released quickly simply by pressing down on the pressure indicator rod or lever. Read the manufacturer's instruction manual to learn how this should be done for your particular model. Take care, as the steam that is released can be extremely hot – you may want to use a wooden spoon to hold down the indicator, or cover your hand with an oven mitt or tea towel.

One of the benefits of this steam-release mechanism is that pressure can be released quickly without causing the pot to lose too much heat. This is perfect for recipes with ingredients that have different cooking times, as cooking can be interrupted and extra ingredients added. Because the pot retains most of its heat, the lid can be locked back in place and the cooker brought back up to pressure quickly to complete the final stage of cooking. This means vegetables better retain their shape.

The quick-release option also makes pressure cooking safer, as it reduces the need to carry a hot, heavy cooker to the sink, as is required for the cold-water release method (the only quick-release option in the old-style cookers). Some recipes still recommend you use the cold-water release method, but only when absolutely necessary.

COLD-WATER RELEASE METHOD

The cold-water release method is the only way to quickly release the pressure when using an older model pressure cooker. To release the pressure using this method, carefully carry the cooker over to the sink and hold the edge of the lid underneath cold running water. Take care that the water does not get sucked into the centre pressure-release valve – this can cause a sudden drop in pressure inside the pot that could in turn cause the lid to buckle.

The benefit of the cold-water release method is that it causes the temperature to drop quickly inside the pot – in comparison, the quick-release method releases the pressure quickly, without dropping the temperature too much. This quick drop in temperature is ideal when cooking needs to be stopped immediately, as when cooking delicate foods such as vegetables and fish – with these foods, an extra minute of cooking can be the difference between a perfectly cooked meal and a plate of mushy vegetables and dry seafood.

ADAPTING RECIPES

It is easy to prepare many of your favourite recipes in the pressure cooker. Traditional recipes that require liquid or steam to cook, as when braising, stewing, steaming or boiling, can be easily adapted to the pressure cooker. In addition, recipes that are cooked in a water bath, and some that are baked, can be successfully adapted to the pressure cooker.

Adapting your favourite recipes for the pressure cooker is quite simple once you know how.

KEY THINGS TO CONSIDER

Preparation

Consider cooking times of individual ingredients, and refer to timing charts (pages 17–23) as a guide. Cooking times may need to be staggered, with ingredients such as vegetables added later (using the quick-release method to release the pressure) so they are not overcooked. Vegetables may also need to be cut into larger pieces so that they hold their shape.

Liquid Level

Using the correct amount of liquid in your pressure cooker is a key step in adapting your favourite recipes.

Remember, the pressure cooker lid has an expandable rubber seal that locks in steam, causing the vessel to pressurise. Little or no liquid escapes in the form of steam – unlike with more conventional forms of cooking. Therefore, you will almost always need to decrease the quantity of liquid used when adapting recipes for a pressure cooker.

However, a minimum amount of liquid is required to bring your cooker up to pressure. Most modern pressure cookers have a minimum-fill level between ½ cup (125 ml/4 fl oz) and 1 cup (250 ml/8½ fl oz). Refer to your manufacturer's guidelines for the requirements of your particular model.

As the cooker reaches very high temperatures, it is important that this minimum liquid component consists of one of, or a combination of, the following: water, stock, wine, beer or juice. Thick liquids and sauces (such as passata and marinades) can be added for flavour, but they are not counted as part of the minimum liquid requirement – if used alone, they will stick to and scorch the bottom of the pot.

When using tinned tomatoes, you need to factor them into your total liquid quantity. For example, a 400-g (14-oz) can of chopped tomatoes is equivalent to 1 cup (250 ml/8½ fl oz) of liquid. So if the recipe you are adapting requires 1½ cups (375 ml/12½ fl oz) of liquid, you could use one can of tomatoes plus ½ cup (125 ml/4 fl oz) of water or stock.

When using fresh vegetables with a high water content, such as cabbage and tomatoes, you need to reduce the liquid quantity slightly due to the amount of water released when the vegetables are cooked.

More liquid is required for longer cooking times. In general, add an extra ½ cup (125 ml/4 fl oz) of liquid for each additional 15 minutes of cooking time. Liquid requirements, however, will depend on the cooking technique (braising, stewing, steaming or boiling) and the pressure level (high or low).

Pressure Level

Some cookers come with only one pressure setting, limiting slightly the variety of recipes you can adapt for pressure cooking.

The main dishes that require the low-pressure setting are:

- puddings and cakes (which require a lower pressure in order to rise)
- seafood (except octopus) and fish, chicken breasts and some vegetables.

Time

As a general rule, reduce conventional cooking times by two-thirds. For example, a dish that would normally cook in 1 hour will cook in 20 minutes in a pressure cooker. Refer to the timing charts on pages 17–23 as a guide. Cooking times, as with minimum-fill levels, vary depending on the model of your pressure cooker. Refer to the timing charts provided by the manufacturer, either online or in the instruction manual.

Release Method

For meat dishes, it is usually best to release the pressure using the natural-release method. This is particularly important for beef, which otherwise will become tough and chewy.

Some delicate meats – such as chicken, and pork and lamb chops and tenderloins – require the quick-release method so they don't become overcooked and tough. Some vegetables, grains and desserts also require this method.

When steaming fish and delicate vegetables, use the cold-water release method. This drops the temperature inside the pot and stops the cooking process very quickly, avoiding overcooking. If you are using an electric cooker, you'll have to make do with the quick-release method.

Thickeners

A thickener, such as a roux (flour and butter mixture), is often added at the beginning of the process when making a stew using a conventional cooking method. However, when using a pressure cooker, thickeners should always be added at the end of the cooking time. Stirring is not possible when using a pressure cooker, so a thickener added at the beginning of the cooking time is likely to cause the sauce to stick to and scorch the bottom of the pot.

To thicken a dish, mix a tablespoon or two of flour with a little water to make a slurry, and add this to the cooker after the lid is removed at the end of the cooking time. Cook, uncovered, for a further 5–10 minutes until the raw flour taste is gone. This will thicken the dish without altering the flavour. For a richer flavour, use equal quantities of flour and butter instead.

Flavours

The flavours of a dish can be more intense when cooked in a pressure cooker, due to the sealed environment. Some recipes may therefore require smaller quantities of spice or herbs when cooked this way. Season your dish with salt and pepper *after* it has finished cooking, and always taste-test before adding seasoning.

PRESSURE COOKING TIME CHARTS

POULTRY & RABBIT

POULTRY & RABBIT	LIQUID	PRESSURE LEVEL	COOKING TIME	RELEASE METHOD
chicken breasts 4	1–2 cups (250–500 ml/8½–17 fl oz)	low	10 minutes	natural
chicken thighs or pieces on the bone 1–1.5 kg (2 lb 3 oz–3 lb 5 oz)	1–2 cups (250–500 ml/8½–17 fl oz)	high	10 minutes	quick
duck marylands 3–4	1–2 cups (250–500 ml/8½–17 fl oz)	high	10 minutes	natural
rabbit pieces on the bone 1.5 kg (3 lb 5 oz)	1–2 cups (250–500 ml/8½–17 fl oz)	high	10 minutes	quick
whole chicken 1.5 kg (3 lb 5 oz)	1 cup (250 ml/8½ fl oz)	high	20 minutes	natural

BEEF & VEAL

- The natural-release method must be used when cooking beef and veal, to prevent the meat from becoming tough.

- Note that cooking times remain the same when quantities are multiplied – one lamb shank will cook in the same time as eight, once the specified pressure has been reached.

- Liquid quantities can be adjusted (as long as the manufacturer's recommended minimum requirement is met), depending on how much gravy/sauce is desired.

BEEF & VEAL	LIQUID	PRESSURE LEVEL	COOKING TIME	RELEASE METHOD
beef mince 750 g–1 kg (1 lb 10 oz–2 lb 3 oz)	1–2 cups (250–500 ml/8½–17 fl oz)	high	10–30 minutes	natural
corned beef 1.5 kg (3 lb 5 oz)	1 L (34 fl oz)	low	45 minutes	natural
osso bucco 2 kg (4 lb 6 oz)	2 cups (500 ml/17 fl oz)	high	20 minutes	natural
stewing beef, such as cheek, shin or blade, cut into 4-cm (1½-in) cubes 750 g–1 kg (1 lb 10 oz–2 lb 3 oz)	1–2 cups (250–500 ml/8½–17 fl oz)	high	20 minutes	natural
veal shanks 8	2 cups (500 ml/17 fl oz)	high	20–25 minutes	natural
veal shoulder, cut into 4-cm (1½-in) cubes 750 g–1 kg (1 lb 10 oz–2 lb 3 oz)	1–2 cups (250–500 ml/8½–17 fl oz)	high	20 minutes	natural

LAMB & GOAT

- The quick-release method can be used for lamb and goat if you're in a hurry.

LAMB & GOAT	LIQUID	PRESSURE LEVEL	COOKING TIME	RELEASE METHOD
goat shin or shoulder, on the bone, cut into chunks 1–2 kg (2 lb 3 oz–4 lb 6 oz)	1–2½ cups (250–625 ml/8½–21 fl oz)	high	15 minutes	natural
lamb leg or shoulder, cut into 3-cm (1¼-in) chunks 750 g– 1 kg (1 lb 10 oz–2 lb 3 oz)	1–2½ cups (250–625 ml/8½–21 fl oz)	high	15 minutes	natural
lamb mince 750 g–1 kg (1 lb 10 oz–2 lb 3 oz)	1–1½ cups (250–375 ml/8½–12½ fl oz)	high	10–15 minutes	natural
lamb neck, cut into 3-cm (1¼-in) thick chops 750 g–1 kg (1 lb 10 oz–2 lb 3 oz)	1½ cups (375 ml/12½ fl oz)	high	15 minutes	natural
lamb shanks 8	2 cups (500 ml/17 fl oz)	high	20–25 minutes	natural
leg of lamb, on the bone 1.5 kg (3 lb 5 oz)	1½ cups (375 ml/12½ fl oz)	high	30–35 minutes	natural

PORK !

PORK	LIQUID	PRESSURE LEVEL	COOKING TIME	RELEASE METHOD
boneless pork belly, in one piece 1.2 kg (2 lb 10 oz)	2–3 cups (500–750 ml/17–25 fl oz)	high	40 minutes	natural
boneless pork belly, cut into six pieces 1.2 kg (2 lb 10 oz)	2–3 cups (500–750 ml/17–25 fl oz)	high	25 minutes	natural
boneless pork loin roast 1.2 kg (2 lb 10 oz)	1 cup (250 ml/8½ fl oz)	high	30 minutes	natural
boned pork shoulder, cut into 3-cm (1¼ in) chunks 750 g–1 kg (1 lb 10 oz–2 lb 3 oz)	1–1½ cups (250–375 ml/8½–12½ fl oz)	high	15 minutes	natural
pork chops 200 g (7 oz)	1 cup (250 ml/8½ fl oz)	high	10 minutes	quick
pork spare ribs, cut into 6-cm (2¼-in) pieces 1.5–2 kg (3 lb 5 oz–4 lb 6 oz)	1½–2 cups (375–500 ml/12½–17 fl oz)	high	10–15 minutes	natural
stuffed pork neck 900 g (2 lb)	2 cups (500 ml/17 fl oz)	high	25–30 minutes	natural

VEGETABLES

- Steam in a basket or on a rack over ½–2 cups (125–500 ml/4–17 fl oz) boiling water on high pressure. (Use the minimum liquid level recommended by the manufacturer.)

- If you have an electric pressure cooker, use the quick-release method instead of the cold-water method.

VEGETABLES	COOKING TIME	RELEASE METHOD
artichokes, globe	7–8 minutes	natural
Asian vegetables	1–2 minutes	cold-water
asparagus	1 minute	cold-water
beans, green or yellow	1–2 minutes	cold-water
beetroots	20 minutes	natural
broccoli, cut into large florets	2–3 minutes	cold-water
brussels sprouts	1–2 minutes	cold-water
cabbage, red or white, thickly sliced	2 minutes	cold-water
carrots or parsnips, thickly sliced	2–3 minutes	cold-water
cauliflower, cut into large florets	2–3 minutes	cold-water
corn on the cob	3 minutes	cold-water
eggplant, cubed	2–3 minutes	quick
fennel, quartered	4–5 minutes	quick
kale or cavolo nero, thickly sliced	2 minutes	cold-water
peas	1-2 minutes	cold-water
potatoes, cubed	4–5 minutes	natural
potatoes, whole (small–medium)	5–10 minutes	natural
pumpkin or sweet potato, cubed	3–4 minutes	natural
turnips, cubed	3–4 minutes	natural
zucchini, thickly sliced	1 minute	cold-water

RICE & OTHER GRAINS

- All liquid measurements are for 1 cup of rice or grains.

- Add 1 tablespoon (20 ml/¾ fl oz) oil per 1 cup rice or grains, to help prevent foaming.

- Grains hold their shape best when lightly toasted in a dry pan prior to cooking.

RICE & OTHER GRAINS	LIQUID (FOR 1 CUP RICE/GRAIN)	PRESSURE LEVEL	COOKING TIME	RELEASE METHOD
arborio or other short-grain white rice	4½–5 cups (1.1–1.25 L/2 pt 6–2 pt 10 fl oz)	low	4–6 minutes	quick
basmati, jasmine or other long-grain white rice	1½ cups (375 ml/12½ fl oz)	high	3 minutes	natural
brown rice	1½ cups (375 ml/12½ fl oz)	high	15–20 minutes	natural
white French millet	2 cups (500 ml/17 fl oz)	high	45 minutes	natural
millet (hulled)	1½ cups (375 ml/12½ fl oz)	high	10–12 minutes	natural
moghrabieh	2 cups (500 ml/17 fl oz)	high	7 minutes	natural
pearl barley or farro	3¼–3½ cups (810–875 ml/27–30 fl oz)	high	15–20 minutes	quick
quinoa	1¼ cups (310 ml/10½ fl oz)	low	1 minute	natural
whole buckwheat	2 cups (500 ml/17 fl oz)	high	3–5 minutes	natural
wild rice	2–3 cups (500–750 ml/17–25 fl oz)	high	20–22 minutes	quick

BEANS & PULSES

- All cooking times are based on beans that have been soaked – using either the pre-soak or quick-soak method (see page 218) – unless otherwise stated.

- For all beans, the bean to water ratio should be 1 cup dried beans to 3 cups (750 ml/25 fl oz) water, plus 1 tablespoon (20 ml/¾ fl oz) oil.

- For all lentils, the lentil to water ratio should be 1 cup lentils to 2 cups (500 ml/17 fl oz) water.

- Always use the natural-release method when cooking beans and pulses.

DRIED BEANS & PULSES	COOKING TIME	PRESSURE LEVEL
adzuki beans	4–6 minutes	high
black-eyed peas (no soaking)	8–10 minutes	high
black turtle beans	7–8 minutes	high
borlotti beans	6–8 minutes	high
broad beans	12–14 minutes	high
brown lentils (no soaking)	3–5 minutes	high
cannellini beans	6–8 minutes	high
chickpeas	12–15 minutes	high
haricot/navy beans	4–6 minutes	high
lima beans	4–6 minutes	low
mung beans (no soaking)	3–5 minutes	high
pinto beans	4–6 minutes	high
Puy lentils (no soaking)	2–4 minutes	high
red kidney beans	8–10 minutes	high
red lentils (no soaking)	2–4 minutes	high

STOCKS & SOUPS

A nourishing soup is the perfect comfort food on a cold winter's day. Often made with just a handful of ingredients, soups are easy to prepare and now, with the help of your pressure cooker, they can be on the table in next to no time.

The key to any soup is using quality ingredients; most importantly, quality stock. Home-made stock can be prepared easily in the pressure cooker. The recipes provided here make enough stock for two average-sized batches of soup. Stock can be made in advance and stored in the refrigerator for 4–5 days, or frozen for a later date. If you're pressed for time or your freezer supply has run out, good-quality liquid stocks can be sourced from super-markets, selected delis, butchers and fishmongers. Failing that, a good-quality powdered stock can be used.

In this chapter you will find hearty old-fashioned favourites such as Scotch broth (page 33), minestrone (page 34), and pea and ham soup (page 31), plus classics like French onion (page 48), borscht (page 32), and potato and leek (page 44). For a lighter option, to be enjoyed even in the warmer months, try your hand at the more exotic Thai chicken, coconut and galangal soup (page 49) or the aromatic Chinese broth with pork wontons (page 50).

Make a big pot of soup, divide it into small containers and freeze for an easy after-work meal or for unexpected dinner guests.

TIPS FOR MAKING STOCK

When making stock, remember never to exceed your cooker's recommended fill level.

Bones & Carcasses

Beef bones and chicken carcasses can be purchased from fresh food markets or your local butcher. If time allows, brown beef bones in a hot oven before adding them to the cooker – this will add a rich flavour and depth of colour.

To save money, buy a whole chicken (instead of pieces) and bone it yourself. Portion up the meat and refrigerate or freeze until required. Remove and discard skin and fat from the carcass, then rinse under cold running water to remove any blood, which can cause the stock to turn cloudy and bitter.

For fish stock, buy whole fish from the market and have your fishmonger fillet them for you. Use the bones immediately, or freeze them for a later date. Fish bones need to be rinsed well to wash off any blood, and the gills must be removed. Fish stock requires a much shorter cooking time than beef and chicken stock. Don't be tempted to cook it for longer, as it will become bitter.

Vegetables

Using vegetable scraps to make stock cuts down on waste. Peelings and trimmings of carrots, onions, celery, leeks and herbs can be substituted for, or added to, the vegetables in the stock recipes here.

Tomatoes make a nice addition to beef stock, giving it a rich colour, as do mushroom peelings. To make a smaller quantity or a stronger-flavoured stock, simply reduce the quantity of liquid by 2–4 cups.

Storage

It is best to refrigerate homemade stock overnight before use if time permits. This allows the fat to float to the surface and solidify, making it easy to remove and discard. It also gives the sediment time to sink to the bottom of the container, where it can be left behind when the stock is poured out.

To make a more concentrated stock, strain the liquid into a clean saucepan and simmer, uncovered, until it is reduced by up to half. Refrigerate overnight and remove the fat. The stock can then be frozen in portions, and diluted with water to the desired strength when required.

CHICKEN STOCK

MAKES 12 CUPS (3 L /6 PT 6 FL OZ)

1 kg (2 lb 3 oz) chicken bones, necks and wings
1 medium-sized onion, unpeeled, quartered
1 medium-sized carrot, unpeeled, coarsely chopped
1 small leek, coarsely chopped
1 stick celery (including leaves), coarsely chopped

5 stalks parsley
4 sprigs thyme
1 clove garlic, unpeeled
5 black peppercorns
2 bay leaves

Rinse the chicken pieces under cold water.

Place the chicken and all other ingredients in a large pressure cooker and add enough water to just cover – about 12 cups (3 L/6 pt 6 fl oz) – ensuring you do not exceed the maximum fill level recommended by the manufacturer. Lock the lid in place and bring to high pressure over high heat. Cook for 30 minutes, adjusting the heat as necessary to maintain a high pressure.

Release the pressure using the natural-release method.

Line a large sieve or colander with a piece of muslin. Strain the stock into a container, discarding the solids. Skim any fat from the surface and use the stock immediately. Alternatively, set aside to cool, then cover and refrigerate overnight. Remove and discard the layer of fat that forms on top, and use the stock as required.

Chicken stock can be stored in the refrigerator for up to 3 days or frozen for up to 4 months.

BEEF STOCK

MAKES 12 CUPS (3 L/6 PT 6 FL OZ)

1.5 kg (3 lb 5 oz) beef bones, cut to fit in your cooker (your butcher can do this for you)

350 g (12 oz) beef shin or stewing beef, cut into chunks

1 medium-sized leek, coarsely chopped

1 large onion, unpeeled, quartered

1 medium-sized carrot, unpeeled, coarsely chopped

1 medium-sized tomato

1 cup (250 ml/8½ fl oz) red wine

2 sticks celery (including leaves), coarsely chopped

5 stalks parsley

4 sprigs thyme

2 cloves garlic, unpeeled

5 black peppercorns

2 bay leaves

Preheat the oven to 200°C (390°F).

Place the bones, meat, leek, onion, carrot and tomato in a large baking dish. Cook in the oven for 45 minutes, or until well browned. Transfer to a large pressure cooker.

Pour the wine into the hot baking dish and stir, scraping the base to remove any bits of cooked meat and vegetables. Pour the liquid into the pressure cooker.

Add the remaining ingredients to the cooker, plus enough water to just cover – about 12 cups (3 L/6 pt 6 fl oz) – ensuring you do not exceed the maximum fill level recommended by the manufacturer.

Lock the lid in place and bring to high pressure over high heat. Cook for 45 minutes, adjusting the heat as necessary to maintain a high pressure.

Release the pressure using the natural-release method.

Line a large sieve or colander with a piece of muslin. Strain the stock into a container, discarding the solids. Skim any fat from the surface and use the stock immediately. Alternatively, set aside to cool, then cover and refrigerate overnight. Remove and discard the layer of fat that forms on top, and use the stock as required.

Beef stock can be stored in the refrigerator for up to 3 days or frozen for up to 4 months.

FISH STOCK

MAKES 12 CUPS (3 L /6 PT 6 FL OZ)

1.5 kg (3 lb 5 oz) fish heads and bones (from firm white fish), gills and skin removed
½ cup (125 ml/4 fl oz) dry white wine
1 medium-sized onion, unpeeled, quartered
1 small leek (white part only), coarsely chopped

1 stick celery (including leaves), coarsely chopped
3 stalks parsley
3 sprigs thyme
5 black peppercorns
1 bay leaf

Rinse the fish heads and bones under cold water.

Place the fish and all other ingredients in a large pressure cooker and add enough water to just cover – about 12 cups (3 L /6 pt 6 fl oz) – ensuring you do not exceed the maximum fill level recommended by the manufacturer.

Lock the lid in place and bring to high pressure over high heat. Cook for 10 minutes, adjusting the heat as necessary to maintain a high pressure.

Release the pressure using the natural-release method.

Line a large sieve or colander with a piece of muslin. Strain the stock into a container, discarding the solids, and use as required.

Fish stock can be stored in the refrigerator for up to 3 days or frozen for up to 3 months.

VEGETABLE STOCK

MAKES 12 CUPS (3 L /6 PT 6 FL OZ)

1 large onion, unpeeled, quartered
1 large carrot, unpeeled, halved
1 large parsnip, unpeeled, halved
1 large leek, halved
3 sticks celery (including leaves), halved
125 g (4½ oz) button mushrooms or mushroom stalks

1 medium-sized tomato
6 stalks parsley
5 sprigs thyme
2 cloves garlic, unpeeled
1 teaspoon sea salt
5 black peppercorns
2 bay leaves

Place all the ingredients in a large pressure cooker and add enough water to just cover – about 12 cups (3 L /6 pt 6 fl oz) – ensuring you do not exceed the maximum fill level recommended by the manufacturer.

Lock the lid in place and bring to high pressure over high heat. Cook for 15 minutes, adjusting the heat as necessary to maintain a high pressure.

Release the pressure using the natural-release method.

Line a large sieve or colander with a piece of muslin. Strain the stock into a container, discarding the solids, and use as required.

Vegetable stock can be stored in the refrigerator for 3–5 days or frozen for up to 3 months.

PEA & HAM SOUP

SERVES 8

2 tablespoons (40 g/1½ oz) butter
1 medium-sized onion, coarsely chopped
2 cloves garlic, coarsely chopped
450 g (1 lb) dried green split peas
1 medium-sized leek (white part only), coarsely chopped
1 medium-sized carrot, coarsely chopped

2 sticks celery, coarsely chopped
1 tablespoon finely chopped fresh thyme
1 × 1-kg (2 lb 3-oz) smoked ham hock
1 tablespoon (20 ml/¾ fl oz) freshly squeezed lemon juice
freshly ground black pepper
crusty bread, to serve

Melt the butter in a large pressure cooker over low–medium heat. Add the onion and garlic, and sauté until golden. Add the split peas, vegetables and thyme, and stir to combine. Add the ham hock and 8 cups (2 L/4 pt 4 fl oz) water, then lock the lid in place and bring to high pressure over high heat. Cook for 25 minutes, adjusting the heat as necessary to maintain a high pressure.

Release the pressure using the natural-release method.

Remove the ham hock from the soup and set aside to cool slightly.

Purée the soup using a hand-held blender or food processor, until smooth. Stir in the lemon juice.

Dice the ham, discarding any fat or sinew, and return to the soup. Season with freshly ground black pepper.

Serve with crusty bread.

BORSCHT

2 tablespoons (40 ml/1½ fl oz) olive oil
500 g (1 lb 2 oz) beef short ribs, cut into 6-cm
(2¼-in) pieces
1 large onion, finely chopped
3 cloves garlic, finely chopped
1 teaspoon caraway seeds
¼ small white cabbage, finely shredded
2 large carrots, grated
1 large potato, grated

3 medium-sized beetroots, unpeeled, washed
and stems trimmed
6 cups (1.5 L/3 pt 3 fl oz) beef stock (page 28)
½ cup (125 ml/4 fl oz) red-wine vinegar
½ cup coarsely chopped dill,
plus extra for garnish
1 tablespoon (15 g/½ oz) caster sugar
salt and freshly ground black pepper
sour cream, to serve

Heat the oil in a pressure cooker over medium–high heat. Add the beef and cook, stirring occasionally, until browned. Decrease the heat to low, then add the onion, garlic and caraway seeds, and sauté until golden. Add the cabbage, carrot and potato, and stir to combine. Finally, add the beetroots and pour in the stock. Lock the lid in place and bring to high pressure over high heat. Cook for 20 minutes, adjusting the heat as necessary to maintain a high pressure.

Release the pressure using the natural or quick-release method.

Remove the beef and beetroots from the pot. Remove the meat from the bones and shred (discard the bones). Wearing food-handling gloves (to prevent staining), peel the beetroots. Coarsely grate two of the beetroots and dice the remaining one.

Return the meat and beetroot to the soup. Stir in the vinegar, dill and sugar, and simmer gently, uncovered, for 5 minutes. Season with salt and pepper.

Serve with a dollop of sour cream and garnish with dill.

For a vegetarian version, substitute vegetable stock for the beef stock and omit the ribs.

SCOTCH BROTH

SERVES 8

2 tablespoons (40 ml/1½ fl oz) olive oil
3 lamb shanks
2 medium-sized carrots, halved lengthways and sliced
1 medium-sized swede, diced
1 medium-sized potato, diced
1 medium-sized onion, chopped
1 medium-sized leek (white part only), thickly sliced
2 sticks celery, sliced

1 clove garlic, finely chopped
¾ cup pearl barley
2 bay leaves
4 sprigs thyme
7 cups (1.75 L/3 pt 11 fl oz) chicken stock (page 27)
¼ cup finely chopped flat-leaf parsley
salt and freshly ground black pepper
crusty bread, to serve

Heat the oil in a large pressure cooker over medium–high heat. Add the lamb shanks and cook until browned all over. Decrease the heat to low, then add the vegetables, garlic, barley, bay leaves and thyme, and stir to combine. Pour in the stock, then lock the lid in place and bring to high pressure over high heat. Cook for 20 minutes, adjusting the heat as necessary to maintain a high pressure.

Release the pressure using the natural-release method.

Remove the shanks from the pot, remove the meat from the bones and shred (discard the bones). Return the meat to the soup. Stir in the parsley and season with salt and pepper.

Serve with crusty bread.

MINESTRONE

1 cup dried borlotti beans
2 tablespoons (40 ml/1½ fl oz) olive oil
150 g (5 oz) pancetta, diced
1 medium-sized onion, diced
3 cloves garlic, finely chopped
2 medium-sized potatoes, diced
2 medium-sized carrots, diced
¼ small white cabbage, shredded
1 medium-sized leek (white part only), sliced
2 sticks celery, diced
7 cups (1.75 L/3 pt 11 fl oz) chicken stock (page 27)

2 × 400-g (14-oz) cans chopped tomatoes
125 g (4½ oz) ditalini or other small pasta
200 g (7 oz) cavolo nero, stem removed and leaves shredded
1 medium-sized zucchini, thickly sliced
2 tablespoons tomato paste
1 tablespoon (15 g/½ oz) caster sugar
salt and freshly ground black pepper
shaved parmesan cheese, to serve
crusty bread, to serve

Soak the beans in a large bowl of cold water for at least 4 hours (or overnight). Drain and rinse.

Heat the oil in a large pressure cooker over low–medium heat. Add the pancetta, onion and garlic, and sauté until golden. Add the potato, carrot, cabbage, leek, celery and borlotti beans, and stir to combine. Pour in the stock, then lock the lid in place and bring to high pressure over high heat. Cook for 25 minutes, adjusting the heat as necessary to maintain a high pressure.

Release the pressure using the natural-release method.

Add the tomatoes, pasta, cavolo nero, zucchini, tomato paste and caster sugar. Cook, uncovered, stirring occasionally, over medium–high heat for 10 minutes or until the pasta is al dente. Season with salt and black pepper.

Serve scattered with parmesan cheese, with crusty bread alongside.

LENTIL, SPINACH & YOGHURT SOUP

SERVES 4-6

1 cup dried brown lentils
2 tablespoons (40 ml/1½ fl oz) olive oil
1 medium-sized onion, diced
2 cloves garlic, finely chopped
1 teaspoon ground cumin,
plus extra for garnish
1 teaspoon ground coriander
3 small potatoes, sliced into rounds
6 cups (1.5 L/3 pt 3 fl oz) chicken stock
(page 27) or vegetable stock (page 30)

1 bunch spinach, washed, stalks removed
and leaves shredded
1½ cups (375 ml/12½ fl oz) natural yoghurt
½ cup chopped coriander
¼ cup chopped flat-leaf parsley
juice of 1 lemon
salt and freshly ground black pepper
extra-virgin olive oil, to serve

Soak the lentils in a large bowl of cold water for at least 2 hours (or overnight). Drain and rinse.

Heat the olive oil in a pressure cooker over low–medium heat. Add the onion and garlic, and cook until clear and softened. Add the spices and potato slices, and cook, stirring, for 30 seconds or until fragrant. Pour in the stock, then lock the lid in place and bring to high pressure over high heat. Cook for 20 minutes, adjusting the heat as necessary to maintain a high pressure.

Release the pressure using the natural or quick-release method.

Add the spinach, half the yoghurt, the herbs and lemon juice to the soup. Cook, uncovered, over medium heat for 1–2 minutes, until the spinach wilts. Season with salt and pepper.

Serve with a dollop of the remaining yoghurt, a drizzle of extra-virgin olive oil and a sprinkle of cumin.

MOROCCAN SPICED LAMB & CHICKPEA SOUP

SERVES 8

¾ cup dried chickpeas
2 tablespoons (40 ml/1½ fl oz) olive oil
2 lamb shanks
salt and freshly ground black pepper
1 large onion, diced
1 medium-sized carrot, finely diced
2 sticks celery, diced
1 clove garlic, finely chopped
1 teaspoon ground turmeric
1 teaspoon ground cinnamon

1 teaspoon ground ginger
¼ cup dried split red lentils, rinsed
7 cups (1.75 L/3 pt 11 fl oz) chicken stock
  (page 27)
2 × 400-g (14-oz) cans chopped tomatoes
1 tablespoon tomato paste
1 cup finely chopped coriander,
  plus extra for garnish
juice of 1 lemon

Soak the chickpeas in cold water for at least 4 hours (or overnight). Drain and rinse.

Heat the oil in a large pressure cooker over medium–high heat. Season the lamb shanks with salt and pepper, and cook until browned all over. Decrease the heat to medium, then add the vegetables and spices, and cook, stirring occasionally, for 2–3 minutes, until the onions are soft and the spices fragrant. Add the chickpeas and lentils, and stir to combine. Pour in the stock, then lock the lid in place and bring to high pressure over high heat. Cook for 20 minutes, adjusting the heat as necessary to maintain a high pressure.

Release the pressure using the natural-release method.

Remove the shanks from the pot, strip the meat from the bones and shred (discard the bones). Return the meat to the soup. Add the tomatoes and tomato paste, and simmer, uncovered, over medium heat for 5–10 minutes. Stir in the coriander and lemon juice, and season with salt and pepper.

Serve sprinkled with coriander.

JERUSALEM ARTICHOKE SOUP

SERVES 6

2 tablespoons (40 g/1½ oz) butter
1 medium-sized onion, coarsely chopped
1 medium-sized leek (white part only),
coarsely chopped
1 stick celery, coarsely chopped
2 cloves garlic, coarsely chopped
900 g (2 lb) Jerusalem artichokes, halved
2 medium-sized potatoes, coarsely chopped

6 cups (1.5 L/3 pt 3 fl oz) chicken stock
(page 27)
salt and ground white pepper
truffle oil, to serve (optional)
JERUSALEM ARTICHOKE CHIPS
2 Jerusalem artichokes, peeled
2 cups (500 ml/17 fl oz) vegetable oil,
for deep-frying

Melt the butter in a pressure cooker over low–medium heat. Add the onion, leek, celery and garlic, and cook until the onion is clear and softened. Add the Jerusalem artichokes, potatoes and stock. Lock the lid in place and bring to high pressure over high heat. Cook for 10 minutes, adjusting the heat as necessary to maintain a high pressure.

Meanwhile, to make the chips, use a vegetable peeler to peel the artichokes into wafer-thin strips. Pat the strips dry with paper towel. Heat the oil in a small saucepan over medium–high heat. Fry the artichoke strips for about 30 seconds, turning frequently, until crisp and golden. Remove using a slotted spoon and drain on paper towel.

Release the cooker's pressure using the natural or quick-release method.

Purée the soup using a hand-held blender or food processor, until smooth. Season with salt and white pepper.

To serve, drizzle with truffle oil if desired and scatter with artichoke chips.

TOMATO & TARRAGON SOUP

SERVES 6

1.5 kg (3 lb 5 oz) vine-ripened tomatoes
2 tablespoons (40 ml/1½ fl oz) olive oil
1 large onion, coarsely chopped
1 clove garlic, coarsely chopped
1 tablespoon tomato paste
2 teaspoons caster sugar

5 cups (1.25 L/2 pt 10 fl oz) vegetable stock
  (page 30) or chicken stock (page 27)
2 tablespoons finely chopped tarragon
salt and freshly ground black pepper
crème fraîche, to serve

Score a cross in the base of each tomato, then blanch them in boiling water for 20 seconds. Drain and peel the tomatoes, then cut each in half horizontally and remove the seeds. Coarsely chop the flesh and set aside.

Heat the oil in a pressure cooker over low–medium heat. Add the onion and garlic, and cook until clear and softened. Add the chopped tomato, tomato paste and sugar, and stir to combine. Pour in the stock, then lock the lid in place and bring to high pressure over high heat. Cook for 10 minutes, adjusting the heat as necessary to maintain a high pressure.

Release the pressure using the natural or quick-release method.

Purée the soup using a hand-held blender or food processor, until smooth. Stir in the tarragon and season with salt and pepper.

Serve with a dollop of crème fraîche and some cracked black pepper.

FISH & CORN CHOWDER

SERVES 4

1 corn cob

3 tablespoons (60 g/2 oz) softened butter

1 large onion, diced

2 sticks celery, diced

1 large green chilli, deseeded and finely sliced

2 cloves garlic, finely chopped

2 medium-sized potatoes, cut into 2.5-cm (1-in) chunks

2 bay leaves

2 cups (500 ml/17 fl oz) fish stock (page 29)

1 tablespoon (15 g/½ oz) plain flour

2 cups (500 ml/17 fl oz) milk

500 g (1 lb 2 oz) skinless firm white fish fillets, cut into 4-cm (1½-in) chunks

¼ cup coarsely chopped flat-leaf parsley

¼ cup coarsely chopped coriander

salt and freshly ground black pepper

Cut the kernels off the corn cob and set aside. Melt 2 tablespoons (40 g/1½ oz) of the butter in a pressure cooker over low–medium heat. Cook the onion, celery, chilli and garlic, until the onion is clear and softened. Add the potato, corn and bay leaves, and stir to combine. Pour in the stock, then lock the lid in place and bring to high pressure over high heat. Cook for 4 minutes, adjusting the heat as necessary to maintain a high pressure.

Release the pressure using the quick-release method.

Combine the remaining butter and the flour in a small bowl. Add 2 tablespoons (40 ml/1½ fl oz) of the cooking liquid and stir to make a smooth paste. Stir the paste into the soup. Pour in the milk and simmer, uncovered, stirring occasionally, over medium heat for 5–10 minutes, until thickened.

Add the fish and fresh herbs and cook for a further 3–5 minutes, until the fish is white and cooked through. Season with salt and pepper, and serve.

BOUILLABAISSE

SERVES 6

12 raw (green) prawns, shelled and deveined but tails left on (shells and heads reserved)
⅓ cup (80 ml/3 fl oz) Pernod or white wine
2 tablespoons (40 ml/1½ fl oz) olive oil
1 medium-sized onion, coarsely chopped
1 baby fennel bulb, finely chopped
1 small leek (white part only), coarsely chopped
1 stick celery, finely chopped
2 cloves garlic, finely chopped
1 × 400-g (14-oz) can chopped tomatoes
1 tablespoon tomato paste
1 bay leaf
1 teaspoon saffron threads
2 cups (500 ml/17 fl oz) fish stock (page 29)

2 tablespoons (40 ml/1½ fl oz) freshly squeezed lemon juice
salt and freshly ground black pepper
500 g (1 lb 2 oz) skinless firm white fish fillets, cut into 4-cm (1½-in) chunks
12 mussels, scrubbed and debearded
½ cup finely chopped flat-leaf parsley
croutons made from baguette, to serve

ROUILLE
4 slices white bread (crusts removed), coarsely torn
¼ cup roasted red capsicum
3 cloves garlic, coarsely chopped
1 small red chilli, deseeded and finely chopped
⅓ cup (80 ml/3 fl oz) olive oil
salt

Preheat the oven to 200°C (390°F).

Spread the prawn shells in a baking dish and cook in the oven for 20 minutes, or until dark-orange and fragrant. Pour the Pernod or wine into the dish and scrape the shells and juices off the base using a wooden spoon.

Heat the oil in a pressure cooker over low–medium heat. Cook the onion, fennel, leek, celery and garlic until the onion is clear and softened. Add the prawn shells and Pernod, and bring to the boil. Add the tomatoes, tomato paste, bay leaf and saffron, and stir to combine. Pour in the stock, then lock the lid in place and bring to high pressure over high heat. Cook for 20 minutes, adjusting the heat as necessary to maintain a high pressure.

Meanwhile, to make the rouille, place the bread in a bowl, cover with cold water and set aside for 2 minutes. Squeeze the excess water out of the bread, then place the bread, capsicum, garlic and chilli in a small food processor, and blend to make a coarse paste. Gradually pour in the oil, blending to make a creamy sauce (the texture should be similar to mayonnaise). Season with salt.

Release the cooker's pressure using the quick-release method.

Line a large sieve or colander with a piece of muslin. Strain the soup, pressing down on the solids to squeeze out all the flavour. Discard the solids.

Return the soup to the pot and simmer, uncovered, over medium heat for 5 minutes. Add the lemon juice and season with salt and pepper, then add the fish, mussels and prawns. Cover with the lid but do not lock in place. Cook for 3–5 minutes, until the mussels are open, the fish is white and the prawns have turned pink.

Stir in the parsley and serve topped with croutons and rouille.

VIETNAMESE BEEF & NOODLE SOUP

SERVES 6

600 g (1 lb 5 oz) rump beef
1 large onion, quartered
5-cm (2-in) piece ginger, bruised
1 cinnamon stick
4 cardamom pods, bruised
3 star anise
5 cloves
1 teaspoon coriander seeds
7 cups (1.75 L/3 pt 11 fl oz) beef stock (page 28)
2½ tablespoons (50 ml/1¾ fl oz) fish sauce

2½ tablespoons (50 ml/1¾ fl oz) soy sauce
1 tablespoon (15 g/½ oz) coarsely grated palm sugar
250 g (9 oz) fresh thin rice noodles
100 g (3½ oz) bean sprouts
250 g (9 oz) beef fillet, thinly sliced
3 spring onions, finely sliced
1 cup coriander leaves
1 cup Vietnamese mint leaves
2 red bird's eye chillies, finely sliced
lime wedges, to serve

Place the rump beef, onion, ginger and spices in a pressure cooker. Pour in the stock, then lock the lid in place and bring to high pressure over high heat. Cook for 30 minutes, adjusting the heat as necessary to maintain a high pressure.

Release the pressure using the natural or quick-release method. Remove the beef from the pot and slice thinly across the grain. Set aside.

Strain the stock through a sieve, discarding the solids. Return the stock to the pot and add the fish sauce, soy sauce and sugar.

Soak the noodles in boiling water until softened, or prepare following the packet instructions. Drain.

Divide the noodles and cooked beef between serving bowls. Scatter with bean sprouts, slices of raw beef fillet, fresh herbs and chilli. Ladle the hot broth over.

Serve with lime wedges.

If substituting dried noodles for the fresh, use half the specified amount.

SPANISH-STYLE SAUSAGE & WHITE BEAN SOUP

SERVES 6

1 cup dried cannellini beans
2 tablespoons (40 ml/1½ fl oz) olive oil
1 large red onion, diced
3 cloves garlic, finely chopped
2 chorizo sausages, thinly sliced
1 teaspoon dried chilli flakes
1 teaspoon smoked paprika
1 teaspoon fennel seeds
5 cups (1.25 L/2 pt 10 fl oz) chicken stock
(page 27)

2 × 400-g (14-oz) cans chopped tomatoes
1 tablespoon tomato paste
2 teaspoons caster sugar
1 cup finely chopped flat-leaf parsley
salt and freshly ground black pepper
extra-virgin olive oil, to serve
GRILLED GARLIC TOASTS
6 slices ciabatta
olive oil, for drizzling
1 clove garlic, halved

Soak the beans in a large bowl of cold water for at least 4 hours (or overnight). Drain and rinse.

Heat the oil in a pressure cooker over low–medium heat. Add the onion and garlic, and cook until clear and softened. Add the chorizo and cook until golden brown. Add the spices and beans, and stir to combine. Pour in the stock, then lock the lid in place and bring to high pressure over high heat. Cook for 10 minutes, adjusting the heat as necessary to maintain a high pressure.

Release the pressure using the natural-release method.

Add the tomatoes, tomato paste and sugar, and cook, uncovered, for 5–10 minutes until thickened slightly. Stir in the parsley and season with salt and pepper.

To make the garlic toasts, preheat a grill pan over high heat. Drizzle the bread with olive oil and grill for 1–2 minutes on each side, until marked with lines. Rub the toasts with garlic.

Serve the soup drizzled with extra-virgin olive oil and with a piece of grilled garlic toast alongside.

POTATO & LEEK SOUP WITH SMOKED SALMON

SERVES 6

3 tablespoons (60 g/2 oz) butter
3 medium-sized leeks (white part only), coarsely chopped
1 medium-sized onion, coarsely chopped
1 clove garlic, coarsely chopped
800 g (1 lb 12 oz) potatoes, coarsely chopped
5 cups (1.25 L/2 pt 10 fl oz) chicken stock (page 27)

salt and ground white pepper
¾ cup (180 ml/6 fl oz) cream
4 slices smoked salmon, finely sliced
crème fraîche, to serve
chives, cut into short lengths, for garnish

Melt the butter in a pressure cooker over low–medium heat. Add the leek, onion and garlic, and cook until clear and softened. Add the potato and stock, then lock the lid in place and bring to high pressure over high heat. Cook for 10 minutes, adjusting the heat as necessary to maintain a high pressure.

Release the pressure using the natural or quick-release method.

Purée the soup using a hand-held blender or food processor, until smooth. Season with salt and white pepper. Strain through a fine mesh sieve, discarding the solids. Return the soup to the pot and stir in the cream.

Serve the soup topped with slices of smoked salmon and a dollop of crème fraîche. Garnish with chives.

HOT & SPICY INDIAN CHICKEN SOUP

SERVES 4–6

2 tablespoons (40 ml/1½ fl oz) melted ghee or vegetable oil

1 large onion, halved and sliced

3 cloves garlic, finely chopped

1 teaspoon finely grated ginger

10 fresh curry leaves

2 small dried red chillies

½ cinnamon stick

½ tablespoon ground cumin

½ tablespoon ground coriander

½ teaspoon ground turmeric

1 teaspoon freshly ground black pepper

4 skinless chicken thigh fillets, diced

2 medium-sized tomatoes, diced

½ cup basmati rice

4 cups (1 L/34 fl oz) chicken stock (page 27)

1 × 400-ml (13½-fl oz) can coconut milk

2 tablespoons (40 ml/1½ fl oz) freshly squeezed lemon juice

1 cup chopped coriander

salt

Heat the ghee or oil in a pressure cooker over medium heat. Add the onion, garlic and ginger, and cook until the onion is clear and softened. Add the curry leaves, chillies and remaining spices, and cook, stirring, for 30 seconds or until fragrant. Add the chicken, tomato and rice, and stir to coat. Pour in the stock, then lock the lid in place and bring to high pressure over high heat. Cook for 10 minutes, adjusting the heat as necessary to maintain a high pressure.

Release the pressure using the natural-release method.

Add the coconut milk and lemon juice to the soup and cook, uncovered, over low–medium heat for 3 minutes, or until warmed through. Stir in the coriander and season with salt before serving.

THAI RED CURRY, SWEET POTATO & ROAST CAPSICUM SOUP

SERVES 6

3 red capsicums
1 tablespoon (20 ml/¾ fl oz) vegetable oil
1 large onion, coarsely chopped
4 sweet potatoes, coarsely chopped
4 cups (1 L/34 fl oz) chicken stock (page 27) or vegetable stock (page 30)
1 × 400-ml (13½-fl oz) can coconut milk
2 tablespoons (40 ml/1½ fl oz) lime juice
2 tablespoons (40 ml/1½ fl oz) fish sauce
1 tablespoon (15 g/½ oz) coarsely grated palm sugar or soft brown sugar
finely sliced spring onions, for garnish

RED CURRY PASTE
2 teaspoons coriander seeds
1 teaspoon cumin seeds
½ teaspoon black peppercorns
1 teaspoon ground hot paprika
2 shallots, finely chopped
3 large red chillies, deseeded and chopped
3 cloves garlic, finely chopped
4-cm (1½-in) piece ginger, coarsely chopped
1 stem lemongrass, chopped
2 tablespoons (40 ml/1½ fl oz) vegetable oil

Preheat the griller to high. Place the capsicums on a baking tray and grill, turning occasionally, until the skins are blackened and blistered. Transfer to a bowl, cover with cling wrap and set aside to cool.

To make the curry paste, dry-fry the coriander and cumin seeds and the peppercorns in a small frying pan over low–medium heat for 1 minute, or until fragrant. Transfer to a mortar and pestle or spice grinder and grind to a fine powder. Add the paprika, shallots, chilli, garlic, ginger and lemongrass, and blend to a coarse paste. Add the oil and blend until combined.

For the soup, heat the oil in a pressure cooker over low–medium heat. Add the onion and cook until it is clear and softened. Add the curry paste and cook, stirring, for 30 seconds or until fragrant. Add the sweet potato and stir to combine. Pour in the stock, then lock the lid in place and bring to high pressure over high heat. Cook for 5 minutes, adjusting the heat as necessary to maintain a high pressure.

Release the pressure using the natural or quick-release method.

Peel and deseed the capsicums and coarsely chop the flesh. Add the capsicum to the soup and purée using a hand-held blender or food processor, until smooth.

Add the coconut milk, lime juice, fish sauce and sugar to the soup. Cook, uncovered, over low–medium heat for 3 minutes, or until warmed through.

Serve garnished with spring onions.

Soy sauce can be substituted for the fish sauce.

FRENCH ONION SOUP

SERVES 6

80 g (3 oz) butter
6 large onions, halved and thinly sliced
2 teaspoons soft brown sugar
1 tablespoon (15 g/½ oz) plain flour
5 cups (1.25 L/2 pt 10 fl oz) beef stock (page 28)
1 bay leaf
½ cup (125 ml/4 fl oz) dry white vermouth or dry white wine

2 tablespoons (40 ml/1½ fl oz) Cognac
salt and freshly ground black pepper
CHEESY CROUTES
½ large baguette, sliced into six rounds 1½-cm (⅝-in) thick
90 g (3 oz) coarsely grated gruyère cheese

Melt the butter in a pressure cooker over low–medium heat. Add the onion and sugar, and cook, stirring occasionally, for 20 minutes or until caramelised and golden brown. Sprinkle the flour over and cook, stirring with a wooden spoon, for 1 minute. Gradually add 2 cups (500 ml/17 fl oz) of the stock, stirring continuously until incorporated. Pour in the remaining stock, and add the bay leaf, vermouth and Cognac. Lock the lid in place and bring to high pressure over high heat. Cook for 10 minutes, adjusting the heat as necessary to maintain a high pressure.

Meanwhile, to make the cheesy croutes, preheat a griller to medium–high. Place the bread slices on a baking tray and grill for 1–2 minutes on each side, until crisp and golden. Sprinkle the cheese over the bread and grill for a further 2 minutes, or until the cheese is melted and golden brown.

Release the cooker's pressure using the natural or quick-release method.

To serve, top each bowl of soup with a cheesy croute.

THAI CHICKEN, COCONUT & GALANGAL SOUP

SERVES 4

2 × 400-ml (13½-fl oz) cans coconut milk
4 cups (1 L/34 fl oz) chicken stock (page 27) or vegetable stock (page 30)
4 skinless chicken thigh fillets
3 tablespoons (60 ml/2 fl oz) fish sauce
2 tablespoons (30 g/1 oz) coarsely grated palm sugar or soft brown sugar
3 shallots, coarsely chopped
3 stems lemongrass (white parts only), bruised

4-cm (1½-in) piece galangal or ginger, peeled and sliced
2 red bird's eye chillies, halved lengthways
3 coriander roots, coarsely chopped
2 cloves garlic, coarsely chopped
8 kaffir lime leaves
3 tablespoons (60 ml/2 fl oz) lime juice
coriander leaves, for garnish

Place the coconut milk in a pressure cooker over medium heat and bring to the boil. Decrease the heat and simmer for 3–4 minutes, until the milk splits. Add the remaining ingredients (except the lime juice and coriander leaves). Lock the lid in place and bring to high pressure over high heat. Decrease the heat to maintain a low pressure and cook for 5 minutes.

Release the pressure using the natural or quick-release method.

Remove the chicken from the pot and slice thinly.

Strain the soup through a fine mesh sieve, then return the soup to the pan. Return the galangal or ginger slices to the soup and discard the remaining solids.

Return the chicken to the pan and stir in the lime juice.

Serve garnished with coriander leaves.

AROMATIC CHINESE BROTH WITH PORK WONTONS

SERVES 4

60 g (2 oz) dried shiitake mushrooms
4 cups (1 L/34 fl oz) chicken stock (page 27)
2.5-cm (1-in) piece ginger, thinly sliced
2 red bird's eye chillies, deseeded and
thinly sliced
2 tablespoons (40 ml/1½ fl oz) soy sauce
1 tablespoon (20 ml/¾ fl oz) rice-wine vinegar
2 teaspoons sesame oil
2 star anise
1 teaspoon Sichuan peppercorns, wrapped in a
piece of muslin
1 bunch Chinese broccoli, coarsely chopped
2 spring onions, thinly sliced, for garnish

PORK WONTONS
250 g (9 oz) pork mince
3 spring onions (white parts only),
finely chopped
1 tablespoon (20 ml/¾ fl oz) soy sauce
1 tablespoon (20 ml/¾ fl oz) rice-wine vinegar
2 teaspoons finely grated ginger
1 clove garlic, crushed
1 teaspoon sesame oil
1 teaspoon cornflour, plus extra for dusting
24 wonton wrappers
1 egg white, lightly beaten

Soak the shiitake mushrooms in boiling water for 30 minutes, or until soft. Drain and slice thinly.

To make the pork wontons, place all ingredients (except the wrappers and egg white) in a small bowl and stir to combine. Spread the wonton wrappers on a clean kitchen surface. Place a heaped teaspoon of filling in the centre of each wrapper and brush the edges with egg white. Bring the corners of the wrappers together in the middle and pinch along the edges to secure, squeezing out the air as you go. (Your dumplings should have four ridges running from the centre to each corner.) Place the wontons on a tray that has been lightly dusted with cornflour, cover and refrigerate until required.

Place the shiitakes, stock and remaining ingredients (except the Chinese broccoli and spring onions) in a pressure cooker. Pour in 2 cups (500 ml/17 fl oz) water, then lock the lid in place and bring to high pressure over high heat. Cook for 5 minutes, adjusting the heat as necessary to maintain a high pressure.

Release the pressure using the natural or quick-release method.

Bring the stock back to the boil, uncovered. Add the wontons and cook, uncovered, over medium heat for 3 minutes, stirring gently to ensure even cooking. Add the broccoli and cook for a further 3 minutes or until the wontons are cooked through and the broccoli is tender.

Serve garnished with spring onions.

CHICKEN DUMPLING, RICE & LEMON SOUP

SERVES 6

5 cups (1.25 L/2 pt 10 fl oz) chicken stock (page 27)
½ cup arborio or other short-grain white rice
1 tablespoon (20 ml/¾ fl oz) olive oil
2 large eggs, lightly beaten
juice of 1 lemon
salt and freshly ground black pepper
coarsely chopped flat-leaf parsley, for garnish

CHICKEN DUMPLINGS
1 tablespoon (20 ml/¾ fl oz) vegetable oil
1 small onion, finely chopped
1 clove garlic, crushed
600 g (1 lb 5 oz) chicken mince
1 tablespoon finely chopped flat-leaf parsley
½ tablespoon chopped dill
salt and freshly ground black pepper

To make the dumplings, heat the oil in a small frying pan over low–medium heat, add the onion and garlic, and cook until clear and softened. Set aside to cool.

Combine the onion mixture, chicken mince and herbs in a bowl, and season with salt and pepper. Shape the mince into 24 equal-sized balls. Place balls on a tray, cover and refrigerate for 1 hour.

Place the stock, rice, oil and dumplings in a pressure cooker. Lock the lid in place and bring to high pressure over high heat. Decrease the heat to maintain a low pressure and cook for 5 minutes.

Release the pressure using the natural or quick-release method.

Combine the eggs and lemon juice in a medium-sized bowl. Gradually whisk 1 cup (250 ml/8½ fl oz) of the soup into the egg mixture, then stir this into the soup. Season with salt and pepper.

Serve immediately, garnished with parsley.

VEGETABLE SOUP WITH PESTO

SERVES 6–8

¾ cup dried cannellini beans
2 medium-sized tomatoes
5 cups (1.25 L/2 pt 10 fl oz) vegetable stock (page 30)
2 medium-sized potatoes, diced
2 medium-sized carrots, diced
1 medium-sized leek (white part only), halved lengthways and sliced
1 medium-sized zucchini, halved lengthways and sliced
200 g (7 oz) green beans, trimmed and cut into pieces

1 cup fresh or frozen peas
salt and freshly ground black pepper
PESTO
¼ cup pine nuts, lightly toasted
2 cloves garlic, coarsely chopped
¼ cup coarsely grated parmesan cheese
½ cup (125 ml/4 fl oz) extra-virgin olive oil
2 cups basil leaves
salt and freshly ground black pepper

Soak the cannellini beans in a large bowl of cold water for at least 4 hours (or overnight). Drain and rinse.

Score a cross in the base of each tomato, then blanch them in boiling water for 20 seconds. Drain and peel the tomatoes, then cut each in half horizontally and remove the seeds. Dice the flesh and set aside.

Place the cannellini beans, stock, potato, carrot, leek and tomato in a pressure cooker. Lock the lid in place and bring to high pressure over high heat. Cook for 25 minutes, adjusting the heat as necessary to maintain a high pressure.

Meanwhile, to make the pesto, place the pine nuts and garlic in a food processor and blend to a coarse paste. Add the cheese and half the oil and blend to combine. Add the basil leaves and pulse, scraping down the sides occasionally, until blended. Gradually add the remaining oil and blend to combine. Season with salt and pepper.

Release the cooker's pressure using the natural-release method.

Add the zucchini and green beans to the soup, and cook, uncovered, over medium heat for 2–3 minutes, until just tender. Add the peas and cook for a further 1–2 minutes, until tender. Season with salt and pepper.

Serve the soup with a dollop of pesto. (Any remaining pesto can be stored in an airtight container in the refrigerator for 4–5 days.)

MEXICAN BLACK BEAN SOUP

SERVES 4–6

1½ cups dried black turtle beans
3 tablespoons (60 ml/2 fl oz) olive oil
1 medium-sized onion, finely chopped
2 rashers smoked bacon, finely chopped
1 small leek (white part only), halved
lengthways and finely sliced
2 cloves garlic, finely chopped
2 chipotle chillies in adobo sauce,
finely chopped

2 teaspoons ground cumin
½ teaspoon ground chilli
1 bay leaf
4 cups (1 L/34 fl oz) beef stock (page 28)
or chicken stock (page 27)
2 tablespoons (40 ml/1½ fl oz) lime juice
salt and freshly ground black pepper
sour cream, to serve
coriander leaves, for garnish

Soak the beans in cold water for at least 4 hours (or overnight). Drain and rinse.

Heat the oil in a pressure cooker over low–medium heat. Add the onion, bacon, leek and garlic, and cook until the onion is clear and softened. Add the chipotle chilli and remaining spices, and cook for 30 seconds or until fragrant. Add the beans and bay leaf, and stir to combine. Pour in the stock, then lock the lid in place and bring to high pressure over high heat. Cook for 20 minutes, adjusting the heat as necessary to maintain a high pressure.

Release the pressure using the natural-release method.

Using a slotted spoon, transfer approximately half of the cooked beans to a food processor. Blend the beans, adding a little of the cooking liquid to make a smooth paste. Return the bean paste to the pot and stir to combine. Add the lime juice and season with salt and pepper.

Serve with a dollop of sour cream and a sprinkling of coriander.

SEAFOOD LAKSA

SERVES 6

2 tablespoons (40 ml/1½ fl oz) peanut or vegetable oil
2 × 400-ml (13½-fl oz) cans coconut milk
4 kaffir lime leaves
1½ cups (375 ml) fish stock (page 29)
2 tablespoons (40 ml/1½ fl oz) fish sauce
2 tablespoons (40 ml/1½ fl oz) lime juice
1 teaspoon coarsely grated palm sugar
400 g (14 oz) hokkien noodles
350 g (12 oz) skinless firm white fish fillets, cut into 4-cm (1½-in) chunks
12 raw (green) prawns, shelled and deveined but tails left on
6 cubes fried tofu, halved
100 g (3½ oz) bean shoots

¼ cup coriander leaves, for garnish
¼ cup Vietnamese mint leaves, for garnish
sambal ulek, to serve

LAKSA PASTE

2 shallots, coarsely chopped
4 cloves garlic, coarsely chopped
60 g (2 oz) candlenuts, coarsely chopped
2 stems lemongrass (white parts only), coarsely chopped
4 dried red bird's eye chillies, coarsely chopped
2 coriander roots, coarsely chopped
1 tablespoon coarsely grated ginger
1 tablespoon dried shrimp
1 teaspoon ground turmeric

To make the laksa paste, place all the ingredients in a large mortar and pestle or small food processor and blend to a paste.

Heat the oil in a pressure cooker over low–medium heat. Cook the laksa paste for 30 seconds or until fragrant. Add the coconut milk and lime leaves, and bring to the boil. Decrease the heat and simmer for 3–4 minutes, until the milk splits. Pour in the stock, then lock the lid in place and bring to high pressure over high heat. Cook for 5 minutes, adjusting the heat as necessary to maintain a high pressure.

Release the pressure using the quick-release method.

Add the fish sauce, lime juice and palm sugar to the pot, stir to combine, then simmer, uncovered, for 5 minutes. Add the noodles, fish, prawns and tofu, and simmer for a further 3–5 minutes, until the noodles are cooked, the fish turns white and the prawns are pink.

Divide the noodles between four deep serving bowls and scatter with bean shoots. Ladle the broth over the top, distributing the fish, prawns and tofu evenly. Garnish with fresh herbs and serve with sambal ulek.

POULTRY & RABBIT

Chicken, duck and rabbit are so versatile. They are easily prepared using various cooking techniques and they embrace flavours, whether strong spices or more subtle aromatics, with ease.

Cooked in a pressure cooker, chicken remains succulent, moist and tender. It can be braised, stewed, poached and even steamed. Use thigh meat and marylands in braises and stews, as they are more flavoursome and provide a better result when cooked under pressure. Use the more delicate breast meat for steaming. In this chapter you will find recipes for cooking a whole chicken, perhaps stuffed with spiced rice or a tangy couscous, in just 20 minutes! There is a creamy chicken korma (page 64), a rich and warming Mexican chicken mole (page 67), as well as a few familiar favourites such as coq au vin (page 65) and chicken cacciatore (page 69).

There are also recipes for duck and rabbit. Duck is a wonderful game meat that can carry robust flavours, such as those in the duck ragu (page 77) and duck leg coconut curry (page 78). Rabbit can be purchased from select butchers and food markets. It is an inexpensive, lean meat that takes particularly well to pressure cooking. Rabbit can be easily substituted for chicken in many recipes, such as the Spanish-style chicken with lentils (page 70), and the sweet and sticky chicken with onions, sherry and raisins (page 71).

SELECTING CHICKEN AND RABBIT

CHICKEN

Nowadays chicken may be labelled as free-range, organic, chemical free, hormone free or corn fed. But what does it all mean?

Factory-farmed

Most chicken in Australia comes from factory-farmed birds. These chickens live in large, crowded sheds under artificial lights. Birds are de-beaked and often have their toes trimmed, to prevent pecking and scratching. Factory-farmed chickens are routinely treated with antibiotics.

Free-range

Any company can label their chicken 'free range', so it's important to look for certification to ensure what you're buying really is free range. Certified free-range chickens are housed in large sheds until the age of 21 days, after which they have access to an outside area. They have slightly more space than factory-farmed chickens. Birds are not de-beaked, do not have their toes trimmed, and are not given antibiotics.

Organic

Certified organic chickens are allowed outside from the age of 10 days, and have twice the space of free-range chickens. Artificial light is not permitted, and the birds' life span is longer than that of factory-farmed or free-range chickens. Birds are not de-beaked, do not have their toes trimmed, and are not given antibiotics. Their feed must be 95% organic. Unlike the factory-farmed and free-range industries, the certification process is independently regulated.

Chemical Free

These chickens have not been sanitised in chlorine-treated water after slaughtering, as is done with most factory-farmed and some free-range chicken.

Hormone Free

All chicken produced in Australia is hormone free – the use of hormones has been banned since the 1960s.

Corn Fed

These chickens are raised using factory-farming methods, but are fed a high level of corn, which gives their flesh a yellow tinge and slightly different flavour.

RABBIT

Wild rabbit meat is tougher than farmed rabbit, as the animals have a higher muscle mass. It is a darker meat and has a stronger game flavour. Both wild and farmed rabbits are suitable for pressure cooking; however, a slightly longer cooking time is required for wild rabbit.

CORIANDER CHICKEN STUFFED WITH PRESERVED LEMON & GREEN OLIVE COUSCOUS

SERVES 4

1 × 1.5-kg (3 lb 5-oz) chicken
3 tablespoons (60 g/2 oz) softened butter
¼ cup finely chopped coriander
1 clove garlic, crushed
salt and freshly ground black pepper
tomato salad or green salad, to serve
COUSCOUS STUFFING
200 g (7 oz) couscous
1 cup (250 ml/8½ fl oz) chicken stock
(page 27), hot
1 tablespoon (20 g/¾ oz) butter

½ small red onion, sliced
1 clove garlic, finely chopped
½ teaspoon ground ginger
½ teaspoon ground cumin
¼ teaspoon ground turmeric
½ preserved lemon, pulp discarded
and skin finely sliced
¼ cup pitted green olives, finely sliced
1 tablespoon finely chopped coriander
salt and freshly ground black pepper

To make the couscous stuffing, place the couscous in a large bowl and pour the hot stock over. Stir with a fork, cover the bowl with cling wrap and set aside for 10 minutes.

Meanwhile, heat the butter in a medium-sized frying pan over low–medium heat. Cook the onion and garlic until the onion is clear and softened. Add the spices, preserved lemon and olives, and stir to combine.

Fluff the couscous with a fork, then stir through the spiced onion mixture and coriander. Season with salt and pepper, and set aside.

Preheat the oven to 200°C (390°F). Wash the chicken, including the cavity, under cold running water. Drain, and pat dry with paper towel.

Combine the butter, coriander and garlic in a small bowl and season with salt and pepper. Smear the coriander butter under the skin of the chicken, taking care not to tear the skin.

Stuff the chicken with the prepared couscous and truss the legs together using kitchen string.

Place the trivet in the pressure cooker and pour in 1 cup (250 ml/8½ fl oz) water. Place the chicken on top of the trivet, lock the lid in place and bring to high pressure over high heat. Cook for 20 minutes, adjusting the heat as necessary to maintain a high pressure.

Release the pressure using the natural-release method.

Transfer the chicken to a baking dish and roast in the oven for 10 minutes or until golden brown. Test whether the chicken is cooked by piercing the thickest part of the chicken thigh: if the juice that runs out is clear, it is cooked; if not, return to the oven and cook for a further 5 minutes.

Carve the chicken and serve with the stuffing and salad.

CHICKEN STUFFED WITH SPICED WALNUT & CURRANT RICE

SERVES 4

1 × 1.5-kg (3 lb 5-oz) chicken
1 tablespoon (20 g/¾ oz) butter
1 tablespoon (20 ml/¾ fl oz) olive oil
salt and freshly ground black pepper
steamed green beans, to serve

RICE STUFFING
1 tablespoon (20 g/¾ oz) butter
½ small onion, finely chopped
1 clove garlic, finely chopped
½ teaspoon ground sweet paprika
½ teaspoon ground coriander

¼ teaspoon ground cumin
¼ teaspoon ground cinnamon
¼ teaspoon ground cardamom
¼ teaspoon freshly ground black pepper
½ cup long-grain white rice, rinsed
¾ cup (180 ml/6 fl oz) chicken stock (page 27)
½ cup walnuts, lightly toasted and coarsely chopped
¼ cup currants
1 tablespoon finely chopped flat-leaf parsley
salt

To make the rice stuffing, melt the butter in a pressure cooker over low–medium heat. Cook the onion, garlic and spices until the onion has softened and the spices are fragrant. Add the rice and stir to coat. Pour in the stock, then lock the lid in place and bring to high pressure over high heat. Cook for 3 minutes, adjusting the heat as necessary to maintain a high pressure.

Release the pressure using the quick-release method.

Spread the rice out on a tray and fluff using a fork, then stir in the walnuts, currants and parsley. Season with salt and set aside.

Remove the skin from the chicken. Wash the chicken, including the cavity, under cold running water. Drain and pat dry with paper towel.

Heat the butter and oil in the pressure cooker over medium–high heat. Season the chicken with salt and pepper, and cook, breast side down first, until golden brown all over. Remove the chicken from the cooker and stuff with the prepared rice. Truss the legs together using kitchen string.

Rinse out the pressure cooker, then insert the trivet and pour in 1 cup (250 ml/8½ fl oz) water. Place the chicken on top of the trivet, lock the lid in place and bring to high pressure over high heat. Cook for 25 minutes, adjusting the heat as necessary to maintain a high pressure.

Release the pressure using the natural-release method.

Test whether the chicken is cooked by piercing the thickest part of the thigh: if the juice that runs out is clear, it is cooked; if not, lock the lid in place, bring back up to high pressure and cook for a further 5 minutes.

Carve the chicken and serve with the stuffing and steamed green beans.

CHICKEN KORMA

SERVES 6

½ cup cashew nuts

⅓ cup (80 ml/3 fl oz) melted ghee or vegetable oil

2 large onions, finely chopped

4 cloves garlic, crushed

1 tablespoon finely grated ginger

5 cardamom pods, bruised

1 cinnamon stick

4 cloves

2 teaspoons ground coriander

1 teaspoon ground cumin

½ teaspoon ground chilli

½ teaspoon ground turmeric

6 skinless chicken thigh fillets, halved

½ cup (125 ml/4 fl oz) natural yoghurt

½ cup (125 ml/4 fl oz) coconut milk

salt

naan bread or steamed basmati rice, to serve

Place the cashews in a small bowl and pour in enough boiling water to just cover. Set aside to soak for 15 minutes. Drain the nuts, reserving the liquid. Place the cashews in a food processor and blend, gradually adding a little of the reserved liquid to make a smooth paste.

Heat half the ghee or oil in a pressure cooker over medium heat and sauté the onion until golden. Add the garlic and ginger, and cook for 2 minutes or until golden brown. Transfer to a bowl.

Heat the remaining ghee or oil in the pressure cooker over medium heat and fry the cardamom, cinnamon and cloves for 30 seconds, or until fragrant. Add the remaining spices and chicken pieces, and cook for 2–3 minutes, until golden brown. Add ⅓ cup (80 ml/3 fl oz) water and bring to the boil. Stir in the cashew paste, yoghurt and coconut milk. Lock the lid in place and bring to high pressure over high heat. Cook for 10 minutes, adjusting the heat as necessary to maintain a high pressure.

Release the pressure using the quick-release method.

Remove the chicken pieces from the pot and place in a baking dish. Cover and keep warm.

Simmer the sauce, uncovered, over medium heat for a further 5–10 minutes, until thickened. Return the chicken to the pot and heat through. Season with salt.

Serve with naan bread or rice.

COQ AU VIN

SERVES 4–6

2 tablespoons (40 ml/1½ fl oz) olive oil

1 × 1.5-kg (3 lb 5-oz) chicken, skin removed, cut into 10 pieces

salt and freshly ground black pepper

4 rashers bacon, cut into thin strips

400 g (14 oz) small pickling onions, peeled

250 g (9 oz) baby button mushrooms, stalks removed

1 stick celery, finely sliced

2 cloves garlic, crushed

6 sprigs thyme

2 bay leaves

2 tablespoons (40 ml/1½ fl oz) Cognac

1½ cups (375 ml/12½ fl oz) red wine

½ cup (125 ml/4 fl oz) chicken stock (page 27)

1 tablespoon (20 g/¾ oz) softened butter

1 tablespoon (15 g/½ oz) plain flour

mashed potato (page 179), to serve

Heat the oil in a pressure cooker over medium heat. Season the chicken with salt and pepper, and cook, in batches, for 4–5 minutes, until browned all over. Transfer to a plate and set aside.

Add the bacon, onions and mushrooms to the pot and sauté over low–medium heat until golden brown. Add the celery, garlic and herbs, and cook for 1 minute or until garlic has softened. Pour in the Cognac and bring to the boil. Pour in the wine and stock, and return the chicken to the pot. Lock the lid in place and bring to high pressure over high heat. Cook for 10 minutes, adjusting the heat as necessary to maintain a high pressure.

Release the pressure using the quick-release method.

Remove the chicken from the pot and place in a baking dish. Cover and keep warm.

Combine the butter and flour in a small bowl. Stir in 2 tablespoons (40 ml/1½ fl oz) of the cooking liquid to make a smooth paste. Pour the paste into the sauce and cook over medium heat, stirring constantly, for 3–5 minutes, until the sauce thickens and the raw flour taste is gone.

Return the chicken to the pot and heat through. Season with salt and pepper.

Serve with mashed potato.

CHINESE RED CHICKEN

SERVES 4

1 × 1.5-kg (3 lb 5-oz) chicken
about 6 cups (1.5 L/3 pt 3 fl oz) chicken stock
(page 27)
steamed long-grain white rice and Asian
vegetables, to serve
RED BRAISING STOCK
¾ cup (180 ml/6 fl oz) Shaoxing rice wine
or dry sherry
¾ cup (180 ml/6 fl oz) dark soy sauce
½ cup (125 ml/4 fl oz) light soy sauce

½ cup (110 g/4 oz) firmly packed
soft brown sugar
2 cloves garlic, bruised
4-cm (1½-in) piece ginger, sliced
3 spring onions, ends trimmed
2 small dried red chillies
2 star anise
1 cinnamon stick
3 strips orange zest

To make the red braising stock, combine all the ingredients in a pressure cooker. Add the chicken and pour in enough chicken stock to cover. Lock the lid in place and bring to high pressure over high heat. Cook for 20 minutes, adjusting the heat as necessary to maintain a high pressure.

Release the pressure using the natural-release method. Remove the lid and leave the chicken to cool in the stock for 2 hours to allow the flavours to fully develop.

Remove the chicken from the pot, draining off any excess liquid. Cut the chicken in half lengthways along the breastbone, remove each thigh and leg and cut in half. Remove the wings, then slice the remaining flesh into thick strips.

Serve with steamed rice and Asian vegetables.

Red braising stock can be used numerous times. Simply strain the stock through a large colander lined with a piece of muslin and store in an airtight container in the freezer. Defrost and bring back to the boil to use again, topping up with extra flavouring ingredients and stock as required.

CHICKEN MOLE

SERVES 6

1 large onion, coarsely chopped
3 cloves garlic, coarsely chopped
1 teaspoon dried oregano
½ teaspoon ground chilli
1 teaspoon ground cinnamon
½ teaspoon ground cumin
¼ teaspoon ground cloves
⅓ cup (80 ml/3 fl oz) olive oil
1 × 400-g (14-oz) can chopped tomatoes

3 chipotle chillies in adobo sauce,
  finely chopped
6 skinless chicken thigh fillets, halved
30 g (1 oz) Mexican or unsweetened dark
  chocolate, coarsely chopped
1 cup (250 ml/8½ fl oz) chicken stock (page 27)
salt
flour tortillas or steamed long-grain white rice,
  to serve

Place the onion, garlic, oregano and spices in a small food processor and blend to a coarse paste. Add half the oil and blend until smooth. Transfer to a small bowl and set aside.

Place the tomatoes and chilli in a food processor and blend to combine. Transfer to a small bowl and set aside.

Heat the remaining oil in a pressure cooker over medium–high heat. Cook the chicken pieces for 2 minutes on each side, or until browned. Transfer to a plate.

Sauté the spiced onion mixture in the cooker over low–medium heat until golden brown. Add the tomato purée and chocolate, and stir to combine. Pour in the stock and return the chicken to the pan, stirring to coat. Lock the lid in place and bring to high pressure over high heat. Cook for 10 minutes, adjusting the heat as necessary to maintain a high pressure.

Release the pressure using the natural or quick-release method.

Transfer the chicken to a plate, cover to keep warm and set aside.

Simmer the sauce, uncovered, over medium heat for a further 5–10 minutes, until thickened. Return the chicken to the pot and heat through. Season with salt.

Serve with flour tortillas or rice.

CHICKEN WITH PANCETTA, FENNEL & OLIVES

SERVES 4

2 tablespoons (40 ml/1½ fl oz) olive oil
6 skinless chicken thighs
salt and freshly ground black pepper
1 medium-sized onion, sliced
150 g (5 oz) pancetta, thinly sliced
2 cloves garlic, crushed
½ cup (125 ml/4 fl oz) dry white wine
2 medium-sized fennel bulbs, trimmed and thickly sliced lengthways
¾ cup kalamata olives
2 bay leaves

1½ cups (375 ml/12½ fl oz) chicken stock (page 27)
rocket and tomato salad, to serve

HERBED BREADCRUMBS

2 cups coarsely chopped fresh breadcrumbs
a few fennel fronds, chopped
2 tablespoons coarsely chopped flat-leaf parsley
2 teaspoons finely grated lemon zest
1 clove garlic, crushed
2 tablespoons (40 ml/1½ fl oz) extra-virgin olive oil
salt and freshly ground black pepper

Preheat the oven to 200°C (390°F).

To make the herbed crumbs, combine all the ingredients in a small baking dish. Bake for 10–15 minutes, stirring occasionally, until crisp and golden brown.

Heat the oil in a pressure cooker over medium heat. Season the chicken with salt and pepper, and cook for 2–3 minutes on each side, until browned. Transfer to a plate and set aside.

Add the onion, pancetta and garlic to the pot and sauté over low–medium heat until golden brown. Pour in the wine and bring to the boil. Return the chicken to the pot. Add the fennel, olives, bay leaves and stock, then lock the lid in place and bring to high pressure over high heat. Cook for 10 minutes, adjusting the heat as necessary to maintain a high pressure.

Release the pressure using the quick-release method. Remove the chicken from the pot and place in a baking dish. Cover and keep warm. Simmer the sauce, uncovered, over medium heat for 5 minutes or until thickened slightly. Return the chicken to the pot and heat through. Season with salt and pepper. Sprinkle with the breadcrumbs and serve with salad.

CHICKEN CACCIATORE

SERVES 4

3 tablespoons (60 ml/2 fl oz) olive oil
4 chicken marylands
salt and freshly ground black pepper
250 g (9 oz) button mushrooms, sliced
1 medium-sized onion, diced
1 stick celery, finely chopped
2 cloves garlic, crushed
⅓ cup (80 ml/3 fl oz) dry white wine

½ cup (125 ml/4 fl oz) chicken stock (page 27)
1 × 800-g (1 lb 12-oz) can chopped tomatoes
1 teaspoon caster sugar
1 sprig rosemary
2 bay leaves
2 tablespoons finely chopped oregano,
  for garnish
mashed potato (page 179), to serve

Heat half the oil in a pressure cooker over medium heat. Season the chicken with salt and pepper, and cook, in batches, for 3–4 minutes on each side, until browned all over. Transfer to a plate and set aside.

Add the remaining oil to the pot, decrease the heat to low–medium and sauté the mushrooms, onion, celery and garlic until golden brown. Pour in the wine and bring to the boil. Add the stock, tomatoes, sugar, rosemary and bay leaves, and stir to combine. Return the chicken to the pot, lock the lid in place and bring to high pressure over high heat. Cook for 10 minutes, adjusting the heat as necessary to maintain a high pressure.

Release the pressure using the quick-release method.

Remove the chicken from the pot and place in a baking dish. Cover and keep warm.

Simmer the sauce, uncovered, over medium heat for 5 minutes, or until thickened. Return the chicken to the pot and heat through. Season with salt and pepper.

Sprinkle with oregano and serve with mashed potato.

SPANISH-STYLE CHICKEN WITH LENTILS

SERVES 4–6

3 tablespoons (60 ml/2 fl oz) olive oil
1 × 1.5-kg (3 lb 5-oz) chicken, skin removed, cut into 10 pieces
salt and freshly ground black pepper
2 medium-sized onions, halved and thickly sliced
2 cloves garlic, crushed
1 chorizo sausage, thinly sliced
3 red capsicums, sliced lengthways
4 medium-sized tomatoes, cut into wedges

½ cup dried brown lentils, rinsed
2 tablespoons sweet paprika
2 bay leaves
pinch of saffron threads
½ cup (125 ml/4 fl oz) dry white wine
1½ cups (375 ml/12½ fl oz) chicken stock (page 27)
½ cup coarsely chopped flat-leaf parsley
crusty bread, to serve

Heat half the oil in a pressure cooker over medium heat. Season the chicken with salt and pepper, and cook, in batches, for 4–5 minutes, until browned all over. Transfer to a plate and set aside.

Add the remaining oil to the pot, decrease the heat to low–medium and cook the onion and garlic until the onion is clear and softened. Add the chorizo and capsicum, and cook for 3–4 minutes, until golden brown. Stir in the tomatoes, lentils, paprika, bay leaves and saffron. Pour in the wine and bring to the boil, then pour in the stock and return the chicken to the pot. Lock the lid in place and bring to high pressure over high heat. Cook for 10 minutes, adjusting the heat as necessary to maintain a high pressure.

Release the pressure using the natural-release method.

Remove the chicken from the pot and place in a baking dish. Cover and keep warm.

Simmer the sauce, uncovered, over medium heat for 5 minutes or until thickened slightly. Return the chicken to the pot and heat through. Stir in the parsley and season with salt and pepper.

Serve with crusty bread.

SWEET & STICKY CHICKEN WITH ONIONS, SHERRY & RAISINS

SERVES 4

2 tablespoons (40 ml/1½ fl oz) olive oil
6 skinless chicken thigh fillets
salt and freshly ground black pepper
2 tablespoons (40 g/1½ oz) butter
2 large onions, halved and sliced
2 cloves garlic, crushed
4 sprigs thyme
2 bay leaves

½ cup raisins
3 tablespoons (60 ml/2 fl oz) red wine
½ cup (125 ml/4 fl oz) sweet Spanish sherry
1½ cups (375 ml/12½ fl oz) chicken stock (page 27)
1 tablespoon (20 ml/¾ fl oz) red-wine vinegar
mashed potato (page 179), to serve

Heat the oil in a pressure cooker over medium heat. Season the chicken with salt and pepper, and cook for 2–3 minutes on each side, until browned. Transfer to a plate and set aside.

Add the butter to the pot and sauté the onion, garlic, thyme and bay leaves over low–medium heat for 15 minutes, or until golden brown. Stir in the raisins, pour in the wine and bring to the boil. Add the sherry and boil until the liquid has reduced by half. Return the chicken to the pot and stir to coat. Pour in the stock and vinegar, lock the lid in place and bring to high pressure over high heat. Cook for 10 minutes, adjusting the heat as necessary to maintain a high pressure.

Release the pressure using the quick-release method.

Remove the chicken from the pot and place in a baking dish. Cover and keep warm.

Simmer the sauce, uncovered, over medium heat for 5 minutes, or until thickened slightly. Return the chicken to the pot and heat through. Season with salt and pepper.

Serve with mashed potato.

FRAGRANT FIVE-SPICE CHICKEN WITH FAT RICE NOODLES

SERVES 4

4 cups (1 L/34 fl oz) chicken stock (page 27)
3 tablespoons (60 ml/2 fl oz) light soy sauce
3 tablespoons (60 ml/2 fl oz) Shaoxing rice wine
or dry sherry
1 tablespoon (15 g/½ oz) soft brown sugar
2 cloves garlic, thinly sliced
4-cm (1½-in) piece ginger, sliced
3 spring onions, cut into 5-cm (2-in) lengths
1 large red chilli, deseeded and thinly
sliced into strips

1 teaspoon Sichuan peppercorns
1 teaspoon fennel seeds
1 teaspoon sesame oil
1 cinnamon stick
1 star anise
5 cloves
4 skinless chicken breast fillets
450 g (1 lb) fresh fat rice noodles
2 bunches baby bok choy, halved lengthways
fried shallots, to serve

Combine all the ingredients (except the chicken, noodles and bok choy) in a pressure cooker. Add the chicken breasts, then lock the lid in place and bring to low pressure over medium heat. Cook for 10 minutes, adjusting the heat as necessary to maintain a low pressure.

Release the pressure using the natural-release method.

Remove the chicken from the pot and set aside. Add the noodles and bok choy to the stock and cook, uncovered, over medium heat for 2–3 minutes, until tender.

Slice the chicken crossways into thick strips. Divide the noodles, bok choy and chicken evenly between shallow serving bowls, garnish with spring onion pieces from the poaching liquid and sprinkle with fried shallots.

Reserve the poaching liquid and use at a later date as the base for a soup such as the aromatic Chinese broth with wontons (page 50).

CHICKEN WITH POMEGRANATE & ALMOND SAUCE

SERVES 4

2 tablespoons (40 ml/1½ fl oz) olive oil
4 chicken marylands, skin removed
salt and freshly ground black pepper
1 tablespoon (20 g/¾ oz) butter
1 medium-sized onion, finely chopped
1 cinnamon stick
½ teaspoon ground cardamom
½ teaspoon ground cumin

3 tablespoons honey
2 tablespoons (40 ml/1½ fl oz) pomegranate
  molasses
1 cup (250 ml/8½ fl oz) pomegranate juice
½ cup (125 ml/4 fl oz) chicken stock (page 27)
½ cup (80 g/3 oz) almond meal
couscous, to serve
¼ cup flaked almonds, lightly toasted

Heat the oil in a pressure cooker over medium heat. Season the chicken with salt and pepper, and cook, in batches, for 3–4 minutes on each side until browned all over. Transfer to a plate and set aside.

Add the butter to the pot and sauté the onion and spices over low–medium heat until the onion has softened and the spices are fragrant. Add the honey and pomegranate molasses, and stir to combine. Pour in the pomegranate juice and chicken stock. Return the chicken to the pot, lock the lid in place and bring to high pressure over high heat. Cook for 10 minutes, adjusting the heat as necessary to maintain a high pressure.

Release the pressure using the quick-release method.

Remove the chicken from the pot and place in a baking dish. Cover and keep warm.

Combine the almond meal and ⅓ cup (80 ml/3 fl oz) of the cooking liquid in a small bowl, stirring to make a smooth paste. Add the paste to the pot and cook the sauce over medium heat, uncovered and stirring continuously, for 5 minutes or until thickened. Return the chicken to the pot and heat through. Season with salt and pepper.

Serve with couscous, sprinkled with toasted almonds.

MEXICAN SPICED CHICKEN LASAGNE

SERVES 4–6

1 × 375-g (13-oz) packet dried lasagne sheets
45 g (1½ oz) coarsely grated cheddar cheese
paprika, for sprinkling
garden salad, to serve

CHICKEN FILLING

1 × 1.5-kg (3 lb 5-oz) chicken
3 red capsicums, coarsely chopped
2 large onions, halved and thickly sliced
4 medium-sized tomatoes, cut into wedges
⅓ cup (80 ml/3 fl oz) chicken stock (page 27)
4 cloves garlic, finely sliced
3 red bird's eye chillies, deseeded and finely sliced
1 tablespoon hot paprika
1 tablespoon finely chopped oregano

1 teaspoon onion powder
1 teaspoon garlic powder
½ teaspoon ground chilli
1 bay leaf
1 × 400-g (14-oz) can kidney beans, drained and rinsed
2 tablespoons tomato paste
1 cup coarsely chopped coriander

BÉCHAMEL SAUCE

2½ tablespoons (50 g/1¾ oz) butter
⅓ cup (50 g/1½ oz) plain flour
3½ cups (875 ml/30 fl oz) milk, hot
45 g (1½ oz) coarsely grated cheddar cheese
½ teaspoon freshly grated or ground nutmeg
salt and ground white pepper

To make the chicken filling, place all the ingredients (except the kidney beans, tomato paste and coriander) in a pressure cooker. Lock the lid in place and bring to high pressure over high heat. Cook for 25 minutes, adjusting the heat as necessary to maintain a high pressure.

Release the pressure using the natural or quick-release method.

Test whether the chicken is cooked by piercing the thickest part of the thigh: if the juice that runs out is clear, it is cooked; if not, lock the lid in place, bring back up to high pressure and cook for a further 5 minutes.

Remove the chicken from the pot and coarsely shred the flesh, discarding the skin and bones.

Return the shredded chicken to the pot. Add the beans and tomato paste, and stir to combine. Simmer gently, uncovered, over medium heat for 5–10 minutes, until the liquid has reduced to make a thick and chunky sauce. Remove the bay leaf, stir in the coriander and set aside.

Preheat the oven to 180°C (355°F). Lightly grease a deep 23-cm × 35-cm (9-in × 14-in) ovenproof dish.

To make the béchamel sauce, melt the butter in a medium-sized saucepan over low heat. Add the flour and cook, stirring, for 2 minutes or until the flour becomes white. Gradually whisk in the hot milk. Cook, stirring continuously with a wooden spoon, over low–medium heat for 10–15 minutes, until thick and the raw flour taste is gone. Stir in the cheese and season with nutmeg and salt and pepper. Cover with a piece of baking paper to prevent a skin from forming and set aside.

Spread a layer of chicken filling in the prepared dish, then cover with a layer of lasagne sheets. Repeat twice more to create three layers. Spread béchamel sauce over the top and scatter with the grated cheese. Sprinkle with paprika.

Cover the tray with aluminium foil and bake in the oven for 30 minutes. Remove the foil and cook for a further 15 minutes, or until the pasta is tender and the top is golden brown.

Serve with a garden salad.

CHICKEN COOKED IN YOGHURT

SERVES 4

3 tablespoons (60 ml/2 fl oz) olive oil
4 skinless chicken breast fillets
salt and freshly ground black pepper
1 large onion, halved and thinly sliced
3 cloves garlic, crushed
1 teaspoon cumin seeds
½ teaspoon ground cumin

½ teaspoon ground cinnamon
1½ cups (375 ml/12½ oz) natural yoghurt
90 g (3 oz) baby spinach
¼ cup finely chopped mint
2 tablespoons (40 ml/1½ fl oz) freshly squeezed lemon juice
couscous, to serve

Heat half the oil in a pressure cooker over medium–high heat. Season the chicken with salt and pepper, and cook for 2–3 minutes on each side, until golden brown. Transfer to a plate and set aside.

Heat the remaining oil in the pot and sauté the onion and garlic over low–medium heat until clear and softened. Add the spices and cook for 30 seconds or until fragrant. Add the yoghurt and ½ cup (125 ml/ 4 fl oz) water, and stir to combine. Return the chicken to the pot, lock the lid in place and bring to low pressure over medium heat. Cook for 10 minutes, adjusting the heat as necessary to maintain a low pressure.

Release the pressure using the natural-release method.

Add the spinach, mint and lemon juice to the sauce and stir until the spinach wilts. Season with salt and pepper.

Serve with couscous.

DUCK RAGU

SERVES 6

2 tablespoons (40 ml/1½ fl oz) olive oil
3 duck marylands
salt and freshly ground black pepper
1 large onion, halved and thinly sliced
2 cloves garlic, finely chopped
150 g (5 oz) pancetta, finely chopped
1 medium-sized carrot, finely diced
1 stick celery, finely chopped

2 tablespoons finely chopped oregano
4 sprigs thyme
2 bay leaves
1 cup (250 ml/8½ fl oz) dry white wine
1 × 400-g (14-oz) can whole peeled tomatoes
⅓ cup (80 ml/3 fl oz) cream
potato gnocchi, to serve
shaved parmesan cheese, to serve

Heat half the oil in a pressure cooker over medium heat. Season the duck marylands with salt and pepper, and cook for 3–4 minutes on each side, until golden brown. Transfer to a plate and set aside.

Heat the remaining oil in the pot and sauté the onion and garlic over low–medium heat, until clear and softened. Add the pancetta, carrot, celery and herbs, and cook until golden brown. Pour in the wine and bring to the boil. Return the duck to the pot and add the tomatoes. Lock the lid in place and bring to high pressure over high heat. Cook for 25 minutes, adjusting the heat as necessary to maintain a high pressure.

Release the pressure using the natural-release method.

Remove the duck from the pot and set aside to cool slightly.

Add the cream to the pot and simmer, uncovered, over medium heat for 5–10 minutes, until thickened to a sauce consistency.

Coarsely shred the duck, discarding the skin and bones. Return the meat to the sauce and stir to combine. Discard the bay leaves and thyme stems, and season with salt and pepper.

Serve over gnocchi, scattered with parmesan cheese.

DUCK-LEG COCONUT CURRY

SERVES 4

1 tablespoon (20 ml/¾ fl oz) vegetable oil
4 duck marylands, cut in half
salt
1 × 400-ml (13½-fl oz) can coconut milk
3 kaffir lime leaves
½ cup (125 ml/ 4 fl oz) chicken stock (page 27)
½ cup coarsely chopped coriander
steamed jasmine rice, to serve
lime wedges, to serve

CURRY PASTE

4 shallots, coarsely chopped
6 cloves garlic, coarsely chopped
3 large red chillies, deseeded and
  coarsely chopped
4-cm (1½-in) piece ginger, coarsely chopped
1 stem lemongrass, coarsely chopped
1 teaspoon ground turmeric
2 tablespoons (40 ml/1½ fl oz) vegetable oil

To make the curry paste, place the shallots, garlic, chilli, ginger and lemongrass in a food processor and blend to a coarse paste. Add the turmeric and oil, and continue blending to make a smooth paste. Transfer to a small bowl and set aside.

For the curry, heat the oil in a pressure cooker over medium heat. Season the duck marylands with salt and cook for 3–4 minutes on each side, until golden brown. Transfer to a plate and set aside.

Add the curry paste to the pot and cook over low–medium heat until softened and fragrant. Pour in the coconut milk and bring to the boil. Decrease the heat and simmer for 3–4 minutes, until the milk splits. Return the duck to the pot and add the lime leaves. Pour in the stock, then lock the lid in place and bring to high pressure over high heat. Cook for 10 minutes, adjusting the heat as necessary to maintain a high pressure.

Release the pressure using the natural-release method.

Remove the duck from the pot and place in a baking dish. Cover and keep warm.

Simmer the sauce, uncovered, over medium heat for 5–10 minutes, until thickened slightly. Return the duck to the pot and heat through. Stir in the coriander and season with salt.

Serve with steamed rice and lime wedges.

RABBIT WITH ORANGE, JUNIPER & THYME

SERVES 4

3 tablespoons (60 ml/2 fl oz) olive oil
1 × 1.5-kg (3 lb 5-oz) farmed rabbit, jointed
(ask your butcher to do this for you)
salt and freshly ground black pepper
1 large onion, diced
2 cloves garlic, finely chopped
2 sticks celery, sliced
1 medium-sized carrot, sliced into rounds
½ cup (125 ml/4 fl oz) dry white wine

1½ cups (375 ml/12½ fl oz) chicken stock
(page 27)
juice and peeled zest of 1 orange
5 juniper berries, crushed
2 bay leaves
4 sprigs thyme
1 tablespoon (20 g/¾ oz) butter
1 tablespoon (15 g/½ oz) plain flour
mashed potato (page 179), to serve

Heat half the oil in a pressure cooker over medium heat. Season the rabbit with salt and pepper, and cook, in batches, for 4–5 minutes until browned all over. Transfer to a plate and set aside.

Add the remaining oil to the pot, decrease the heat to low–medium and cook the onion and garlic until the onion is clear and softened. Add the celery and carrot, and cook for a further 3–4 minutes, until softened and golden. Pour in the wine and bring to the boil. Add the stock, orange juice and zest, and herbs. Return the rabbit to the pot, lock the lid in place and bring to high pressure over high heat. Cook for 10 minutes, adjusting the heat as necessary to maintain a high pressure.

Release the pressure using the quick-release method.

Remove the rabbit from the pot and place in a baking dish. Cover and keep warm.

Combine the butter and flour in a small bowl. Gradually stir in 2 tablespoons (40 ml/1½ fl oz) of the cooking liquid to make a smooth paste. Pour the paste into the sauce and cook over medium heat, stirring constantly, for 3–5 minutes, until the sauce thickens and the raw flour taste is gone. Return the rabbit to the pot and heat through. Season with salt and pepper.

Serve with mashed potato.

RABBIT STEW WITH PRUNES & CINNAMON

SERVES 4

3 tablespoons (60 ml/2 fl oz) olive oil
1 × 1.5-kg (3 lb 5-oz) farmed rabbit, jointed
(ask your butcher to do this for you)
salt and freshly ground black pepper
2 medium-sized onions, halved and
thickly sliced
1 rasher bacon, finely diced
2 cloves garlic, finely chopped
1 stick cinnamon
150 g (5 oz) dried pitted prunes

2 tablespoons (40 ml/1½ fl oz) brandy
1½ cups (375 ml/12½ fl oz) chicken stock
(page 27)
2 tablespoons (40 ml/1½ fl oz) vegetable oil
¼ cup whole blanched almonds
1 tablespoon (20 g/¾ oz) softened butter
1 tablespoon (15 g/½ oz) plain flour
1 tablespoon (20 ml/¾ fl oz) freshly squeezed
lemon juice
couscous, to serve

Heat the olive oil in a pressure cooker over medium heat. Season the rabbit with salt and pepper, and cook, in batches, for 4–5 minutes, until browned all over. Transfer to a plate and set aside.

Add the onion, bacon and garlic to the pot and cook over low–medium heat until clear and softened. Add the cinnamon and prunes, and stir to combine. Pour in the brandy and bring to the boil. Pour in the stock and return the rabbit to the pot. Lock the lid in place and bring to high pressure over high heat. Cook for 10 minutes, adjusting the heat as necessary to maintain a high pressure.

Meanwhile, heat the vegetable oil in a small frying pan over medium heat. Fry the almonds for 2 minutes or until golden brown. Remove using a slotted spoon and drain on paper towel.

Release the cooker's pressure using the quick-release method.

Remove the rabbit from the pot and place in a baking dish. Cover and keep warm.

Combine the butter and flour in a small bowl. Gradually stir in 2 tablespoons (40 ml/1½ fl oz) of the cooking liquid and the lemon juice, to make a smooth paste. Pour the paste into the sauce and cook over medium heat, stirring constantly, for 3–5 minutes, until the sauce thickens and the raw flour taste is gone. Return the rabbit to the pot and heat through. Season with salt and pepper.

Serve with couscous and garnish with the fried almonds.

BEEF & VEAL

Tougher, generally inexpensive, cuts of meat such as veal shanks, beef shin, blade, cheek and rump tenderise beautifully when cooked under pressure. These cuts, which would usually take hours of cooking on the stove top or in the oven to become tender, can be falling off the bone in as little as 20 minutes when prepared in a pressure cooker.

In this chapter you'll find a selection of recipes to suit everyone's taste. There are comforting wintry stews such as beef and Guinness stew (page 92), and family favourites like bolognese (page 87), Hungarian goulash (page 90) and Italian meatballs in tomato sauce (page 93) – all perfect for those on a budget. Tender veal shanks make hearty winter fare, while chilli con carne (page 88) infused with the addictive slow warmth of chipotle chillies is certain to become a regular on your menu.

Stews, curries and chillies can be prepared a day or two in advance – they just get tastier as their flavours develop over time. Divide a large batch into portions and freeze for convenient after-work meals.

Browning meats before stewing adds depth to the flavour; however, if you are running short on time this step can be skipped. Remember when cooking beef to always use the natural-release method to release the pressure, otherwise the meat will become tough and stringy.

CORNED BEEF WITH MUSTARD SAUCE

SERVES 4–6

1.5 kg (3 lb 5 oz) corned beef (silverside)
1 medium-sized onion, peeled and studded
with 5 cloves
1 medium-sized carrot, coarsely chopped
1 small leek (white part only), coarsely chopped
1 stick celery, coarsely chopped
4 parsley stalks
3 sprigs thyme
2 bay leaves
4 peppercorns
1 tablespoon (20 ml/¾ fl oz) malt vinegar
1 tablespoon (15 g/½ oz) soft brown sugar

650 g (1 lb 7 oz) small new potatoes
8–10 baby carrots, trimmed
1 small cabbage, coarsely chopped
¼ cup coarsely chopped flat-leaf parsley
salt and freshly ground black pepper

MUSTARD SAUCE
1½ tablespoons (30 g/1 oz) butter
3 tablespoons (45 g/1½ oz) plain flour
2 tablespoons Dijon mustard
1 tablespoon (20 ml/¾ fl oz) malt vinegar
salt and freshly ground black pepper

Place the trivet in the base of the pressure cooker. Put the beef on top and add the onion, chopped carrot, leek, celery, herbs and peppercorns. Pour in 4 cups (1 L/34 fl oz) water and add the malt vinegar and sugar. Lock the lid in place and bring to low pressure over high heat. Cook for 45 minutes, adjusting the heat as necessary to maintain a low pressure.

Release the pressure using the natural-release method.

Remove the beef from the pot and place on a plate. Cover and keep warm.

Skim and discard any scum from the surface of the stock, then strain through a fine mesh sieve, discarding the solids.

To make the mustard sauce, melt the butter in a medium-sized saucepan over medium heat. Add the flour and cook, stirring continuously, for 1–2 minutes, until it becomes white. Remove from the heat and gradually whisk in 2 cups (500 ml/17 fl oz) of the reserved stock, until a smooth sauce is formed. Return the saucepan to the heat and cook, stirring continuously, for a further 5 minutes or until the raw flour taste is gone and the sauce has thickened. Stir in the mustard and vinegar, and season with salt and pepper. Cover with a piece of baking paper to prevent a skin from forming, and set aside.

Rinse out the pressure cooker, then pour in the remaining stock. Add the potatoes, lock the lid in place and bring to low pressure over high heat. Cook for 6 minutes, adjusting the heat as necessary to maintain a low pressure.

Release the pressure using the natural-release method.

Add the baby carrots and cabbage, and cover, but do not lock the lid in place. Cook for 3–4 minutes, until tender. Stir in the parsley, and season with salt and pepper.

Thickly slice the beef, and reheat the sauce if necessary.

Serve the corned beef with the vegetables and mustard sauce.

OSSO BUCCO WITH GREMOLATA

SERVES 4–6

⅓ cup (80 ml/3 fl oz) olive oil

2 kg (4 lb 6 oz) osso bucco (veal shank cut into slices 3 cm/1¼ in thick)

salt and freshly ground black pepper

2 medium-sized onions, coarsely chopped

2 cloves garlic, finely chopped

2 sticks celery, coarsely chopped

2 medium-sized carrots, coarsely chopped

1 cup (250 ml/8½ fl oz) red wine

1 × 400-g (14-oz) can chopped tomatoes

1½ cups (375 ml/12½ fl oz) chicken stock (page 27)

3 sprigs thyme

2 bay leaves

1 tablespoon (20 g/¾ oz) softened butter

2 tablespoons (30 g/1 oz) plain flour

1 tablespoon (20 ml/¾ fl oz) freshly squeezed lemon juice

mashed potato (page 179) or crusty bread, to serve

GREMOLATA

¼ cup finely chopped flat-leaf parsley

2 tablespoons finely chopped lemon zest

1 small clove garlic, crushed

Heat half the oil in a pressure cooker over medium–high heat. Season the veal with salt and pepper, and cook, in batches, for 2–3 minutes on each side, until browned. Transfer to a plate and set aside.

Add remaining oil to the pot and sauté the onion and garlic until clear and softened. Add celery and carrot, and cook for a further 3–4 minutes, until golden brown. Pour in the wine and bring to the boil. Return meat to the pot. Add the tomatoes, stock, thyme and bay leaves, then lock the lid in place and bring to high pressure over high heat. Cook for 20 minutes, adjusting the heat as necessary to maintain a high pressure.

Meanwhile, to make the gremolata, combine the parsley, lemon zest and garlic in a small bowl.

Release the cooker's pressure using the natural-release method.

Remove the meat from the pot and place in a baking dish. Cover and keep warm.

Combine the butter and flour in a small bowl. Gradually stir in 2 tablespoons (40 ml/1½ fl oz) of the cooking liquid to make a smooth paste. Pour the paste into the pot and cook over medium heat, stirring constantly, for 3–5 minutes, until the sauce thickens and the raw flour taste is gone. Return the meat to the pot, add the lemon juice, and heat through. Season with salt and pepper.

Serve with mashed potato or crusty bread, sprinkled with the gremolata.

SPAGHETTI BOLOGNESE

SERVES 6

2 tablespoons (40 ml/1½ fl oz) extra-virgin olive oil
1 large onion, finely diced
2 sticks celery, finely diced
1 large carrot, finely chopped
3 cloves garlic, finely chopped
500 g (1 lb 2 oz) pork mince
500 g (1 lb 2 oz) veal mince
¾ cup (180 ml/6 fl oz) red wine

2 × 400-g (14-oz) cans chopped tomatoes
2 tablespoons tomato paste
2 tablespoons finely chopped oregano
1 teaspoon sugar
2 bay leaves
salt and freshly ground black pepper
freshly cooked spaghetti, to serve
grated parmesan cheese, to serve

Heat the oil in a pressure cooker over low–medium heat. Sauté the onion, celery, carrot and garlic until the onion is clear and softened. Increase the heat to medium–high, add the pork and veal mince, and cook, stirring occasionally, until the meat is well browned and all the liquid has evaporated. Pour in the wine and bring to the boil. Stir in the tomatoes, tomato paste, oregano, sugar and bay leaves. Pour in ½ cup (125 ml/4 fl oz) water, lock the lid in place and bring to high pressure over high heat. Cook for 30 minutes, adjusting the heat as necessary to maintain a high pressure.

Release the pressure using the natural-release method.

Simmer the bolognese, uncovered, over medium heat for 5–10 minutes, or until thick. Remove the bay leaves and season with salt and pepper.

Serve over freshly cooked spaghetti, scattered with parmesan cheese.

Bolognese ragu can be used to make a meat lasagne: refer to the Mexican Spiced Chicken Lasagne (page 74) for method and béchamel sauce recipe.

CHILLI CON CARNE

SERVES 6–8

1 cup dried red kidney beans
⅓ cup (80 ml/3 fl oz) olive oil
750-g (1 lb 10-oz) piece beef rump
salt and freshly ground black pepper
2 medium-sized onions, finely chopped
3 cloves garlic, finely chopped
2 small dried red chillies, finely chopped
2 ancho chillies, finely chopped
1 cinnamon stick
2 teaspoons dried oregano
2 bay leaves
2 teaspoons ground cumin

2 teaspoons ground paprika
¼ teaspoon ground cloves
1 cup (250 ml/8½ fl oz) beef stock (page 28)
1 × 400-g (14-oz) can chopped tomatoes
2 tablespoons tomato paste
2 tablespoons (40 ml/1½ fl oz) cider vinegar
30 g (1 oz) Mexican chocolate or unsweetened
  dark chocolate, coarsely chopped
steamed long-grain white rice, to serve
sour cream, to serve
chopped chives, for garnish

Soak the beans in cold water for at least 4 hours (or overnight). Drain and rinse.

Place the beans, 3 cups (750 ml/25 fl oz) water and 2 tablespoons (40 ml/1½ fl oz) of the oil in a pressure cooker. Lock the lid in place and bring to high pressure over high heat. Cook for 10 minutes, adjusting the heat as necessary to maintain a high pressure.

Release the pressure using the natural-release method. Drain the beans and set aside.

Heat the remaining oil in the pressure cooker over medium–high heat. Season the beef with salt and pepper, and sear until well browned on all sides. Transfer to a plate.

Add the onion and garlic to the pot and sauté over low–medium heat until golden brown. Add the chillies, cinnamon, oregano, bay leaf and remaining spices, and cook for 30 seconds or until fragrant. Pour in the beef stock and bring to the boil. Add the tomatoes, tomato paste and cider vinegar. Return the beef to the pot, lock the lid in place and bring to high pressure over high heat. Cook for 40 minutes, adjusting the heat as necessary to maintain a high pressure.

Release the pressure using the natural-release method.

Remove the meat from the pot and place in a large bowl. Set aside to cool. When cool enough to handle, shred the beef – it should easily come apart into small chunks.

Return the meat to the pot and simmer, uncovered, over medium heat for 5–10 minutes, or until the sauce is thick. Add the beans and chocolate, and stir to combine.

Serve with steamed rice and sour cream, garnished with chives.

HUNGARIAN GOULASH

SERVES 4–6

3 tablespoons (60 ml/2 fl oz) olive oil
1 kg (2 lb 3 oz) stewing beef (such as cheek, shin or blade), cut into 4-cm (1½-in) cubes
salt and freshly ground black pepper
2 medium-sized onions, halved and thinly sliced
2 cloves garlic, finely chopped
3 medium-sized potatoes, quartered
2 medium-sized tomatoes, coarsely chopped
1 tablespoon tomato paste

1 tablespoon Hungarian sweet paprika
1 teaspoon caraway seeds
¼ teaspoon ground cloves
1 bay leaf
1 cup (250 ml/8½ fl oz) beef stock (page 28)
1 tablespoon (15 g/½ oz) plain flour
crusty bread, to serve
sour cream, to serve
chopped chives, for garnish

Heat 2 tablespoons (40 ml/1½ fl oz) of the oil in a pressure cooker over medium–high heat. Season the beef with salt and pepper, and cook, in batches, for 3–4 minutes, until browned. Transfer to a plate.

Add the remaining oil to the pot, decrease the heat to low–medium and sauté the onion and garlic until golden brown. Return the meat to the pot. Add the potato, tomato, tomato paste, paprika, caraway seeds, cloves and bay leaf, and stir to combine. Pour in the stock, then lock the lid in place and bring to high pressure over high heat. Cook for 20 minutes, adjusting the heat as necessary to maintain a high pressure.

Release the pressure using the natural-release method.

Combine the flour with 1 tablespoon (20 ml/¾ fl oz) of the cooking liquid, stirring to make a smooth paste. Stir the paste into the goulash and simmer, uncovered, over medium heat for 5 minutes, or until the raw flour taste is gone and the sauce has thickened. Remove the bay leaf and season with salt and pepper.

Serve with crusty bread. Top with a dollop of sour cream and garnish with chives.

CHINESE BRAISED BEEF SHIN

SERVES 4

3 tablespoons (60 ml/2 fl oz) peanut oil
750 g (1 lb 10 oz) beef shin (on the bone),
cut into slices 3 cm (1¼ in) thick
1 leek (white part only), quartered lengthways
4 spring onions, cut into thirds crossways
3 cloves garlic, thinly sliced
5-cm (2-in) piece ginger, sliced into
thin matchsticks
2 large red chillies, deseeded and finely sliced
1 star anise

1 cinnamon stick
½ teaspoon Sichuan peppercorns, crushed
½ cup (125 ml/4 fl oz) beef stock (page 28)
¼ cup (55 g/2 oz) firmly packed soft
brown sugar
3 tablespoons (60 ml/2 fl oz) Shaoxing rice wine
or dry sherry
2 tablespoons (40 ml/1½ fl oz) dark soy sauce
2 tablespoons (40 ml/1½ fl oz) light soy sauce
steamed rice and Chinese cabbage, to serve

Heat 2 tablespoons (40 ml/1½ fl oz) of the oil in a pressure cooker over medium–high heat. Sear the beef shin for 5–6 minutes, until browned all over. Transfer to a plate.

Add the remaining oil to the pot, decrease the heat to low–medium and cook the leek, spring onions, garlic, ginger and chilli until softened. Add the spices and cook for 30 seconds or until fragrant. Add the remaining ingredients and bring to the boil. Return the beef to the pot, lock the lid in place and bring to high pressure over high heat. Cook for 40 minutes, adjusting the heat as necessary to maintain a high pressure.

Release the pressure using the natural-release method.

Test whether the beef is ready by inserting a fork into the flesh; the meat should be tender and easily come away from the bone. If it's not done, lock the lid in place and cook for a further 3–5 minutes at high pressure.

Remove the beef from the pot and place in a baking dish. Cover to keep warm and set aside.

Simmer the sauce, uncovered, for 5 minutes or until the liquid reduces slightly. Return the beef to the pot and turn to coat it in sauce.

Serve with steamed rice and Chinese cabbage.

BEEF & GUINNESS STEW

SERVES 4–6

3 tablespoons (60 ml/2 fl oz) olive oil
1 kg (2 lb 3 oz) stewing beef (such as cheek, shin or blade), cut into 4-cm (1½-in) cubes
salt and freshly ground black pepper
1 large onion, coarsely chopped
2 sticks celery, coarsely chopped
2 cloves garlic, finely chopped
250 g (9 oz) small button mushrooms, stems removed

4 sprigs thyme
2 bay leaves
1 tablespoon tomato paste
1 tablespoon (15 g/½ oz) soft brown sugar
1½ cups (375 ml/12½ fl oz) Guinness
1 cup (250 ml/8½ fl oz) beef stock (page 28)
1 tablespoon (20 g/¾ oz) softened butter
1 tablespoon (15 g/½ oz) plain flour
mashed potato (page 179), to serve

Heat 2 tablespoons (40 ml/1½ fl oz) of the oil in a pressure cooker over medium–high heat. Season the beef with salt and pepper, and cook, in batches, for 3–4 minutes, until browned. Transfer to a plate.

Add the remaining oil to the pot, decrease the heat to low–medium and sauté the onion, celery and garlic until clear and softened. Add the mushrooms, thyme and bay leaves, and cook until the mushrooms are golden brown.

Return the meat to the pot. Add the tomato paste and sugar, and stir to combine. Pour in the Guinness and bring to the boil. Add the stock, then lock the lid in place and bring to high pressure over high heat. Cook for 20 minutes, adjusting the heat as necessary to maintain a high pressure.

Release the pressure using the natural-release method.

Combine the butter and flour in a small bowl. Add 1 tablespoon (20 ml/¾ fl oz) of the cooking liquid and stir to make a smooth paste. Stir the paste into the stew and cook, uncovered, over medium heat for 5–10 minutes, until the raw flour taste is gone and the sauce has thickened. Remove the bay leaves and thyme stems, and season with salt and pepper.

Serve with mashed potato.

ITALIAN MEATBALLS IN TOMATO SAUCE

SERVES 4

2 tablespoons (40 ml/1½ fl oz) olive oil
1 medium-sized onion, finely chopped
2 cloves garlic, finely chopped
1 tablespoon tomato paste
1 teaspoon sugar
2 bay leaves
2 × 400-g (14-oz) cans chopped tomatoes
salt and freshly ground black pepper
grated parmesan cheese, to serve
finely chopped flat-leaf parsley,
for garnish

MEATBALLS
90 g (3 oz) fresh white breadcrumbs
⅓ cup (80 ml/3 fl oz) milk
500 g (1 lb 2 oz) veal or beef mince
250 g (9 oz) pork mince
⅓ cup finely grated parmesan cheese
2 tablespoons finely chopped parsley
2 tablespoons finely chopped oregano
1 large egg, lightly beaten
2 cloves garlic, crushed
zest of 1 lemon
salt and freshly ground black pepper

To prepare the meatballs, soak the breadcrumbs in the milk for 5 minutes or until softened. Squeeze out excess moisture and combine the breadcrumbs with all the other meatball ingredients (except the salt and pepper) in a bowl. Mix thoroughly and season with salt and pepper. Shape the mixture into golfball-sized balls and place on a tray.

To make the sauce, heat the oil in a pressure cooker over low–medium heat and cook the onion and garlic until clear and softened. Pour in ⅓ cup (80 ml/3 fl oz) water, then stir in the tomato paste and sugar, and add the bay leaves. Arrange the meatballs in a single layer on top and pour the chopped tomatoes over. Lock the lid in place and bring to low pressure over high heat. Cook for 20 minutes, adjusting the heat as necessary to maintain a low pressure.

Release the pressure using the natural-release method.

Remove the meatballs from the sauce using a slotted spoon, place in a dish and cover to keep warm.

Simmer the sauce, uncovered, for 5 minutes, until it thickens. Remove the bay leaves and season with salt and pepper.

Serve the meatballs covered in sauce and scattered with parmesan cheese. Sprinkle with parsley to garnish.

BEEF & RED WINE STEW

SERVES 6

3 tablespoons (60 ml/2 fl oz) olive oil
1 kg (2 lb 3 oz) stewing beef (such as cheek, shin or blade), cut into 4-cm (1½-in) cubes
salt and freshly ground black pepper
2 tablespoons (40 g/1½ oz) softened butter
12 small pickling onions
2 cloves garlic, finely chopped
1 medium-sized carrot, diced

1 tablespoon tomato paste
3 sprigs thyme
2 bay leaves
2 cups (500 ml/17 fl oz) red wine
½ cup (125 ml/4 fl oz) beef stock (page 28)
1 tablespoon (15 g/½ oz) plain flour
¼ cup coarsely chopped flat-leaf parsley
boiled new potatoes and steamed peas, to serve

Heat 2 tablespoons (40 ml/1½ fl oz) of the oil in a pressure cooker over medium–high heat. Season the beef with salt and pepper, and cook, in batches, for 3–4 minutes, until browned. Transfer to a plate.

Add the remaining oil and 1 tablespoon (20 g/¾ oz) of the butter to the pot and sauté the onions and garlic over low–medium heat until golden. Add the carrot, tomato paste, thyme and bay leaves, and stir to combine. Pour in the wine and bring to the boil. Add the stock, then lock the lid in place and bring to high pressure over high heat. Cook for 20 minutes, adjusting the heat as necessary to maintain a high pressure.

Release the pressure using the natural-release method.

Combine the flour and remaining butter in a small bowl. Add 2 tablespoons (40 ml/1½ fl oz) of the cooking liquid and stir to make a smooth paste. Stir the paste into the stew and cook, uncovered, over medium heat for 5–10 minutes, until the raw flour taste is gone and the sauce has thickened. Remove the bay leaves and thyme stems, stir in the parsley and season with salt and pepper.

Serve with boiled potatoes and peas.

HOT & SOUR BEEF CHEEKS

SERVES 4

3 tablespoons tamarind pulp
3 tablespoons (60 ml/2 fl oz) vegetable oil
4 beef cheeks (about 800 g/1 lb 12 oz in total)
2 medium-sized red onions, halved and
thinly sliced
4 cloves garlic, finely chopped
4-cm (1½-in) piece ginger, finely sliced
3 large red chillies, deseeded and finely sliced

1 stem lemongrass, finely sliced
4 medium-sized vine-ripened tomatoes,
coarsely chopped
2 tablespoons (30 g/1 oz) soft brown sugar
1 teaspoon ground turmeric
1½ cups (375 ml/12½ fl oz) beef stock (page 28)
2 tablespoons (40 ml/1½ fl oz) fish sauce
steamed rice and Asian vegetables, to serve

Combine the tamarind with ⅓ cup (80 ml/3 fl oz) water in a small bowl and set aside for 15 minutes, to soften. Stir to make a paste, then pass through a fine mesh sieve, discarding the solids.

Heat 2 tablespoons (40 ml/1½ fl oz) of the oil in a pressure cooker over medium–high heat and cook the beef for 3–4 minutes, until browned. Transfer to a plate.

Add the remaining oil to the pot, decrease the heat to low–medium and cook the onion, garlic, ginger, chilli and lemongrass until the onion is clear and softened. Add the tomato, tamarind purée, sugar and turmeric, and stir to combine. Pour in the stock and return the beef to the pot. Lock the lid in place and bring to high pressure over high heat. Cook for 30 minutes, adjusting the heat as necessary to maintain a high pressure.

Release the pressure using the natural-release method.

Test whether the beef is ready by inserting a fork into the flesh; the meat should be tender and break apart easily. If it's not done, lock the lid in place and cook for a further 3–5 minutes at high pressure.

Remove the beef from the pot and place in a baking dish. Cover to keep warm and set aside.

Simmer the sauce, uncovered, for 5 minutes or until the liquid reduces slightly. Stir in the fish sauce. Return the beef to the pot and turn to coat in sauce.

Serve with steamed rice and Asian vegetables.

MASSAMAN BEEF CURRY

SERVES 4–6

1 tablespoon tamarind pulp
2 tablespoons (40 ml/1½ fl oz) vegetable oil
5 cardamom pods
4 cloves
900 g (2 lb) beef rump, cut into
4-cm (1½-in) cubes
1 × 400-ml (13½-fl oz) can coconut cream
3 medium-sized potatoes, quartered
½ cup unsalted roasted peanuts,
coarsely chopped
2 tablespoons (30 g/1 oz) coarsely grated
palm sugar
2 tablespoons (40 ml/1½ fl oz) fish sauce

2 tablespoons (40 ml/1½ fl oz) lime juice
steamed jasmine rice, to serve
MASSAMAN CURRY PASTE
½ cinnamon stick, broken into pieces
2 teaspoons coriander seeds
1 dried long red chilli
1 teaspoon cumin seeds
2 shallots, coarsely chopped
2 cloves garlic, coarsely chopped
1 stem lemongrass, coarsely chopped
2 teaspoons finely grated ginger
1 teaspoon shrimp paste
2 tablespoons (40 ml/1½ fl oz) vegetable oil

Combine the tamarind with 3 tablespoons (60 ml/2 fl oz) water in a small bowl and set aside for 15 minutes, to soften. Stir to make a paste and pass through a fine mesh sieve. Discard the solids.

To make the curry paste, dry-fry the cinnamon, coriander, chilli and cumin seeds in a frying pan over medium heat for 30 seconds or until fragrant. Transfer to a mortar or spice grinder and blend to a fine powder. Combine the spices with remaining ingredients in a small food processor and blend to a smooth paste.

Heat the oil in a pressure cooker over medium heat. Add the curry paste, cardamom pods and cloves, and cook for 1 minute or until the paste is softened and fragrant. Add the beef and cook for 3–5 minutes or until browned. Pour in the coconut cream and bring to the boil. Decrease the heat and simmer for 3–4 minutes, until the cream splits. Pour in ½ cup (125 ml/4 fl oz) water and the tamarind purée, and stir to combine. Add the potato and peanuts, lock the lid in place and bring to high pressure over high heat. Cook for 15 minutes, adjusting the heat as necessary to maintain a high pressure.

Release the pressure using the natural-release method.

Add the sugar, fish sauce and lime juice to the curry and stir in. Simmer, uncovered, over medium heat for 5–10 minutes, until the sauce thickens. Serve with rice.

BEEF STROGANOFF

SERVES 4

3 tablespoons (60 ml/2 fl oz) olive oil
750 g (1 lb 10 oz) beef sirloin steak, cut against
the grain into thin strips
1½ teaspoons Hungarian paprika
salt and freshly ground black pepper
1 large onion, halved and sliced
2 cloves garlic, finely chopped
250 g (9 oz) Swiss brown mushrooms, sliced
2 tablespoons tomato paste

½ cup (125 ml/4 fl oz) dry white wine
1 cup (250 ml/8½ fl oz) beef stock (page 28)
1 tablespoon (20 g/¾ oz) butter
1 tablespoon (15 g/½ oz) plain flour
½ cup (125 ml/4 fl oz) sour cream,
plus extra to serve
¼ cup coarsely chopped flat-leaf parsley,
plus extra for garnish
mashed potato (page 179), to serve

Heat 2 tablespoons (40 ml/1½ fl oz) of the oil in a pressure cooker over medium–high heat. Toss the beef in the paprika and season with salt and pepper, then cook, in batches, for 2 minutes or until browned. Transfer to a plate.

Add the remaining oil to the pot, decrease the heat to low–medium and cook the onion and garlic until softened. Add the mushrooms and cook for 3–4 minutes, until golden brown. Stir in the tomato paste, pour in the wine and bring to the boil. Return the beef to the pot and pour in the stock. Lock the lid in place and bring to low pressure over high heat. Cook for 8 minutes, adjusting the heat as necessary to maintain a low pressure.

Release the pressure using the natural-release method.

Combine the butter and flour in a small bowl. Gradually stir in 2 tablespoons (40 ml/1½ fl oz) of the cooking liquid to make a smooth paste. Pour the paste into the pot and cook over medium heat, stirring constantly, for 3–5 minutes, until the sauce thickens and the raw flour taste is gone. Stir in the sour cream and parsley, and season with salt and pepper.

Serve with mashed potato and garnish with parsley.

CREAMY VEAL WITH MUSHROOM & BACON

SERVES 6

1 kg (2 lb 3 oz) veal shoulder, cut into 4-cm (1½-in) cubes
18 pickling onions, peeled
1 stick celery, coarsely chopped
1 medium-sized carrot, coarsely chopped
1 small leek (white part only), coarsely chopped
4 parsley stalks
3 sprigs thyme
1 bay leaf
4 peppercorns
4 cups (1 L/34 fl oz) chicken stock (page 27)
1 tablespoon (20 g/¾ oz) butter

3 rashers bacon, coarsely chopped
150 g (5 oz) small button mushrooms, thinly sliced
2 tablespoons (30 g/1 oz) plain flour
½ cup (125 ml/4 fl oz) cream
1 large egg yolk
¼ cup coarsely chopped flat-leaf parsley
2 tablespoons (40 ml/1½ fl oz) freshly squeezed lemon juice
salt and freshly ground black pepper
freshly cooked pappardelle, to serve
shaved parmesan cheese, to serve

Place the veal, onions, celery, carrot, leek, herbs and peppercorns in a pressure cooker. Pour in the stock, then lock the lid in place and bring to low pressure over medium heat. Cook for 20 minutes, adjusting the heat as necessary to maintain a low pressure.

Release the pressure using the natural-release method.

Remove the veal and baby onions from the stock and place in a bowl. Cover and set aside.

Skim and discard any scum from the surface of the stock. Strain through a fine mesh sieve, discarding the solids.

Melt the butter in a medium-sized saucepan over medium heat. Add the bacon and mushrooms, and cook until golden brown. Add the flour and cook, stirring continuously, for 1–2 minutes, until it becomes white. Remove from the heat and gradually whisk in 3 cups (750 ml/25 fl oz) of the reserved stock, until a smooth sauce is formed. Return to the heat and cook, stirring continuously, for a further 5 minutes, or until the raw flour taste is gone and the sauce has thickened.

Combine the cream and egg yolk in a small bowl. Add ½ cup (125 ml/4 fl oz) of the hot sauce and stir to combine. Pour the yolk mixture into the sauce and stir to combine. Stir in the parsley and lemon juice, and season with salt and pepper. Return the veal and onions to the pan and heat through.

Serve over freshly cooked pappardelle, scattered with parmesan cheese.

VEAL PAPRIKA

3 tablespoons (60 ml/2 fl oz) olive oil
1 kg (2 lb 3 oz) veal shoulder, cut into 4-cm (1½-in) cubes
salt and freshly ground black pepper
1 large onion, coarsely chopped
1 clove garlic, finely chopped
3 medium-sized tomatoes, coarsely chopped
1 red capsicum, sliced lengthways
1 tablespoon Hungarian sweet paprika

1 bay leaf
1 cup (250 ml/8½ fl oz) chicken stock (page 27) or water
1 cup (250 ml/8½ fl oz) sour cream, plus extra to serve (optional)
salt and freshly ground black pepper
freshly cooked fettuccine, to serve
finely chopped parsley, for garnish

Heat 2 tablespoons (40 ml/1½ fl oz) of the oil in a pressure cooker over medium–high heat. Season the veal with salt and pepper, and cook, in batches, for 3–4 minutes until browned. Transfer to a plate.

Add the remaining oil to the pot, decrease the heat to low–medium and cook the onion and garlic until softened. Add the tomato, capsicum, paprika and bay leaf, and stir to combine. Pour in the stock or water, then lock the lid in place and bring to high pressure over high heat. Cook for 20 minutes, adjusting the heat as necessary to maintain a high pressure.

Release the pressure using the natural-release method.

Stir the sour cream into the stew and cook, uncovered, for 5–10 minutes, until the sauce thickens. Remove the bay leaf and season with salt and pepper.

Serve with fettuccine and an extra dollop of sour cream, if desired. Garnish with parsley.

VEAL SHANKS WITH SAGE & PANCETTA

SERVES 4

3 tablespoons (60 ml/2 fl oz) olive oil
8 French-trimmed veal shanks
salt and freshly ground black pepper
200 g (7 oz) pancetta, thinly sliced
20 sage leaves
2 medium-sized onions, halved and sliced
3 cloves garlic, finely chopped

250 g (9 oz) cherry tomatoes
½ cup (125 ml/4 fl oz) dry white wine
1½ cups (375 ml/12½ fl oz) chicken stock (page 27)
1 tablespoon (20 g/¾ oz) butter
1 tablespoon (15 g/½ oz) plain flour
apple and celeriac mash (page 181), to serve

Heat 2 tablespoons (40 ml/1½ fl oz) of the olive oil in a pressure cooker over medium–high heat. Season the veal shanks with salt and pepper, and cook for 3–5 minutes, until browned all over. Transfer to a plate.

Add the pancetta and sage to the pot and cook for 3–4 minutes, until crisp and golden brown. Set aside with the veal.

Add the remaining oil to the pot and decrease the heat to low–medium. Cook the onion and garlic until softened, then return the shanks and pancetta to the pot and stir to coat. Add the tomatoes and pour in the wine and stock. Lock the lid in place and bring to high pressure over high heat. Cook for 20 minutes, adjusting the heat as necessary to maintain a high pressure.

Release the pressure using the natural-release method.

Test whether the veal is ready by inserting a fork into the flesh; the meat should be tender and almost falling off the bone. If it's not, lock the lid in place and cook for a further 5 minutes at high pressure.

Remove the veal from the pot and place in a baking dish. Cover to keep warm and set aside.

Combine the butter and flour in a small bowl. Stir in 2 tablespoons (40 ml/1½ fl oz) of the cooking liquid to make a smooth paste. Pour the paste into the pot and cook over medium heat, stirring constantly, for 3–5 minutes, until the sauce thickens and the raw flour taste is gone. Return the veal to the pot and heat through. Season with salt and pepper.

Serve with apple and celeriac mash.

ACCOMPANIMENTS FOR MEAT DISHES

There are a variety of simple side dishes that you can whip up while you're waiting for the pressure cooker to do its thing. Here are some ideas to get you started.

- **Garlic bread** – cut a baguette into 3-cm (1¼ in) slices, but don't cut all the way through the loaf. Combine crushed garlic with some softened butter and spread between the slices. Wrap the loaf in aluminium foil and bake in a moderate 180°C (355°F) oven until crunchy. Serve with spaghetti bolognese (page 87) or Italian meatballs (page 93).

- **Soft polenta** – combine fine polenta with hot water, stock or milk, and cook until thick, like porridge. Add some parmesan cheese and a dollop of butter. Serve with osso bucco (page 86).

Side Salads

- **Rocket & parmesan salad** – drizzle balsamic dressing over some rocket leaves and top with freshly shaved parmesan cheese. Serve with veal shanks (page 101), Italian meatballs (page 93), creamy veal with mushroom and bacon (page 98), or spaghetti bolognese (page 87).

- **Panzanella salad** – combine tomato wedges, sliced cucumber, thinly sliced red onion and freshly torn basil leaves. Drizzle with red-wine vinegar and olive oil, add torn pieces of day-old country-style bread and toss to combine. Serve with spaghetti bolognese (page 87) or Italian meatballs (page 93).

- **Garden salad** – drizzle a lemon dressing over some mixed lettuce leaves and toss to coat. Serve with veal shanks (page 101), Italian meatballs (page 93), creamy veal with mushroom and bacon (page 98) or spaghetti bolognese (page 87).

- **Mexican salad** – combine diced red and green capsicum, tomato and red onion with some sliced jalapeno chillies and fresh coriander. Drizzle with a lime-juice dressing and toss to coat. Serve with chilli con carne (page 88).

- **Tomato, basil & mozzarella salad** – layer slices of tomato, bocconcini and basil leaves in a shallow dish. Drizzle with extra-virgin olive oil and season with cracked pepper. Serve with spaghetti bolognese (page 87) or Italian meatballs (page 93).

Vegetables

- Steam **baby new potatoes** and toss with a little butter and some chives. Serve with creamy veal with mushroom and bacon (page 98).

- Steam fresh or frozen **peas** with two sprigs of mint until just tender. Serve with beef and red wine stew (page 94) or beef and Guinness stew (page 92).

- Steam some mixed **Asian vegetables** (such as pak choy, bok choy, Chinese cabbage or Chinese broccoli) until just tender. Mix through a handful of bean sprouts and add a drizzle of lime juice. Serve with Chinese braised beef shin (page 91) or hot and sour beef cheeks (page 95).

Pasta

Whether fresh or dried, **pasta** makes a great accompaniment to meat sauces. Try **pappardelle**, **fettuccine**, **linguini**, **spaghetti** or **potato gnocchi**. Pick your favourite and serve with bolognese sauce (page 87), Italian meatballs (page 93), creamy veal with mushroom and bacon (page 98), beef stroganoff (page 97) or veal paprika (page 100).

Cook pasta in a large saucepan of salted boiling water, stirring occasionally, until al dente. (Note that fresh pasta takes less time to cook than dried.) Gnocchi dumplings float to the surface when ready.

LAMB & GOAT

Traditionally slow-cooked favourites such as tender lamb shanks, spiced curries and hearty stews can now be prepared in a fraction of the time using a pressure cooker. Hours of simmering away on the stove top or in the oven are no longer required to create rich flavours and falling-off-the-bone meat. Economical, tough cuts of lamb such as shanks, shoulder and neck are perfect for pressure cooking. Goat meat, too, is tenderised with ease and can be used as a substitute for lamb. Goat is relatively inexpensive in comparison to lamb and is readily available from fresh food markets and select butchers.

In this chapter you will find an array of dishes from around the world. From Greece there's a lamb stew infused with red wine and oregano (page 118), and a cinnamon-spiced moussaka (page 112). Italian-style lamb shanks are cooked with fennel, tomato and caperberries (page 115). For a touch of the Middle East, try the Persian lamb with pumpkin and pomegranate sauce (page 114). Or sample the French classic, lamb navarin (page 119): a stew of vegetables in a creamy sauce. For those who like spices there's a Moroccan lamb and apricot tagine (page 120), or a mouth-watering steamed cumin leg of lamb (page 116) – a great alternative to the traditional Sunday roast. Favourites from India include rogan josh (page 106) and lamb madras (page 110).

ROGAN JOSH

SERVES 4

3 tablespoons (60 ml/2 fl oz) melted ghee or
vegetable oil
750 g (1 lb 10 oz) lamb leg or shoulder, cut into
3-cm (1¼-in) chunks
6 green cardamom pods, bruised
1 cinnamon stick
4 cloves
1 large onion, finely chopped
5 cloves garlic, finely chopped
1 tablespoon finely grated ginger
2 teaspoons paprika

1 teaspoon ground coriander
1 teaspoon ground cumin
½ teaspoon ground chilli
½ teaspoon ground turmeric
¼ teaspoon ground nutmeg
¼ teaspoon freshly ground black pepper
¾ cup (180 ml/6 fl oz) natural yoghurt
½ cup (125 ml/4 fl oz) tomato purée
naan bread or spiced Indian pilaf (page 197),
to serve

Heat the ghee or oil in a pressure cooker over medium–high heat. Cook the lamb, in batches, for 3–4 minutes until browned. Transfer to a plate and set aside.

Fry the cardamom, cinnamon and cloves in the pot for 30 seconds or until fragrant. Add the onion, garlic and ginger, and cook, stirring, until golden brown. Return the lamb and any juices to the pot. Add the remaining spices, yoghurt and tomato purée, and cook, stirring continuously, for 2 minutes. Pour in 1 cup (250 ml/8½ fl oz) water, then lock the lid in place and bring to high pressure over high heat. Cook for 15 minutes, adjusting the heat as necessary to maintain a high pressure.

Release the pressure using the natural-release method.

Simmer the curry, uncovered, over medium heat for 5 minutes, or until the gravy thickens.

Serve with naan bread or spiced Indian pilaf.

MINCED LAMB, POTATO & PEA CURRY

SERVES 4–6

3 tablespoons (60 ml/2 fl oz) melted ghee or vegetable oil

1 large onion, halved and thinly sliced

2 cloves garlic, finely chopped

2 teaspoons finely grated ginger

2 green bird's eye chillies, deseeded and finely chopped

2 teaspoons ground coriander

2 teaspoons ground cumin

½ teaspoon ground chilli

¼ teaspoon freshly ground black pepper

650 g (1 lb 7 oz) lamb mince

3 medium-sized potatoes, cut into 3-cm (1¼-in) cubes

1 cup (250 ml/8½ fl oz) chopped tomatoes

1 bay leaf

1 cup frozen peas

2 tablespoons (40 ml/1½ fl oz) natural yoghurt

1 cup coarsely chopped coriander

chapati bread or steamed basmati rice, to serve

Heat the ghee or oil in a pressure cooker over low–medium heat. Cook the onion, garlic and ginger until the onion is clear and softened. Add the chilli and spices, and cook for 30 seconds or until fragrant. Increase the heat to medium–high, add the mince and cook, stirring frequently, for 4–5 minutes, until browned. Add the potato, tomatoes, ⅓ cup (80 ml/3 fl oz) water and the bay leaf. Lock the lid in place and bring to high pressure over high heat. Cook for 10 minutes, adjusting the heat as necessary to maintain a high pressure.

Release the pressure using the natural-release method

Stir in the peas, yoghurt and coriander, and cook, uncovered, over medium heat for 5 minutes, or until the sauce thickens and the peas are tender.

Serve with chapatis or rice.

LAMB KOFTAS

SERVES 4–6

steamed rice or naan bread, to serve
coriander leaves, for garnish
KOFTAS
750 g (1 lb 10 oz) lamb mince
1 small onion, finely chopped
2 red bird's eye chillies, deseeded and
finely chopped
2 tablespoons finely chopped coriander
1 large egg, lightly beaten
2 cloves garlic, finely chopped
1 teaspoon finely grated ginger
1 teaspoon garam masala
½ teaspoon ground cumin
salt and freshly ground black pepper

CURRY SAUCE
2 tablespoons (40 ml/1½ fl oz) melted ghee
or vegetable oil
1 medium-sized onion, finely chopped
2 cloves garlic, finely chopped
1 teaspoon finely grated ginger
2 teaspoons ground cumin
1 teaspoon ground coriander
1 teaspoon paprika
½ teaspoon ground cardamom
1 teaspoon ground cinnamon
1 teaspoon garam masala
1 teaspoon ground turmeric
½ teaspoon ground chilli
1 × 400-g (14-oz) can chopped tomatoes
⅓ cup (80 ml/3 fl oz) natural yoghurt

To prepare the koftas, combine all the ingredients in a medium-sized bowl. Mix thoroughly and season with salt and pepper. Shape the mixture into golfball-sized balls.

To prepare the curry sauce, heat the ghee or oil in a pressure cooker over low–medium heat. Cook the onion, garlic and ginger until the onion is clear and softened. Add the spices and cook for a further 30 seconds or until fragrant. Pour in ⅓ cup (80 ml/3 fl oz) water and bring to the boil. Add the tomatoes and yoghurt, and stir to combine. Transfer half of the sauce to a bowl.

Arrange the meatballs in a single layer in the pressure cooker. Pour the reserved sauce over the top, then lock the lid in place and bring to low pressure over high heat. Cook for 20 minutes, adjusting the heat as necessary to maintain a low pressure.

Release the pressure using the natural-release method.

Remove the meatballs from the sauce using a slotted spoon. Place in a dish and cover to keep warm.

Simmer the sauce, uncovered, for 5 minutes or until thickened. Return the koftas to the pot and toss to coat in the sauce.

Serve with rice or naan bread. Garnish with coriander.

LAMB MADRAS

SERVES 6

3 tablespoons (60 ml/2 fl oz) melted ghee or
vegetable oil

900 g (2 lb) lamb leg or shoulder, cut into
2.5-cm (1-in) chunks

2 large onions, finely chopped

7 fresh curry leaves

3 medium-sized tomatoes, finely chopped

1 tablespoon tomato paste

¾ cup (180 ml/6 fl oz) coconut milk

1 tablespoon (20 ml/¾ fl oz) freshly squeezed
lemon juice

steamed basmati rice and chapati bread,
to serve

MADRAS CURRY PASTE

¼ cup shredded fresh coconut

4 cloves garlic, coarsely chopped

4 dried red chillies, crumbled

1.5-cm (⅝-in) piece ginger, coarsely chopped

1 tablespoon ground coriander

2 teaspoons ground cumin

1 teaspoon ground turmeric

1 teaspoon ground cinnamon

½ teaspoon fenugreek seeds

½ teaspoon ground chilli

½ teaspoon ground cardamom

¼ teaspoon freshly ground black pepper

To make the curry paste, place all the ingredients in a small food processor and blend to a coarse paste.

Heat half the ghee or oil in a pressure cooker over medium heat. Cook the lamb in batches for 3–4 minutes, until browned. Transfer to a plate and set aside.

Heat the remaining ghee or oil in the pot, decrease the heat to low–medium and cook the onion until golden brown. Add the curry paste and cook, stirring, for 1 minute or until fragrant. Return the lamb and any juices to the pot. Add the curry leaves, tomatoes and tomato paste, and stir to combine. Pour in ⅓ cup (80 ml/ 3 fl oz) water and bring to the boil, then boil until the sauce is reduced by half. Stir in the coconut milk and lemon juice, then lock the lid in place and bring to high pressure over high heat. Cook for 15 minutes, adjusting the heat as necessary to maintain a high pressure.

Release the pressure using the natural-release method.

Simmer the curry, uncovered, over medium heat for 5 minutes, or until the sauce thickens.

Serve with rice and chapatis.

LAMB, PISTACHIO & CURRANT MEATBALLS IN YOGHURT SAUCE

SERVES 4

1 cup (250 ml/8½ fl oz) natural yoghurt
1 tablespoon (20 ml/¾ fl oz) freshly squeezed lemon juice
½ teaspoon ground cinnamon
½ teaspoon ground cumin
salt and freshly ground black pepper
steamed basmati rice, to serve
coarsely chopped coriander, for garnish
MEATBALLS
90 g (3 oz) fresh white breadcrumbs
⅓ cup (80 ml/3 fl oz) milk

750 g (1 lb 10 oz) lamb mince
½ cup pistachios, coarsely chopped
⅓ cup currants
2 tablespoons finely chopped coriander
2 tablespoons finely chopped mint
1 large egg, lightly beaten
1 clove garlic, finely chopped
1 teaspoon ground cinnamon
1 teaspoon ground cumin
salt and freshly ground black pepper

To prepare the meatballs, soak the breadcrumbs in the milk for 5 minutes, or until softened. Squeeze out excess moisture, then combine the bread with the remaining meatball ingredients in a medium-sized bowl. Mix thoroughly and season with salt and pepper. Shape the mixture into golfball-sized balls.

Combine the yoghurt, lemon juice and spices with ¾ cup (180 ml/6 fl oz) water in a bowl. Pour half the yoghurt sauce into a pressure cooker and arrange the meatballs in a single layer on top. Pour the remaining sauce over, then lock the lid in place and bring to low pressure over high heat. Cook for 20 minutes, adjusting the heat as necessary to maintain a low pressure.

Release the pressure using the natural-release method.

Remove the meatballs from the sauce using a slotted spoon. Place in a dish, cover and keep warm. Simmer the sauce, uncovered, for 5 minutes, or until thickened. Season with salt and pepper.

Return the meatballs to the pot and toss to coat in the sauce.

Serve with rice and garnish with coriander.

LAMB MOUSSAKA

SERVES 4–6

3 medium-sized potatoes, peeled and cut lengthways into 5-mm (¼-in) slices
salt and freshly ground black pepper
½ cup (125 ml/4 fl oz) olive oil
2 large eggplants, cut lengthways into 5-mm (¼-in) slices
garden salad, to serve

LAMB FILLING
2 tablespoons (40 ml/1½ fl oz) olive oil
1 medium-sized onion, finely chopped
2 cloves garlic, finely chopped
500 g (1 lb 2 oz) lamb mince
1 tablespoon finely chopped oregano
2 teaspoons ground cinnamon
1 bay leaf
½ cup (125 ml/4 fl oz) red wine
1 × 400-g (14-oz) can chopped tomatoes
½ teaspoon sugar
salt and freshly ground black pepper

BÉCHAMEL SAUCE
2½ tablespoons (50 g/1¾ oz) butter
⅓ cup (50 g/1¾ oz) plain flour
3 cups (750 ml/25 fl oz) milk, hot
½ teaspoon freshly grated or ground nutmeg
salt and ground white pepper

To make the filling, heat the oil in a pressure cooker over low–medium heat. Cook the onion and garlic until the onion is clear and softened. Increase the heat to medium–high, add the mince, oregano, cinnamon and bay leaf, and cook, stirring occasionally, for 5 minutes or until browned. Pour in the wine and bring to the boil. Add the tomatoes and sugar, and stir to combine. Lock the lid in place and bring to high pressure over high heat. Cook for 15 minutes, adjusting the heat as necessary to maintain a high pressure.

Meanwhile, season the potato slices with salt and pepper, and drizzle with a little oil. Cook, covered, in a frying pan over medium heat for 2–3 minutes on each side, until golden brown and cooked through. Transfer to a tray. Fry the eggplant slices in the same pan, adding oil as required, until golden brown and cooked through. Set aside with the potato.

Release the cooker's pressure using the natural or quick-release method.

Cook the sauce, uncovered, over medium heat for 5 minutes more, or until thickened.

Preheat the oven to 180°C (355°F). Lightly grease a deep 20–23 cm (8–9 in) square ovenproof dish.

To make the béchamel sauce, melt the butter in a medium-sized saucepan over low heat. Add the flour and cook, stirring, for 2 minutes or until the flour becomes white. Gradually whisk in the hot milk. Cook, stirring continuously with a wooden spoon, over low–medium heat for 10–15 minutes, until thick and the raw flour taste is gone. Add the nutmeg and season with salt and white pepper. Cover the sauce with a piece of baking paper to prevent a skin from forming, and set aside.

Arrange half the eggplant slices in the base of the prepared dish. Layer all the potato slices on top and spoon over the lamb filling. Arrange a second layer of eggplant on top of the meat, then pour the béchamel sauce evenly over the top.

Bake in the oven for 30–40 minutes, or until the top is golden.

Serve with a garden salad.

PERSIAN LAMB WITH PUMPKIN & POMEGRANATE SAUCE

SERVES 4

3 tablespoons (60 ml/2 fl oz) olive oil
1 large onion, halved and sliced
2 cloves garlic, finely chopped
1 red capsicum, coarsely chopped
3 red bird's eye chillies, deseeded and coarsely chopped
1 teaspoon ground cumin
3 tablespoons (60 ml/2 fl oz) pomegranate molasses

2 teaspoons honey
1 cup (250 ml/8½ fl oz) chicken stock (page 27)
900 g (2 lb) boneless lamb shoulder, cut into 2.5-cm (1-in) chunks
salt and freshly ground black pepper
350 g (12 oz) pumpkin, cut into 4-cm (1½-in) cubes
1 cup coarsely chopped coriander
couscous, to serve

Heat half the oil in a pressure cooker over low–medium heat. Cook the onion and garlic until the onion is clear and softened. Add the capsicum, chilli and cumin, and cook for a further 4–5 minutes, until the capsicum has softened. Add the pomegranate molasses and honey, and stir to combine. Transfer to a food processor and blend while gradually adding 3 tablespoons (60 ml/2 fl oz) of the chicken stock, until the mixture is smooth.

Heat the remaining oil in the pressure cooker over medium–high heat. Season the lamb with salt and pepper, and cook for 3–4 minutes, until browned. Pour in the remaining stock. Add the capsicum purée and pumpkin, and stir to combine. Lock the lid in place and bring to high pressure over high heat. Cook for 15 minutes, adjusting the heat as necessary to maintain a high pressure.

Release the pressure using the natural-release method.

Simmer, uncovered, over medium heat for 5 minutes, or until the sauce thickens. Stir in the coriander and season with salt and pepper.

Serve with couscous.

BRAISED LAMB SHANKS WITH FENNEL, TOMATO & CAPERBERRIES

SERVES 4

3 tablespoons (60 ml/2 fl oz) olive oil
4 French-trimmed lamb shanks
salt and freshly ground black pepper
1 large onion, halved and sliced
2 cloves garlic, finely chopped
2 fennel bulbs, trimmed and quartered
lengthways
2 stalks rosemary
2 bay leaves
½ cup (125 ml/4 fl oz) dry white wine

2 × 400-g (14-oz) cans whole peeled tomatoes
½ cup (125 ml/4 fl oz) chicken stock
  (page 27)
¼ cup caperberries, drained
mashed potato (page 179), to serve
GREMOLATA
2 tablespoons finely chopped flat-leaf parsley
2 teaspoons finely chopped lemon zest
1 clove garlic, crushed

Heat 2 tablespoons (40 ml/1½ fl oz) of the olive oil in a pressure cooker over medium–high heat. Season the lamb shanks with salt and pepper, and cook for 3–5 minutes, until browned all over. Transfer to a plate.

Add the remaining oil to the pot, decrease the heat to low–medium and cook the onion and garlic until softened. Add the fennel, rosemary and bay leaves, and stir to combine. Pour in the wine and bring to the boil. Add the tomatoes, stock and caperberries. Return the shanks to the pot and turn to coat in the sauce. Lock the lid in place and bring to high pressure over high heat. Cook for 20 minutes, adjusting the heat as necessary to maintain a high pressure.

Meanwhile, to make the gremolata, combine all the ingredients in a small bowl. Cover and refrigerate.

Release the cooker's pressure using the natural-release method.

Test whether the lamb is ready by inserting a fork into the flesh; the meat should be tender and almost falling off the bone. If it's not, lock the lid in place and cook for a further 3–5 minutes at high pressure.

Remove the lamb from the pot and place in a baking dish. Cover and keep warm. Simmer the sauce, uncovered, for 5–10 minutes, until thickened. Return the shanks to the pot and turn to coat in the sauce.

Serve with mashed potato and sprinkle with gremolata.

STEAMED CUMIN LEG OF LAMB

SERVES 4–6

1.5 kg (3 lb 5 oz) leg of lamb (on the bone)
3 tablespoons (60 g/2 oz) softened butter
¼ cup finely chopped coriander, plus extra for garnish
½ preserved lemon, pulp discarded and skin finely chopped
2 cloves garlic, crushed
2 teaspoons finely grated ginger

2 teaspoons ground cumin
½ teaspoon ground turmeric
1 teaspoon sea salt
½ teaspoon freshly ground black pepper
1½ cups (375 ml/12½ fl oz) boiling water
couscous and natural yoghurt, to serve
North African root-vegetable stew (page 185), to serve (optional)

Trim the skin off the lamb using a small sharp knife and make about six deep incisions in the flesh.

Place the remaining ingredients (except the water) in a small bowl and mix well to combine. Smear the mixture all over the lamb, pushing it into the incisions.

Place the trivet in the base of the pressure cooker and pour the boiling water into the base of the pot. Sit the lamb on top of the trivet, then lock the lid in place and bring to high pressure over high heat. Cook for 30 minutes, adjusting the heat as necessary to maintain a high pressure.

Release the pressure using the natural-release method.

Test whether the lamb is ready by inserting a fork into the flesh; the meat should be tender and easily come away from the bone. If it's not done, lock the lid in place and cook for a further 5–10 minutes at high pressure.

Remove the lamb from the cooker and slice.

Serve with couscous and natural yoghurt, and garnish with coriander. To complete the meal, you can serve the lamb with North African root-vegetable stew.

BRAISED LAMB NECK WITH ARTICHOKES & BEANS

SERVES 4–6

3 medium-sized globe artichokes
juice of ½ lemon
3 tablespoons (60 ml/2 fl oz) olive oil
1.2 kg (2 lb 10 oz) lamb neck, cut into
3-cm (1¼-in) thick chops (ask your
butcher to do this for you)
salt and freshly ground black pepper
1 large onion, halved and sliced
2 cloves garlic, finely chopped
3 medium-sized vine-ripened tomatoes,
coarsely chopped

4 sprigs thyme
2 bay leaves
zest of 1 lemon
½ cup (125 ml/4 fl oz) verjuice
1 cup (250 ml/8½ fl oz) chicken stock
(page 27)
250 g (9 oz) green beans, trimmed
crusty bread, to serve

To prepare the artichokes, remove the tough outer leaves and trim the stem. Trim off a third of the top, and scoop out and discard the choke. Cut each artichoke in half lengthways and submerge in a large bowl of water with the lemon juice added to it, to prevent discolouration. Set aside.

Heat 2 tablespoons (40 ml/1½ fl oz) of the oil in a pressure cooker over medium–high heat. Season the lamb with salt and pepper, and cook for 2–3 minutes on each side, until browned. Transfer to a plate.

Add the remaining oil to the pot, decrease the heat to low–medium and cook the onion and garlic until softened. Add the artichokes, tomato, herbs and lemon zest, and stir to combine. Pour in the verjuice and bring to the boil. Return the lamb to the pot and pour in the stock. Lock the lid in place and bring to high pressure over high heat. Cook for 15 minutes, adjusting the heat as necessary to maintain a high pressure.

Release the pressure using the natural-release method.

Add the beans to the pot, lock the lid in place and cook at high pressure for a further 2 minutes. Release the pressure using the natural-release method. Transfer the lamb to a baking dish, cover and keep warm.

Simmer the sauce, uncovered, for 5–10 minutes, until thickened. Return the lamb to the pot and toss to coat. Serve with crusty bread.

GREEK LAMB STEW

SERVES 4

3 tablespoons (60 ml/2 fl oz) olive oil
900 g (2 lb) boneless lamb shoulder, cut into 3-cm (1¼-in) chunks
salt and freshly ground black pepper
500 g (1 lb 2 oz) small pickling onions, peeled
3 cloves garlic, finely chopped
1 cinnamon stick, broken into pieces
4 cloves
4 whole allspice berries
2 bay leaves

1 cup (250 ml/8½ fl oz) red wine
½ cup (125 ml/4 fl oz) chicken stock (page 27)
2 medium-sized vine-ripened tomatoes, finely chopped
3 tablespoons (60 ml/2 fl oz) red-wine vinegar
2 tablespoons finely chopped oregano
1 tablespoon tomato paste
crusty bread or mashed potato (page 179), to serve

Heat 2 tablespoons (40 ml/1½ fl oz) of the oil in a pressure cooker over medium–high heat. Season the lamb with salt and pepper, and cook, in batches, for 3–4 minutes, until browned. Transfer to a bowl.

Heat the remaining oil in the pot, add the onions and garlic, and sauté over low–medium heat until golden brown. Add the spices and bay leaves, and cook for 30 seconds or until fragrant. Pour in the red wine and bring to the boil. Add the remaining ingredients, return the lamb to the pot and stir. Lock the lid in place and bring to high pressure over high heat. Cook for 15 minutes, adjusting the heat as necessary to maintain a high pressure.

Release the pressure using the natural-release method.

Simmer, uncovered, for a further 5–10 minutes, until the sauce thickens.

Serve with crusty bread or mashed potato.

LAMB NAVARIN

SERVES 6

4 medium-sized vine-ripened tomatoes
3 tablespoons (60 ml/2 fl oz) olive oil
1.2 kg (2 lb 10 oz) boneless lamb shoulder, cut into 3-cm (1¼-in) chunks
salt and freshly ground black pepper
1 medium-sized leek (white part only), coarsely chopped
1 large onion, coarsely chopped
1 clove garlic, finely chopped
2 medium-sized carrots, coarsely chopped
2 medium-sized turnips, coarsely chopped
2 medium-sized potatoes, quartered
1 tablespoon tomato paste
2 bay leaves
½ cup (125 ml/4 fl oz) dry white wine
1½ cups (375 ml/12½ fl oz) chicken stock (page 27)
150 g (5 oz) green beans, trimmed and halved crossways
1 cup fresh or frozen peas
½ cup (125 ml/4 fl oz) cream
crusty bread, to serve

Score a cross in the base of each tomato, then blanch them in boiling water for 20 seconds. Drain and peel the tomatoes, then cut into quarters and remove the seeds. Set aside.

Heat 2 tablespoons (40 ml/1½ fl oz) of the oil in a pressure cooker over medium–high heat. Season the lamb with salt and pepper, and cook for 3–4 minutes, until browned. Transfer to a bowl.

Add the remaining oil to the pot, decrease the heat to low–medium and cook the leek, onion and garlic until softened. Add the carrot, turnip, potato, tomato paste and bay leaves, and stir to combine. Pour in the wine and bring to the boil. Return the lamb to the pot. Pour in the stock, then lock the lid in place and bring to high pressure over high heat. Cook for 15 minutes, adjusting the heat as necessary to maintain a high pressure.

Release the pressure using the natural-release method.

Add the tomato and beans, and simmer, uncovered, for 5 minutes or until the beans are just tender. Stir in the peas and cream, and simmer, uncovered, for a further 3–5 minutes, until the peas are tender and the sauce has thickened slightly. Season with salt and pepper.

Serve with crusty bread.

LAMB & APRICOT TAGINE

SERVES 4

3 tablespoons (60 ml/2 fl oz) olive oil
900 g (2 lb) boneless lamb shoulder, cut into
3-cm (1¼-in) chunks
salt and freshly ground black pepper
1 large onion, halved and sliced
2 cloves garlic, finely chopped
1 cinnamon stick
1 teaspoon ground cumin
1 teaspoon ground ginger
1 bay leaf

200 g (7 oz) dried apricots
1 teaspoon saffron threads, soaked in
2 tablespoons (40 ml/1½ fl oz) water
1 cup (250 ml/8½ fl oz) chicken stock (page 27)
1 cup coarsely chopped coriander, plus extra
for garnish
1 tablespoon (20 g/¾ oz) butter
160 g (5½ oz) whole blanched almonds
couscous, to serve

Heat 2 tablespoons (40 ml/1½ fl oz) of the oil in a pressure cooker over medium–high heat. Season the lamb with salt and pepper, and cook for 3–4 minutes, until browned. Transfer to a bowl.

Add the remaining oil to the pot, decrease the heat to low–medium and cook the onion and garlic until softened. Add the cinnamon, cumin, ginger and bay leaf, and cook for 30 seconds or until fragrant. Return the lamb to the pot, add the apricots and stir to combine. Pour in the saffron water and stock, then lock the lid in place and bring to high pressure over high heat. Cook for 15 minutes, adjusting the heat as necessary to maintain a high pressure.

Release the pressure using the natural-release method.

Simmer the tagine, uncovered, over medium heat for 5–10 minutes, until the sauce thickens. Stir in the coriander and season with salt and pepper.

Melt the butter in a small saucepan over medium heat. Fry the almonds for 3–4 minutes, until golden brown.

Serve the tagine with couscous. Sprinkle with the fried almonds and garnish with coriander.

INDIAN GOAT CURRY

SERVES 6

3 tablespoons (60 ml/2 fl oz) melted ghee or vegetable oil

2 kg (4 lb 6 oz) goat shin or shoulder (on the bone), cut into chunks (ask your butcher to do this for you)

2 large onions, halved and sliced

3 cloves garlic, finely chopped

1 tablespoon finely grated ginger

5 cardamom pods, bruised

2 small dried red chillies

1 cup (250 ml/8½ fl oz) natural yoghurt

steamed basmati rice, to serve

coriander leaves, for garnish

SPICE MIX

2 small dried red chillies

½ cinnamon stick, broken into pieces

1 teaspoon cumin seeds

½ teaspoon cardamom seeds

1 teaspoon garam masala

To make the spice mix, dry-fry all the spices (except the garam masala) in a small frying pan over medium heat for 30 seconds or until fragrant. Transfer to a mortar or spice grinder and blend to a coarse powder. Add the garam masala and blend to a fine powder.

Heat 2 tablespoons (40 ml/1½ fl oz) of the ghee or oil in a pressure cooker over medium–high heat. Cook the goat, in batches, for 3–4 minutes, until browned. Transfer to a bowl.

Add the remaining ghee or oil to the pot, decrease the heat to low–medium and cook the onion, garlic and ginger until the onion is clear and softened. Add the cardamom pods, chillies and spice mix, and cook for 30 seconds or until fragrant. Return the goat to the pot and stir to combine. Pour in ½ cup (125 ml/4 fl oz) water and bring to the boil. Stir in the yoghurt, then lock the lid in place and bring to high pressure over high heat. Cook for 15 minutes, adjusting the heat as necessary to maintain a high pressure.

Release the pressure using the natural-release method.

Simmer the curry, uncovered, over medium heat for 5–10 minutes, until the gravy thickens.

Serve with steamed rice and garnish with coriander.

JAMAICAN GOAT CURRY

SERVES 6

3 tablespoons (60 ml/2 fl oz) olive oil
2 kg (4 lb 6 oz) goat shin or shoulder (on the bone), cut into chunks (ask your butcher to do this for you)
1 large onion, coarsely chopped
4 cloves garlic, finely chopped
1 Scotch bonnet pepper (see note), deseeded and finely chopped
1 tablespoon finely grated ginger
1 medium-sized tomato, finely chopped
1 × 400-ml (13½-fl oz) can coconut milk
Creole rice and beans (page 196), to serve
lime wedges, to serve

SPICE MIX
1 cinnamon stick, broken into pieces
3 teaspoons coriander seeds
2 teaspoons cumin seeds
2 teaspoons fenugreek seeds
1 teaspoon yellow mustard seeds
½ teaspoon black peppercorns
4 whole pimento berries
4 cloves
2 teaspoons ground turmeric
1 teaspoon ground chilli

To make the spice mix, dry-fry all the spices (except the turmeric and ground chilli) in a small frying pan over medium heat for 30 seconds, or until fragrant. Transfer to a mortar or spice grinder and blend to a coarse powder. Add the turmeric and ground chilli and blend to a fine powder.

Combine the spice mix with 2 tablespoons (40 ml/1½ fl oz) of the oil in a bowl. Add the goat and toss to coat. Cover and refrigerate overnight.

Heat a pressure cooker over medium–high heat and cook the goat, in batches, for 3–4 minutes, until browned. Transfer to a clean bowl.

Add the remaining oil to the pot, decrease the heat to low–medium and cook the onion, garlic, chilli and ginger until softened and golden brown. Add the tomato, return the goat to the pot and stir to combine. Pour in ½ cup (125 ml/4 fl oz) water and bring to the boil. Stir in the coconut milk, then lock the lid in place and bring to high pressure over high heat. Cook for 15 minutes, adjusting the heat as necessary to maintain a high pressure.

Release the pressure using the natural-release method.

Simmer the curry, uncovered, over medium heat for 5–10 minutes, until sauce thickens.

Serve with Creole rice and beans, with lime wedges on the side.

Commonly used in Caribbean and Jamaican cooking, Scotch bonnet peppers are short and fat, and range in colour from yellow to red. They are extremely hot and should be used with caution. It is essential to wear gloves when handling these chillies. They can be found at some supermarkets and fresh food markets. Substitute 2–4 fresh red bird's eye chillies if you can't find Scotch bonnet peppers.

ACCOMPANIMENTS FOR CURRIES

Indian curries – such as minced lamb, potato and pea curry (page 107), rogan josh (page 106), lamb madras (page 110), lamb koftas (page 108) and Indian goat curry (page 121) – are usually served with either rice or bread. Other accompaniments such as raita, pickles, chutney and salad are also often served with curry. Here are some suggestions.

Breads

Flatbread is traditionally used to scoop up curries and their gravy. The following Indian breads are readily available at supermarkets and Indian grocers.

- **Naan** is a flat, oval, yeast-leavened bread. It is traditionally cooked in a tandoor (clay) oven. Simply brush bought naan with a little melted butter and reheat in a hot oven.

- **Roti and chapatis** are unleavened breads, usually round in shape. Reheat in a hot frying pan or in the oven.

- **Pappadums** are thin crackers that are usually made out of ground lentils. Fry them in hot vegetable oil for 10 seconds or heat on high in the microwave for 45 seconds, until they expand and are crisp. Pappadums make excellent starters served with a selection of chutneys, pickles and raitas. They can also be crumbled over the top of curries and rice to add a textural and flavour contrast.

Raitas

Raitas are made from plain yoghurt and are served as dips or as a cooling condiment for curries. Here are some that are quick and easy to make.

- **Tomato and onion raita** – Mix finely diced tomato and red onion with plain yoghurt. Dry-fry some black mustard seeds until they pop, then stir them through the yoghurt and season with salt and pepper.

- **Cucumber raita** – Peel a small Lebanese cucumber, deseed it and coarsely grate the flesh. Mix with plain yoghurt and add a little lemon juice, some finely chopped coriander leaves and a pinch of ground cumin. Stir to combine, and season with salt and pepper.

- **Mint raita** – Finely slice some fresh mint and stir through plain yoghurt.

Pickles & Chutneys

Good-quality spiced Indian pickles and chutneys can be served as a starter with pappadums or as an accompaniment to any curry. The following are the most common varieties; they are readily available at supermarkets and Indian grocers.

- **Lime pickle** is a tart, slightly hot pickle made from salted lime wedges and a mixture of spices.

- **Mango chutney** is a sweet, spiced chutney made from mango.

- **Tamarind chutney** is a sweet, slightly sour, spiced chutney made from tamarind.

Salads

Simple fresh salads, such as the following, make perfect accompaniments to curries.

- **Onion and tomato salad** – Combine tomato wedges with finely sliced onion, then drizzle with lemon juice and olive oil and season with salt and pepper.

- **Cucumber salad** – Peel and deseed two small cucumbers and slice finely. Add some finely chopped coriander, drizzle with olive oil and season with salt and pepper.

PORK

The pressure cooker easily transforms a variety of pork cuts into crowd-pleasing favourites. Rolled pork neck, succulent belly, sticky ribs, tenderised rump and shoulder are all a breeze when prepared in the pressure cooker.

Here you'll find something for every occasion. There are satisfying one-pot meals, such as the lion's head meatballs with tasty broth, cabbage and noodles (page 139). A country-style pork terrine (page 148), on the other hand, is perfect for a spring picnic – prepare it in advance and serve with a fresh baguette, some piquant cornichons and pickled onions. For those who like it spicy, there's vindaloo (page 140) or Burmese curry (page 147), which team nicely with rice or flatbread. Or for a celebration, try the Mexican pork tamale pie wrapped in corn husks (page 130) – it makes an impressive centre piece to any Mexican feast.

The rolled pork stuffed with sage, apricots and pistachios (page 134) cooks in just 25 minutes and makes a fabulous alternative to the traditional Sunday roast. Finger-licking-good pork ribs become ever so tender in the pressure cooker – finish them off on the barbecue for a few minutes to give them a lovely smoky flavour.

Gelatinous pork belly becomes melt-in-the-mouth in no time when prepared in the pressure cooker. Try it with a red bean glaze (page 133), braised in soy and ginger (page 136) or with a chilli–caramel sauce (page 138). Whichever you choose to cook, you're sure to win the approval of even the most discerning palate.

PORK RIBS IN BLACK BEAN SAUCE

SERVES 4

1.5 kg (3 lb 5 oz) pork spare ribs, cut into 6-cm (2¼-in) pieces
2 tablespoons (40 ml/1½ fl oz) white vinegar
2 tablespoons (40 ml/1½ fl oz) soy sauce
steamed long-grain white rice and Asian greens, to serve

BLACK BEAN SAUCE
1 cup (250 ml/8½ fl oz) chicken stock (page 27)
3 tablespoons (60 ml/2 fl oz) black bean sauce
2 tablespoons (40 ml/1½ fl oz) light soy sauce

2 tablespoons honey
1 tablespoon (20 ml/¾ fl oz) Shaoxing rice wine or dry sherry
1 tablespoon salted black beans
2 cloves garlic, crushed
3-cm (1¼-in) piece ginger, finely grated
1 red bird's eye chilli, deseeded and finely chopped
2 teaspoons sesame oil

Place the ribs, vinegar, soy sauce and 2 cups (500 ml/17 fl oz) water in a pressure cooker. Lock the lid in place and bring to high pressure over high heat. Cook for 5 minutes, adjusting the heat as necessary to maintain a high pressure.

Release the pressure using the quick-release method. Remove ribs from the pot and set aside. Discard the cooking liquid.

To make the black bean sauce, combine all the ingredients in the pressure cooker. Add the ribs, then lock the lid in place and bring to high pressure over high heat. Cook for 10 minutes, adjusting the heat as necessary to maintain a high pressure.

Preheat a grill pan over high heat or a barbecue grill to hot.

Release the cooker's pressure using the natural-release method.

Grill the ribs for 5 minutes, or until charred. Serve with steamed rice and Asian greens.

Salted black beans are soy beans that have been fermented in salt, garlic and ginger. They are available from Chinese supermarkets.

BRAISED PORK WITH CABBAGE & PRUNES

SERVES 6

2 tablespoons (40 ml/1½ fl oz) olive oil
1.2-kg (2 lb 10-oz) boneless pork loin roast
salt and freshly ground black pepper
2 tablespoons (40 g/1½ oz) butter
1 large onion, halved and sliced
2 cloves garlic, finely chopped

3 tablespoons (60 ml/2 fl oz) brandy
½ cabbage, shredded
300 g (10½ oz) pitted prunes
4 sprigs thyme
1 bay leaf
¾ cup (180 ml/6 fl oz) chicken stock (page 27)

Heat the oil in a pressure cooker over medium–high heat. Season the pork with salt and pepper, and cook, turning occasionally, until browned all over. Transfer to a plate and set aside.

Add the butter to the pot, decrease the heat to low–medium and sauté the onion and garlic until golden brown. Add the brandy and bring to the boil. Stir in the cabbage, prunes and herbs. Pour in the chicken stock and return the pork and any juices to the pot. Lock the lid in place and bring to high pressure over high heat. Cook for 30 minutes, adjusting the heat as necessary to maintain a high pressure.

Release the pressure using the natural-release method.

To test for doneness, insert a skewer into the pork: if the juices run clear it is cooked; if they're pink, lock the lid in place and cook for a further 5 minutes at high pressure.

Transfer the pork and cabbage to a baking dish. Cover and keep warm.

Cook the remaining liquid, uncovered, over medium heat for 5–10 minutes, until thickened slightly. Season with salt and pepper.

Slice the pork. Serve with the cabbage and drizzle with the sauce.

MEXICAN PORK TAMALE PIE

SERVES 6

corn husks from 6–8 corn cobs
Mexican red rice (page 210), to serve
Mexican-style salsa and sour cream, to serve

PORK FILLING

500 g (1 lb 2 oz) pork rump
1 large onion, quartered
4 cloves garlic, peeled
2 bay leaves
½ teaspoon black peppercorns
70 g (2½ oz) butter
1 teaspoon onion powder

½ teaspoon garlic powder
1 teaspoon hot paprika
½ teaspoon ground chilli
salt and freshly ground black pepper

CORN PASTE

180 g (6½ oz) fine yellow polenta
70 g (2½ oz) butter, cubed
2 teaspoons ground chilli
2 teaspoons ground cumin
salt and freshly ground black pepper

Trim and discard the tough ends of the corn husks. Place the husks in a large bowl and cover with boiling water. Soak for 1 minute, to soften. Drain and set aside.

To prepare the pork filling, place the pork, onion, garlic, bay leaves, peppercorns and 1 L (34 fl oz) water in a pressure cooker. Lock the lid in place and bring to high pressure over high heat. Cook for 30 minutes, adjusting the heat as necessary to maintain a high pressure.

Release the cooker's pressure using the natural-release method.

Remove the pork from the stock, place in a bowl and set aside to cool slightly.

Strain the stock through a fine mesh sieve. Discard the bay leaves and peppercorns. Return the onion and garlic to the stock and blend using a hand-held blender or food processor, until smooth. Set aside.

Finely shred the pork, removing any fat.

Melt the butter in a small frying pan over low heat. Add the onion and garlic powders, paprika and chilli, and cook for 30 seconds, or until fragrant. Pour the spiced butter and ½ cup (125 ml/4 fl oz) of the reserved stock over the shredded pork. Season with salt and pepper and set aside.

To make the corn paste, bring 3 cups (750 ml/25 fl oz) of the reserved stock to the boil in a medium-sized saucepan. Gradually whisk in the polenta. Cook, stirring continuously with a wooden spoon, over low–medium heat for 10–15 minutes, until smooth and beginning to come away from the sides of the pan. Add the butter and spices, and stir to combine.

To assemble the tamale pie, line the base of a 20-cm (8-in) round cake tin with the prepared corn husks. Arrange another layer of husks around the sides of the tin, so that they hang over the edge. Spread half the corn paste over the base, then cover this with the spiced pork filling. Spread the remaining corn paste on top, then fold over the corn husks to enclose the filling. Place a small heatproof plate on top as a weight.

Place the trivet in the base of the pressure cooker. Fold a tea towel into thirds lengthways to make a thick strip. Place the cake tin in the centre of the strip and, using the ends of the towel as handles, lower the tin into the pressure cooker. Fold the ends of the towel over the tin. Pour enough water into the cooker to come halfway up the sides of the cake tin. Lock the lid in place and bring to high pressure over high heat. Cook for 10 minutes, adjusting the heat as necessary to maintain a high pressure.

Release the pressure using the natural or quick-release method.

Lift the cake tin out of the cooker using the tea towel. Carefully invert the tamale onto a serving plate. Unwrap and cut into wedges.

Serve with Mexican red rice, salsa and sour cream.

You can use baking paper to line the cake tin instead of corn husks.

PORK, APPLE & POTATO IN A CREAMY PORT SAUCE

SERVES 4

2 tablespoons (40 ml/1½ fl oz) olive oil
4 pork loin chops (about 200 g/7 oz each)
salt and freshly ground black pepper
1 tablespoon (20 g/¾ oz) butter
1 large onion, halved and sliced
1 clove garlic, finely chopped
1 cinnamon stick
3 cloves

1 bay leaf
½ cup (125 ml/4 fl oz) port
12 baby new potatoes
2 tart green cooking apples (such as Granny Smith), peeled, cored and quartered
½ cup (125 ml/4 fl oz) chicken stock (page 27)
1 tablespoon (20 ml/¾ fl oz) apple-cider vinegar
½ cup (125 ml/4 fl oz) cream

Heat the oil in a pressure cooker over medium–high heat. Season the pork with salt and pepper, and cook for 2 minutes on each side, or until browned. Transfer to a plate and set aside.

Add the butter to the pot, decrease the heat to low–medium heat and cook the onion, garlic, spices and bay leaf until the onion has softened and the spices are fragrant. Pour in the port and bring to the boil. Stir in the potatoes and apple. Pour in the chicken stock and vinegar and return the pork and any juices to the pot. Lock the lid in place and bring to high pressure over high heat. Cook for 10 minutes, adjusting the heat as necessary to maintain a high pressure.

Release the pressure using the quick-release method.

Transfer the pork, potatoes and apple to a baking dish. Cover and keep warm.

Add the cream to the pot and simmer, uncovered, over medium heat for 5–10 minutes, until the sauce has thickened slightly. Season with salt and pepper.

Return the potatoes, apple, pork and any juices to the pot and stir to coat in sauce. Serve.

GLAZED RED BEAN PORK BELLY

SERVES 6

1.2 kg (2 lb 10 oz) boneless pork belly
steamed long-grain white rice and
Chinese broccoli, to serve
RED BEAN BRAISING LIQUID
1½ cups (375 ml/10½ fl oz) chicken stock
(page 27) or water
300 g (10½ oz) red bean paste
½ cup (125 ml/4 fl oz) hoisin sauce

½ cup (150 g/5 oz) honey
½ cup (125 ml/4 fl oz) Shaoxing rice wine
or dry sherry
½ cup (125 ml/4 fl oz) light soy sauce
3 cloves garlic, crushed
2 teaspoons Chinese five-spice

Place the pork in the pressure cooker and pour in enough water to just cover. Lock the lid in place and bring to high pressure over high heat. Once high pressure is reached, remove the pot from the heat and release the pressure using the quick-release method.

Remove the pork from the pot and rinse it under cold running water. Drain and pat dry with paper towel. Discard the cooking liquid.

To make the red bean braising liquid, combine all the ingredients in a bowl.

Place the pork, skin side up, in the pressure cooker and pour in the braising liquid. Lock the lid in place and bring to high pressure over high heat. Cook for 30 minutes, adjusting the heat as necessary to maintain a high pressure.

Release the pressure using the natural-release method.

Remove the pork from the braising liquid and place in a baking dish. Cover and keep warm.

Simmer the braising liquid, uncovered, over medium heat for 5 minutes, or until thickened to a glaze consistency. Brush the glaze over the pork.

Slice the pork and serve it with steamed rice and Chinese broccoli.

ROLLED PORK STUFFED WITH SAGE, APRICOTS & PISTACHIOS

SERVES 4

900-g (2-lb) piece pork neck
salt and freshly ground black pepper
2 tablespoons (40 ml/1½ fl oz) olive oil
2 cups (500 ml/17 fl oz) chicken stock
(page 27)
3 sprigs thyme
1 bay leaf
250 g (9 oz) green beans, trimmed
1 bunch spinach, washed and stalks removed
1 tablespoon (20 g/¾ oz) softened butter
2 tablespoons (30 g/1 oz) plain flour

1 tablespoon (20 ml/¾ fl oz) freshly squeezed
lemon juice

STUFFING
1 tablespoon (20 g/¾ oz) butter
2 shallots, finely chopped
2 cloves garlic, crushed
200 g (7 oz) pork mince
100 g (3½ oz) dried apricots, thinly sliced
⅓ cup pistachios, coarsely chopped
3 tablespoons finely chopped sage
salt and freshly ground black pepper

To prepare the stuffing, melt the butter in a small frying pan over low–medium heat. Sauté the shallot and garlic until golden brown. Transfer to a bowl and set aside to cool slightly. Add the mince, apricots, pistachios and sage to the bowl, and stir to combine. Season with salt and pepper.

Cut the pork lengthways down the centre line, slicing only two-thirds of the way through. Butterfly the meat and spread the stuffing along the centre. Roll up to enclose the stuffing, then tie at 4 cm (1½ in) intervals using kitchen string. Season with salt and pepper.

Heat the oil in a pressure cooker over medium–high heat. Cook the pork, turning occasionally, until browned all over. Transfer to a baking dish and set aside.

Pour the stock into the cooker and scrape the base with a wooden spoon to loosen any bits of cooked meat. Add the herbs, then insert the trivet and place the pork roll on top. Lock the lid in place and bring to high pressure over high heat. Cook for 25 minutes, adjusting the heat as necessary to maintain a high pressure.

Release the pressure using the natural-release method.

To test for doneness, insert a skewer into the pork: if the juices run clear, it is cooked; if they're pink, lock the lid in place and cook for a further 5–10 minutes at high pressure.

Remove the pork from the pot and place in a baking dish. Cover with aluminium foil and set aside to rest for 10 minutes.

Meanwhile, remove the trivet from the pot and add the beans to the stock. Cook, uncovered, over medium heat for 1 minute. Add the spinach and cook for a further 1 minute or until the beans are tender and the spinach is wilted. Remove the vegetables from the stock using a slotted spoon and place in a bowl. Cover and keep warm.

Combine the butter and flour in a small bowl. Gradually stir in 2 tablespoons (40 ml/1½ fl oz) of the cooking liquid to make a smooth paste. Pour the paste into the pot and cook over medium heat, stirring constantly, for 3–5 minutes, until the sauce thickens and the raw flour taste is gone. Stir in the lemon juice and season with salt and pepper.

Slice the pork and serve it with the vegetables and sauce.

SOY & GINGER BRAISED PORK BELLY WITH PICKLED CABBAGE

SERVES 6

1.2 kg (2 lb 10 oz) boneless pork belly, cut into 6 pieces

steamed rice, to serve

SOY BRAISING LIQUID

2 tablespoons tamarind pulp

2 cups (500 ml/17 fl oz) chicken stock (page 27)

⅓ cup (80 ml/3 fl oz) kecap manis (sweet soy sauce)

3 tablespoons (60 ml/2 fl oz) dark soy sauce

3 tablespoons (60 ml/2 fl oz) Shaoxing rice wine or dry sherry

5-cm (2-in) piece ginger, sliced into thin matchsticks

1 large red chilli, deseeded and thinly sliced lengthways

2 cloves garlic, finely chopped

2 teaspoons sesame oil

PICKLED CABBAGE

1 Chinese cabbage, coarsely chopped

2 tablespoons (20 g/¾ oz) sea salt

1 tablespoon (15 g/½ oz) caster sugar

2 tablespoons (40 ml/1½ fl oz) rice-wine vinegar

To prepare the pickled cabbage, place the cabbage, salt and sugar in a medium-sized bowl and toss well to combine. Cover with a plate or cling wrap and set aside for 2 hours. Drain the cabbage, squeezing out any excess moisture. Add the vinegar and toss to coat. Set aside until required.

To make the soy braising liquid, combine the tamarind with ⅓ cup (80 ml/3 fl oz) water in a small bowl and set aside for 15 minutes, to soften. Stir to make a paste, then pass through a fine mesh sieve, discarding the solids. Combine the tamarind liquid with the remaining braising ingredients in a bowl.

Place the pork in the pressure cooker and pour in just enough water to cover. Lock the lid in place and bring to high pressure over high heat. Once high pressure is reached, remove the pot from the heat and release the pressure using the quick-release method.

Remove the pork from the pot and rinse it under cold running water. Drain and pat dry with paper towel. Discard the cooking liquid.

Place the pork, skin side up, in the pressure cooker and pour in the braising liquid. Lock the lid in place and bring to high pressure over high heat. Cook for 15 minutes, adjusting the heat as necessary to maintain a high pressure.

Release the pressure using the natural-release method.

Remove the pork from the braising liquid and place in a baking dish. Cover and keep warm.

Simmer the braising liquid, uncovered, over medium heat for 5–10 minutes, until thickened slightly. Return the pork to the pot and toss to coat in the sauce.

Serve the pork with steamed rice and the pickled cabbage.

PORK BELLY WITH CHILLI–CARAMEL SAUCE

SERVES 6

½ cup (110 g/4 oz) coarsely grated palm sugar or firmly packed soft brown sugar
2 tablespoons (40 ml/1½ fl oz) rice-wine vinegar
1½ cups (375 ml/10½ fl oz) chicken stock (page 27), hot
2 tablespoons (40 ml/1½ fl oz) fish sauce
juice of 1 lime

1.2 kg (2 lb 10 oz) boneless pork belly, cut into 6 pieces
2 red bird's eye chillies, halved lengthways
1 red capsicum, sliced into thin strips
4 spring onions, sliced into thin strips
½ cup coriander leaves
steamed long-grain white rice, to serve

Place the sugar and vinegar in a pressure cooker and cook over low–medium heat, stirring occasionally, until the sugar dissolves. Gently simmer for 5 minutes or until just caramelised. Stir in the stock, fish sauce and lime juice. Add the pork belly and chillies. Lock the lid in place and bring to high pressure over high heat. Cook for 25 minutes, adjusting the heat as necessary to maintain a high pressure.

Meanwhile, combine the capsicum, spring onion and coriander. Set aside.

Release the cooker's pressure using the natural-release method.

Remove the pork from the braising liquid and place in a baking dish. Cover and keep warm.

Simmer the liquid, uncovered, over medium heat for 5–10 minutes, until thickened slightly.

Serve the pork with steamed rice and the chilli–caramel sauce. Garnish with the capsicum, spring onion and coriander.

LION'S HEAD MEATBALLS

SERVES 4

4 dried shiitake mushrooms
⅓ cup (80 ml/3 fl oz) boiling water
2 tablespoons (40 ml/1½ fl oz) vegetable oil
1½ cups (375 ml/12½ fl oz) chicken stock (page 27)
½ Chinese cabbage, thickly sliced lengthways
3 tablespoons (60 ml/2 fl oz) soy sauce
1 teaspoon sugar
100 g (3½ oz) bean thread noodles
1 teaspoon sesame oil

MEATBALLS

450 g (1 lb) pork mince
80 g (3 oz) water chestnuts, finely chopped
2 teaspoons finely grated ginger
1 clove garlic, crushed
3 spring onions, finely chopped
1 large egg white
1 tablespoon (20 ml/¾ fl oz) Shaoxing rice wine
1 tablespoon (20 ml/¾ fl oz) dark soy sauce
1 tablespoon (15 g/½ oz) cornflour

Soak the shiitake mushrooms in the boiling water for 30 minutes, or until soft. Drain, reserving the water, and thinly slice.

To make the meatballs, place the pork, water chestnuts, ginger and garlic in a food processor and blend to combine. Transfer to a medium-sized bowl. Add the spring onion, egg white, rice wine, soy sauce and cornflour, and stir to combine. Divide the mixture into eight equal portions and shape each into a ball.

Heat the vegetable oil in a pressure cooker over medium heat. Cook the meatballs for 2–3 minutes, until browned. Pour in the stock and reserved mushroom liquid. Add the mushrooms, cabbage, soy sauce and sugar, and stir to combine. Lock the lid in place and bring to high pressure over high heat. Cook for 10 minutes, adjusting the heat as necessary to maintain a high pressure.

Meanwhile, place the noodles in a medium-sized bowl and cover with boiling water. Set aside to soak for 1 minute, or until softened. Drain and rinse under cold running water.

Release the cooker's pressure using the quick-release method.

Add the noodles and sesame oil to the pot and stir to combine.

To serve, divide the meatballs, noodles and cabbage among four shallow soup bowls and ladle a little of the broth over.

PORK VINDALOO

SERVES 6

900 g (2 lb) boned pork shoulder, cut into 3-cm (1¼-in) chunks

2 tablespoons (40 ml/1½ fl oz) melted ghee or vegetable oil

2 medium-sized onions, halved and thinly sliced

2 cloves garlic, finely chopped

2 tomatoes, finely chopped

3 tablespoons (60 ml/2 fl oz) white-wine vinegar

1 cup (250 ml/8½ fl oz) chicken stock (page 27)

salt

steamed basmati rice and chapati bread, to serve

VINDALOO CURRY PASTE

2 teaspoons coriander seeds

1 teaspoon cumin seeds

½ teaspoon fenugreek seeds

1 teaspoon cardamom seeds

1 cinnamon stick, broken into pieces

½ teaspoon cloves

½ teaspoon black peppercorns

3 dried red chillies, soaked in hot water until soft

1 teaspoon ground turmeric

3 cloves garlic, coarsely chopped

2-cm (¾-in) piece ginger, coarsely chopped

3 tablespoons (60 ml/2 fl oz) white-wine vinegar

CORIANDER RAITA

1 cup (250 ml/8½ fl oz) natural yoghurt

2 tablespoons finely chopped coriander

1 tablespoon (20 ml/¾ fl oz) freshly squeezed lemon juice

salt

To make the curry paste, dry-fry the coriander, cumin, fenugreek and cardamom seeds, and the cinnamon, cloves and peppercorns together in a small frying pan over low–medium heat for 1 minute or until fragrant. Place in a mortar or spice grinder and blend to a fine powder. Transfer the powder to a small food processor. Drain the chillies, discarding the water. Add the chillies, turmeric, garlic and ginger to the processor and blend to a coarse paste. Gradually add the vinegar, blending to make a smooth paste.

Coat the pork with the spice paste. Cover and refrigerate for at least 2 hours (or overnight).

Heat the ghee or oil in a pressure cooker over low–medium heat and sauté the onion and garlic until golden brown. Add the pork and spice paste, and cook, stirring occasionally, for 3–4 minutes, until browned. Add the tomato, vinegar and stock, and stir to combine. Lock the lid in place and bring to high pressure over high heat. Cook for 15 minutes, adjusting the heat as necessary to maintain a high pressure.

Meanwhile, to make the coriander raita, combine the yoghurt, coriander and lemon juice in a small bowl. Season with salt.

Release the cooker's pressure using the natural-release method.

Simmer the curry, uncovered, over medium heat for 5 minutes, or until the sauce thickens. Season with salt.

Serve with steamed rice, chapatis and the coriander raita.

HOISIN PORK RIBS

SERVES 4

1.5 kg (3 lb 5 oz) pork spare ribs, cut into 6-cm (2¼-in) pieces
2 tablespoons (40 ml/1½ fl oz) white vinegar
steamed long-grain white rice, to serve

HOISIN SAUCE
1 cup (250 ml/8½ fl oz) chicken stock (page 27)
1 cup (250 ml/8½ fl oz) hoisin sauce
3 tablespoons (60 ml/2 fl oz) soy sauce
2 teaspoons sesame oil
2 cloves garlic, crushed
2 teaspoons finely grated ginger
1 teaspoon Chinese five-spice

CUCUMBER AND BEAN SPROUT SALAD
1 Continental cucumber
4 spring onions, thinly sliced
1 stick celery, thinly sliced
1 cup bean sprouts
½ cup coriander leaves
1 teaspoon white sesame seeds, lightly toasted
2 tablespoons (40 ml/1½ fl oz) lime juice
1 tablespoon (20 ml/¾ fl oz) extra-virgin olive oil
1 teaspoon sesame oil

Place the ribs, 2 cups (500 ml/17 fl oz) water and the vinegar in a pressure cooker. Lock the lid in place and bring to high pressure over high heat. Cook for 5 minutes, adjusting the heat as necessary to maintain a high pressure. Release the pressure using the quick-release method. Remove the pork from the pot and set aside. Discard the cooking liquid.

To make the hoisin sauce, combine all the ingredients in the pressure cooker. Return the ribs to the pot, lock the lid in place and bring to high pressure over high heat. Cook for 10 minutes, adjusting the heat as necessary to maintain a high pressure.

Meanwhile, to prepare the salad, cut the cucumber in half lengthways and scrap out the seeds using a spoon. Cut into thirds crossways and then slice into thin strips. Combine the cucumber, spring onion, celery, bean sprouts, coriander leaves and sesame seeds in a medium-sized bowl. Whisk together the lime juice, olive oil and sesame oil, then pour it over the salad and toss to coat.

Preheat a grill pan over high heat.

Release the cooker's pressure using the natural-release method. Remove the ribs from the sauce.

Grill the ribs for 5 minutes, or until charred. Serve with steamed rice and the cucumber salad.

PORK & CORIANDER STEW

SERVES 6

2 tablespoons coriander seeds
½ cinnamon stick, broken into pieces
900 g (2 lb) pork fillet, cut into
4-cm (1½-in) cubes
salt and freshly ground black pepper
1½ cups (375 ml/12½ fl oz) red wine
3 tablespoons (60 ml/2 fl oz) olive oil

1 large onion, halved and sliced
1 clove garlic, crushed
½ cup (125 ml/4 fl oz) chicken stock (page 27)
1 tablespoon (20 g/¾ oz) softened butter
1 tablespoon (15 g/½ oz) plain flour
fried potatoes, to serve

Dry-fry the coriander seeds and cinnamon in a small frying pan over medium heat for 30 seconds or until fragrant. Transfer to a mortar or spice grinder and blend to a coarse powder. Combine the spices and pork in a medium-sized bowl. Season with salt and pepper and toss to coat. Pour in the wine, cover, and refrigerate overnight.

Drain the pork, reserving the marinade.

Heat 2 tablespoons (40 ml/1½ fl oz) of the oil in a pressure cooker over medium–high heat. Cook the pork, in batches, for 3–4 minutes, until browned. Transfer to a bowl.

Add the remaining oil and the onion and garlic to the cooker, and cook over low–medium heat until softened. Return the pork to the pot and stir to combine. Add the reserved marinade and bring to the boil. Pour in the chicken stock, then lock the lid in place and bring to high pressure over high heat. Cook for 15 minutes, adjusting the heat as necessary to maintain a high pressure.

Release the pressure using the natural-release method.

Combine the butter and flour in a small bowl. Stir in 2 tablespoons (40 ml/1½ fl oz) of the cooking liquid to make a smooth paste. Pour the paste into the pot and cook over medium heat for 3–5 minutes, stirring constantly, until the sauce thickens and the raw flour taste is gone. Season with salt and pepper.

Serve the stew with fried potatoes.

PORK & WHITE BEAN CASSOULET

SERVES 4–6

1 cup dried haricot beans
1 tablespoon (20 ml/¾ fl oz) vegetable oil
2 tablespoons (40 ml/1½ fl oz) olive oil
300 g (10½ oz) pork belly, cut into 4-cm (1½-in) cubes
8 good-quality pork sausages
1 large onion, coarsely chopped
2 cloves garlic, finely chopped
1 medium-sized carrot, coarsely chopped
1 stick celery, coarsely chopped
2 bay leaves
4 sprigs thyme
⅓ cup (80 ml/3 fl oz) red wine

1 × 400-g (14-oz) can chopped tomatoes
1 tablespoon tomato paste
½ cup coarsely chopped flat-leaf parsley
salt and freshly ground black pepper

GOLDEN BREADCRUMBS

3 cups (90 g/3 oz) roughly torn day-old sourdough bread
¼ cup finely chopped flat-leaf parsley
2 tablespoons (40 ml/1½ fl oz) melted butter
1 tablespoon (20 ml/¾ fl oz) extra-virgin olive oil
salt and freshly ground black pepper

Soak the beans in a large bowl of cold water for at least 4 hours (or overnight). Drain and rinse.

Preheat the oven to 200°C (390°F).

Place the beans, 3 cups (750 ml/25 fl oz) water and the vegetable oil in a pressure cooker. Lock the lid in place and bring to high pressure over high heat. Cook for 6 minutes, adjusting the heat as necessary to maintain a high pressure.

Release the pressure using the natural-release method.

Drain the beans and transfer to a medium-sized bowl. Rinse and dry the pressure cooker.

Heat half the olive oil in the pressure cooker over medium heat. Add the pork belly and sausages, and cook for 3–5 minutes, until browned all over. Transfer to a plate.

Add the remaining olive oil to the pot, decrease the heat to low–medium and cook the onion and garlic until softened. Add the carrot, celery, bay leaves and thyme, and cook for 2–3 minutes, until golden. Pour in the wine and bring to the boil.

Add the tomatoes and tomato paste to the pot, and stir to combine. Lock the lid in place and bring to high pressure over high heat. Cook for 20 minutes, adjusting the heat as necessary to maintain a high pressure.

Meanwhile, to prepare the breadcrumbs, spread the torn bread and parsley over a baking tray. Drizzle with the butter and olive oil, season with salt and pepper, and toss to coat. Cook in the oven, tossing occasionally, for 15 minutes or until golden brown.

Release the cooker's pressure using the natural-release method.

Stir the beans into the sauce and simmer, uncovered, for 5 minutes or until the sauce thickens. Stir in the parsley and season with salt and pepper.

Serve topped with the golden breadcrumbs.

POLISH HUNTER'S STEW

SERVES 6

2 tablespoons (40 ml/1½ fl oz) olive oil
1 tablespoon (20 g/¾ oz) butter
300 g (10½ oz) venison (or other game meat),
cut into 5-cm (2-in) cubes
250 g (9 oz) pork belly, cut into
5-cm (2-in) cubes
250 g (9 oz) smoked Polish sausage (such as
kabana), thickly sliced
2 large onions, halved and sliced
2 cloves garlic, finely chopped
2 bay leaves

4 juniper berries, crushed
1 teaspoon Hungarian paprika
½ teaspoon caraway seeds
450 g (1 lb) sauerkraut, rinsed and drained
2 medium-sized tart green cooking apples
(such as Granny Smith), peeled, quartered
and sliced
1 × 400-g (14-oz) can chopped tomatoes
1 cup (250 ml/8½ fl oz) chicken stock (page 27)
salt and freshly ground black pepper
crusty bread and sour cream, to serve

Heat the oil and butter in a pressure cooker over medium–high heat. Cook the venison, pork belly and sausage, in batches, for 4–5 minutes, until browned. Transfer to a plate and set aside.

Add the onion and garlic to the pot and cook over low–medium heat until softened. Add the bay leaves and spices, and cook for 30 seconds or until fragrant. Return the meat to the pot. Add the sauerkraut and apple. Pour in the tomatoes and chicken stock. Lock the lid in place and bring to low pressure over high heat. Cook for 25 minutes, adjusting the heat as necessary to maintain a low pressure.

Release the pressure using the natural-release method.

Simmer the stew, uncovered, over medium heat for 5–10 minutes, until the sauce thickens. Discard the bay leaves, and season with salt and pepper.

Serve with crusty bread and sour cream.

BURMESE PORK CURRY

SERVES 4-6

3 tablespoons tamarind pulp
900 g (2 lb) pork belly, cut into 4-cm (1½-in) cubes
2 tablespoons (40 ml/1½ fl oz) vegetable oil
3 shallots, finely sliced
¼ cup roasted peanuts, coarsely chopped
1½ cups (375 ml/12½ fl oz) chicken stock (page 27)
2 tablespoons (40 ml/1½ fl oz) fish sauce
2 tablespoons (30 g/1 oz) coarsely grated palm sugar
salt

steamed jasmine rice, to serve
coriander leaves, for garnish

CURRY PASTE

2 teaspoons coriander seeds
1 teaspoon cumin seeds
½ cinnamon stick, broken into pieces
2 small dried red chillies
1 stem lemongrass, coarsely chopped
5-cm (2-in) piece ginger, coarsely chopped
2 shallots, coarsely chopped
2 cloves garlic, coarsely chopped
1 teaspoon shrimp paste
½ teaspoon ground turmeric

Combine the tamarind with ½ cup (125 ml/4 fl oz) water in a small bowl and set aside for 15 minutes, to soften. Stir to make a paste, then pass through a fine mesh sieve, discarding the solids.

Bring a large saucepan of water to the boil. Blanch the pork for 30 seconds, then drain and set aside.

To make the curry paste, dry-fry the coriander, cumin, cinnamon and chillies in a small frying pan over low–medium heat for 30 seconds or until fragrant. Transfer to a mortar or spice grinder and blend to a fine powder. Combine the spice powder and remaining curry paste ingredients in a small food processor and blend to a coarse paste.

Heat the oil in a pressure cooker over low–medium heat. Cook the shallots until clear and softened. Add the curry paste and cook for 1 minute, or until softened and fragrant. Add the pork and peanuts, and stir to coat. Pour in the tamarind liquid and stock, and stir to combine. Lock the lid in place and bring to high pressure over high heat. Cook for 10 minutes, adjusting the heat as necessary to maintain a high pressure.

Release the pressure using the natural-release method. Stir the fish sauce and sugar into the curry and simmer, uncovered, over medium heat for 5–10 minutes, until the sauce thickens. Season with salt. Serve with steamed rice and garnish with coriander.

COUNTRY-STYLE PORK TERRINE

SERVES 8

TERRINE

250 g (9 oz) pork shoulder, minced (ask your butcher to do this for you)

100 g (3½ oz) pork back fat, minced (ask your butcher to do this for you)

250 g (9 oz) pork belly, diced

200 g (7 oz) chicken livers, finely chopped

1 small onion, finely chopped

1 clove garlic, crushed

2 tablespoons (40 ml/1½ fl oz) Cognac

1 tablespoon finely chopped thyme

2 teaspoons salt

½ teaspoon freshly ground black pepper

½ teaspoon ground cinnamon

½ teaspoon ground nutmeg

½ teaspoon ground allspice

8 thin rashers bacon, rind removed

ACCOMPANIMENTS

French-style baguette

pickled cocktail onions

cornichons

fruit chutney

Dijon mustard

To make the terrine mixture, place all the ingredients (except the bacon) in a medium-sized bowl. Mix well to combine.

Line a 20-cm (8-in) long rectangular terrine dish with bacon, leaving the ends overhanging the edge of the dish. Spoon in the prepared filling, packing it down firmly. Fold the bacon over to enclose the mixture. Cover the dish with a piece of baking paper, followed by a piece of aluminium foil, and tie with string to secure.

Place the trivet in the base of the pressure cooker. Fold a tea towel into thirds lengthways to make a thick strip. Place the terrine in the centre of the strip and, using the ends of the towel as handles, lower it into the pressure cooker. Fold the ends of the towel over the dish. Pour enough boiling water into the cooker to come halfway up the sides of the dish. Lock the lid in place and bring to low pressure over high heat. Cook for 45 minutes, adjusting the heat as necessary to maintain a low pressure.

Release the pressure using the natural-release method.

Lift the terrine out of the cooker using the tea towel and remove the foil and baking paper. Set aside to cool to room temperature.

Invert the terrine onto a plate and discard any cooking liquid from the dish. Return the terrine to the dish, then cover and refrigerate overnight.

To serve, immerse the base of the dish in boiling water for 10 seconds, then invert the terrine onto a serving plate. Slice thickly and serve with accompaniments.

Store the terrine (in its dish) in the refrigerator and eat within 4 days. Or to keep it for 7–10 days, melt 125 g (4½ oz) butter, allow it to cool slightly, then pour over the top of the terrine to cover completely. Cover with cling wrap and refrigerate. Once the terrine has been sliced, serve it within 2 days.

FISH & SEAFOOD

In this chapter you'll find a range of fish and seafood stews from across the globe. For fast entertaining options, try the Spanish seafood stew (page 154) or Mexican fish and chorizo stew (page 159). The Brazilian seafood, peanut and coconut stew (page 163) is sure to please dinner guests – and it's ready in just 10 minutes, leaving you more time for entertaining.

Octopus and squid are ideal cooked in a pressure cooker. Octopus can be tenderised in half the usual time: in only 30 minutes you can make a delicious, rich octopus and red wine stew (page 158), perfect for the winter months. Baby octopus is done in 15 minutes, ready to be marinated for a delicious Greek-style summer salad (page 157). Squid stuffed with rice (page 164) makes an excellent starter for a dinner party or an interesting addition to an antipasto platter.

SELECTING FISH & SEAFOOD

Fish and seafood are best eaten fresh, preferably the day they are caught. Buy from reputable markets or fishmongers that have a high turnover of produce, where the fish is accessible so you can see, smell and touch it. Frozen fish is a suitable substitute when fresh is unavailable. When in doubt, ask your fishmonger for advice and plan or adjust your menu to suit what's on hand.

Selecting Fish

- **Odour** – Fresh fish should have a subtle ocean smell; it should not have a strong fishy odour.

- **Look** – The eyes should be plump, clear and glossy, and the gills should be a deep-red colour. The skin should be vibrant and shiny, and moist but not slimy or oily.

- **Feel** – The flesh should be firm; when pressed gently it should bounce back.

Selecting Shellfish and Other Seafood

- **Mussels and clams** – Shellfish should be alive when you buy them. Tap the shell: if it closes, the animal is alive.

- **Oysters** – When sold on the half-shell, oysters should be plump and moist. They should sit in a little of their own liquid, which should be clear (never milky). They should have a fresh ocean smell.

- **Scallops** – Scallops are most commonly sold loose (shucked) or frozen: dry-frozen are better, as they contain less extra liquid. Fresh scallops on the half-shell should be plump and moist, with an ocean smell.

- **Squid and octopus** – Frozen squid and octopus are common and perfectly acceptable. However, as always, if you can find them fresh, buy them.

- **Prawns and crayfish** – If buying frozen, choose a product where the shells and head are intact. When purchasing live crayfish or lobster (which is of course the superior option), choose the most active specimen.

Sustainable Fish

Overfishing is a worldwide problem. The consumer plays a powerful role in influencing how fisheries are managed. If we make sustainable choices when purchasing fish, we can help preserve our marine environment for the future.

Talk to your fishmonger and ask questions to help you make the best choice. Sustainable fish are usually species that:

- are sourced locally
- are fast growing
- have a short life-cycle
- are caught using methods that don't damage their habitat
- are caught using methods that minimise 'bycatch' (species that are caught incidentally, such as turtles, dolphins, sharks and sea birds).

- **Sustainable options for firm white fish** include: wild barramundi, blue grenadier (hoki), blue-eye trevalla, bream, mullet and ling.

SPANISH SEAFOOD STEW

SERVES 6

3 large tomatoes
⅓ cup (80 ml/3 fl oz) olive oil
4 cloves garlic, coarsely chopped
¼ cup (40 g/1½ oz) almond meal
2 cups flat-leaf parsley leaves
1 medium-sized onion, halved and sliced
1 large red chilli, deseeded and finely chopped
1 teaspoon smoked paprika
2 bay leaves
⅓ cup (80 ml/3 fl oz) dry white wine
2 tablespoons (40 ml/1½ fl oz) brandy
1 teaspoon saffron threads, soaked in
2 tablespoons (40 ml/1½ fl oz) water

1 tablespoon tomato paste
1 cup (250 ml/8½ fl oz) fish stock (page 29)
12 mussels, scrubbed and debearded
350 g (12 oz) blue-eye (or other firm white fish) fillets, cut into 6-cm (2¼-in) chunks
350 g (12 oz) snapper (or other firm white fish) fillets, cut into 6-cm (2¼-in) chunks
300 g (10½ oz) squid, cleaned and cut into 5-cm (2-in) squares
12 raw (green) prawns, shelled and deveined but tails left on
salt and freshly ground black pepper
crusty bread and lemon wedges, to serve

Score a cross in the base of each tomato, then blanch them in boiling water for 20 seconds. Drain, and refresh in cold water. Peel the tomatoes, then cut each in half horizontally and remove the seeds. Dice the flesh and set aside.

Heat half the oil in a pressure cooker over low–medium heat. Cook the garlic until softened. Add the almond meal and cook for 3–4 minutes, until golden brown. Transfer to a bowl and set aside to cool.

Place the almond mixture and half the parsley in a food processor and blend to a paste. Return to the bowl and set aside.

Heat the remaining oil in the pressure cooker over low–medium heat and cook the onion until clear and softened. Add the chilli, paprika and bay leaves, and cook for 30 seconds or until fragrant. Pour in the wine and brandy, and bring to the boil. Add the saffron water, tomato, tomato paste and fish stock, and stir to combine. Lock the lid in place and bring to high pressure over high heat. Cook for 4 minutes, adjusting the heat as necessary to maintain a high pressure.

Release the pressure using the quick-release method.

Add the almond paste to the stew and stir to combine, then add the mussels. Put the lid on the pot but do not lock it in place. Cook over medium heat for 3 minutes, or until the mussels open.

Add the fish, squid and prawns, and cook, uncovered, for a further 2–3 minutes, until the fish and squid are white and just cooked through and the prawns are pink.

Stir in the remaining parsley and season with salt and pepper.

Serve with crusty bread and lemon wedges.

SCALLOP & FENNEL STEW

SERVES 4

3 tablespoons (60 ml/2 fl oz) olive oil
1 medium-sized onion, thinly sliced
3 cloves garlic, finely chopped
2 rashers bacon, cut into thin strips
½ teaspoon dried chilli flakes
2 bay leaves
2 fennel bulbs, trimmed and coarsely chopped
⅓ cup (80 ml/3 fl oz) dry sherry
1 × 400-g (14-oz) can chopped tomatoes

¾ cup (180 ml/6 fl oz) fish stock (page 29)
1 teaspoon saffron threads, soaked in
   2 tablespoons (40 ml/1½ fl oz) water
500 g (1 lb 2 oz) scallops, roe removed
90 g (3 oz) baby spinach
juice of 1 lemon
salt and freshly ground black pepper
crusty bread and lemon wedges, to serve

Heat the oil in a pressure cooker over low–medium heat. Cook the onion and garlic until the onion is clear and softened. Add the bacon, chilli and bay leaves, and cook until the bacon is golden brown. Add the fennel and stir to combine. Pour in the sherry and bring to the boil. Add the tomatoes, fish stock and saffron water, then lock the lid in place and bring to high pressure over high heat. Cook for 4 minutes, adjusting the heat as necessary to maintain a high pressure.

Release the pressure using the quick-release method.

Simmer the stew, uncovered, for 3 minutes, or until thickened slightly. Add the scallops and spinach, and cook for 1–2 minutes, until the scallops are just cooked through. Stir in the lemon juice and season with salt and pepper.

Serve with crusty bread and lemon wedges.

GREEK BABY OCTOPUS SALAD

SERVES 4

650 g (1 lb 7 oz) baby octopus, cleaned
2 cloves garlic, bruised
4 sprigs thyme
2 sprigs rosemary
½ teaspoon black peppercorns
90 g (3 oz) curly endive
3 vine-ripened tomatoes, diced
1 Continental cucumber, diced
1 small red onion, thinly sliced
100 g (3½ oz) fetta cheese, diced

100 g (3½ oz) pitted kalamata olives

MARINADE

2 tablespoons (40 ml/1½ fl oz) freshly squeezed lemon juice
1 tablespoon (20 ml/¾ fl oz) white-wine vinegar
2 cloves garlic, finely chopped
⅓ cup (80 ml/3 fl oz) extra-virgin olive oil
3 tablespoons finely chopped oregano
salt and freshly ground black pepper

Place the octopus, garlic, thyme, rosemary and peppercorns in a pressure cooker and pour in 1 L (34 fl oz) water. Lock the lid in place and bring to high pressure over high heat. Cook for 15 minutes, adjusting the heat as necessary to maintain a high pressure.

Meanwhile, to make the marinade, combine the lemon juice, vinegar and garlic in a small bowl. Whisk in the oil, add the oregano and season with salt and pepper.

Release the cooker's pressure using the natural or quick-release method.

Drain the octopus and set aside to cool slightly.

Pour the marinade over the octopus and toss to coat. Refrigerate for at least 2 hours (or overnight).

To make the salad, drain the octopus (reserving the marinade). Place the octopus and remaining ingredients in a large bowl, pour the marinade over and toss to coat.

OCTOPUS & RED WINE STEW

SERVES 4–6

2 tablespoons (40 ml/1½ fl oz) olive oil

500 g (1 lb 2 oz) small pickling onions, peeled

3 cloves garlic, finely chopped

2 bay leaves

1 cinnamon stick

1 small dried red chilli, finely chopped

1 teaspoon black peppercorns

650 g (1 lb 7 oz) octopus, cleaned and cut into 4-cm (1½-in) pieces

3 vine-ripened tomatoes, quartered

1 cup (250 ml/8½ fl oz) red wine

2 tablespoons (40 ml/1½ fl oz) red-wine vinegar

1 teaspoon sugar

steamed long-grain white rice, to serve

Heat the oil in a pressure cooker over low–medium heat. Cook the onions until golden. Add the garlic and cook until softened. Add the bay leaves and spices, and cook for 30 seconds or until fragrant. Add the octopus and tomato, and stir to combine. Pour in the wine, add the vinegar and sugar, and bring to the boil. Lock the lid in place and bring to low pressure over medium heat. Cook for 30 minutes, adjusting the heat as necessary to maintain a low pressure.

Release the pressure using the natural or quick-release method.

Simmer the stew, uncovered, over medium heat for 5 minutes, until the sauce thickens.

Serve with steamed rice.

MEXICAN FISH & CHORIZO STEW

SERVES 4

2 tablespoons (40 ml/1½ fl oz) olive oil
1 medium-sized onion, halved and thinly sliced
2 cloves garlic, finely chopped
1 chorizo sausage, casing removed, sliced
1–2 chipotle chillies in adobo sauce, finely chopped
1 teaspoon dried oregano
2 teaspoons ground cumin
1 teaspoon hot paprika

4 vine-ripened tomatoes, diced
120 g (4 oz) green olives
2 tablespoons (40 ml/1½ fl oz) lime juice
750 g (1 lb 10 oz) firm white fish fillets, cut into 5-cm (2-in) pieces
1 cup coarsely chopped coriander
salt and freshly ground black pepper
Mexican green rice (page 209), to serve

Heat the oil in a pressure cooker over low–medium heat. Cook the onion and garlic until the onion is clear and softened. Add the chorizo, chilli, oregano and spices, and cook until the sausage is golden brown and the spices are fragrant. Pour in ⅓ cup (80 ml/3 fl oz) water and bring to the boil. Stir in the tomato, olives and lime juice. Lock the lid in place and bring to high pressure over high heat. Cook for 5 minutes, adjusting the heat as necessary to maintain a high pressure.

Release the pressure using the quick-release method.

Add the fish and coriander to the stew and stir to combine. Season with salt and pepper. Place the lid on the pot but do not lock it in place. Cook for 1–2 minutes, until the fish is just cooked through and flakes easily.

Serve with Mexican green rice.

GARLIC FISH & POTATO STEW

SERVES 4

3 tablespoons (60 ml/2 fl oz) olive oil
2 medium-sized onions, halved and sliced
10 cloves garlic, finely chopped
1 tablespoon fresh thyme
salt and freshly ground black pepper
4 medium-sized potatoes, thickly sliced into rounds

3 tablespoons (60 ml/2 fl oz) freshly squeezed lemon juice
4 × 200-g (7-oz) firm white fish cutlets
1 cup coarsely chopped flat-leaf parsley
crusty bread and lemon wedges, to serve

Heat the oil in a pressure cooker over low–medium heat. Cook the onion and garlic until the onion is clear and softened. Add the thyme and 2 teaspoons freshly ground pepper, and cook for 30 seconds or until fragrant. Add the potato and stir to coat. Pour in ½ cup (125 ml/4 fl oz) water and the lemon juice, add the fish and scatter with the parsley. Lock the lid in place and bring to low pressure over medium heat. Cook for 4 minutes, adjusting the heat as necessary to maintain a low pressure.

Release the pressure using the cold-water release method (or the quick-release method if using an electric cooker).

Check whether the fish is cooked; the flesh should flake easily. If it's not ready, cover the pot but do not lock the lid in place, and cook for a further 1–2 minutes. Season with salt and pepper.

Serve with crusty bread and lemon wedges.

ARABIC FISH TAGINE

SERVES 4

2 tablespoons (40 ml/1½ fl oz) olive oil
1 medium-sized onion, diced
2 cloves garlic, finely chopped
2 red bird's eye chillies, deseeded and finely sliced
2 teaspoons paprika
2 teaspoons ground cumin
1 teaspoon ground coriander
½ teaspoon ground turmeric
½ teaspoon cayenne pepper

4 × 200-g (7-oz) firm white fish cutlets
salt and freshly ground black pepper
1 red capsicum, cut into 5-cm (2-in) squares
1 green capsicum, cut into 5-cm (2-in) squares
2 medium-sized vine-ripened tomatoes, cut into wedges
2 tablespoons (40 ml/1½ fl oz) freshly squeezed lemon juice
1 cup coarsely chopped coriander
couscous, to serve

Heat the oil in a pressure cooker over low–medium heat. Cook the onion and garlic until the onion is clear and softened. Add the chilli and spices, and cook for 30 seconds or until fragrant. Season the fish with salt and pepper, then add to the pot and turn to coat in the spices. Transfer to a plate.

Add the red and green capsicum to the pot and cook for 2 minutes, or until just softened. Add the tomato and lemon juice, and stir to combine. Return the fish to the pot and scatter with the coriander. Lock the lid in place and bring to low pressure over medium heat. Cook for 4 minutes, adjusting the heat as necessary to maintain a low pressure.

Release the pressure using the cold-water release method (or the quick-release method if using an electric cooker).

Check whether the fish is cooked; the flesh should flake easily. If it's not ready, cover the pot but do not lock the lid in place, and cook for a further 1–2 minutes. Season with salt and pepper.

Serve with couscous.

PROSCIUTTO-WRAPPED ROCKLING IN CINNAMON BROTH

SERVES 4

4 × 200-g (7-oz) rockling fillets
salt and freshly ground black pepper
8 slices prosciutto
2 tablespoons (40 ml/1½ fl oz) olive oil
2 bay leaves
2 cinnamon sticks, broken into pieces
½ teaspoon cloves

½ teaspoon black peppercorns
½ cup (125 ml/4 fl oz) dry white wine
1½ cups (375 ml/12½ fl oz) chicken stock (page 27)
2 leeks (white parts only), quartered lengthways
steamed kipfler potatoes, to serve

Season the rockling with salt and pepper. Wrap each piece of fish in two slices of prosciutto and secure with a toothpick.

Heat the oil in a pressure cooker over medium heat. Cook the fish for 2–3 minutes, until golden brown all over. Transfer to a plate.

Add the bay leaves and spices to the pot, and cook for 30 seconds or until fragrant. Pour in the wine and bring to the boil. Pour in the chicken stock, then lock the lid in place and bring to high pressure over high heat. Cook for 3 minutes, adjusting the heat as necessary to maintain a high pressure.

Release the pressure using the cold-water release method (or the quick-release method if using an electric cooker).

Add the leek and rockling to the pot, lock the lid in place and bring to low pressure over medium heat. Cook for 8 minutes, adjusting the heat as necessary to maintain a low pressure.

Release the pressure using the quick-release method.

Remove the toothpicks from the fish. Serve with the leek and some kipfler potatoes.

BRAZILIAN SEAFOOD, PEANUT & COCONUT STEW

SERVES 4

2 tablespoons (40 ml/1½ fl oz) olive oil
1 large onion, halved and sliced
2 cloves garlic, finely chopped
1 large red chilli, deseeded and finely sliced
2 teaspoons finely grated ginger
120 g (4 oz) raw peanuts
¼ cup dried shrimp
1 × 400-ml (13½-fl oz) can coconut milk
3 tablespoons (60 ml/2 fl oz) lime juice

500 g (1 lb 2 oz) firm white fish fillets,
   cut into 5-cm (2-in) pieces
250 g (9 oz) raw (green) prawns, shelled
   and deveined but tails left on
1 cup coarsely chopped coriander,
   plus extra to garnish
salt
steamed long-grain white rice and lime wedges,
   to serve

Heat the oil in a pressure cooker over low–medium heat. Add the onion, garlic, chilli and ginger, and cook until softened. Add the peanuts and shrimp, and cook until golden brown. Set aside to cool slightly. Transfer the mixture to a food processor and blend to a coarse paste. Gradually pour in ½ cup (125 ml/4 fl oz) of the coconut milk, blending to make a smooth paste.

Transfer the peanut paste to the pressure cooker, pour in the remaining coconut milk and bring to the boil. Add ½ cup (125 ml/4 fl oz) water and the lime juice, and stir to combine. Lock the lid in place and bring to high pressure over high heat. Cook for 5 minutes, adjusting the heat as necessary to maintain a high pressure.

Release the pressure using the quick-release method.

Simmer the sauce, uncovered, over medium heat for 2–3 minutes, until thickened slightly. Add the fish and prawns, and scatter with the coriander. Cover, but do not lock the lid in place, and cook for 1–2 minutes, until the fish is just cooked through and flakes easily, and the prawns are pink. Season with salt.

Serve with steamed rice and lime wedges. Garnish with coriander.

SQUID STUFFED WITH RICE

SERVES 4

1 kg (2 lb 3 oz) medium-sized squid (about 4 squid), cleaned
2 tablespoons (40 ml/1½ fl oz) olive oil
1 medium-sized onion, finely chopped
2 cloves garlic, finely chopped
1 cup long-grain white rice
¼ cup pitted kalamata olives, finely chopped
¼ cup pine nuts, lightly toasted
¼ cup finely chopped oregano
¼ cup finely chopped flat-leaf parsley
2 teaspoons finely grated lemon zest

salt and freshly ground black pepper
garden salad, to serve

TOMATO SAUCE
2 tablespoons (40 ml/1½ fl oz) olive oil
1 small onion, finely diced
2 cloves garlic, finely chopped
⅓ cup (80 ml/3 fl oz) dry white wine
1 × 400-g (14-oz) can chopped tomatoes
1 tablespoon tomato paste
1 teaspoon sugar
1 cup (250 ml/8½ fl oz) chicken stock (page 27)
salt and freshly ground black pepper

Rinse the squid under cold water. Remove the wings from the hood, and cut off and discard the hard strip of cartilage. Finely chop the wings and tentacles and set them aside with the hoods.

Heat the oil in a medium-sized frying pan over low–medium heat. Cook the onion and garlic until the onion is clear and softened. Add the rice and stir to coat. Remove the pan from the heat and stir in the olives, pine nuts, herbs and lemon zest. Season with salt and pepper. Add the chopped squid and stir to combine.

Stuff the squid hoods three-quarters full with the rice mixture, leaving room for the rice to swell during cooking. Secure the ends of the hoods with toothpicks. Set aside.

To make the tomato sauce, heat the oil in a pressure cooker over low–medium heat. Cook the onion and garlic until the onion is clear and softened. Pour in the wine and bring to the boil. Add the tomatoes, tomato paste and sugar, and stir to combine. Pour in the stock, then lock the lid in place and bring to high pressure over high heat. Cook for 4 minutes, adjusting the heat as necessary to maintain a high pressure.

Release the pressure using the quick-release method.

Season the sauce with salt and pepper. Transfer half the sauce to a bowl.

Arrange the squid parcels in the pressure cooker and pour the reserved sauce over the top. Lock the lid in place and bring to low pressure over medium heat. Cook for 15 minutes, adjusting the heat as necessary to maintain a low pressure.

Release the pressure using the natural-release method.

Slice each squid hood crossways into three or four pieces and serve with the sauce, with a garden salad on the side.

VEGETABLES

From rich Thai curries to spiced North African stews, Italian-style stuffed vegetables to aromatic Indian coconut curries, pressure-cooked vegetable dishes are not only quick and easy to make, they can also be delicious and exotic.

Vegetable dishes are endlessly versatile. Most can be served as an accompaniment to other dishes or as a meal in their own right. Vegetable curries and stews make tasty, satisfying mains, and can be paired with a favourite dish from the Rice and Other Grains chapter. Italian-style stuffed artichokes (page 184) make an excellent starter, while peperonata (page 175) is a tasty addition to an antipasto platter. Braised vegetables such as red cabbage (page 182) and baby leeks (page 179) make great accompaniments to other dishes, as do age-old favourites like mashed potato (page 179).

Vegetable dishes are a great source of nutrition. When vegetables are braised in a pressure cooker, any liquid that seeps out during cooking remains in the pot and becomes part of the sauce served with the dish, ensuring all the vitamins and minerals are retained.

Cooking times are very important when preparing vegetables – an extra minute can turn your brussels sprouts into a soggy mess or cause your steamed vegetables to lose their colour and crispness. Refer to the timing chart on page 21 to ensure perfect steamed vegetables.

When selecting vegetables, be inspired by what is in season. Be sure to check out your local food market and select the freshest produce. The better the quality of the ingredient, the better the result!

SEASONAL VEGETABLES

SPRING	SUMMER	AUTUMN	WINTER
Asian greens	Asparagus	Asian greens	Asian greens
Asparagus	Avocadoes	Avocadoes	Avocadoes
Avocadoes	Borlotti beans	Broccoli	Beetroots
Beetroots	Capsicums	Brussels sprouts	Broad beans
Broad beans	Celery	Capsicums	Broccoli
Broccoli	Chillies	Carrots	Brussels sprouts
Cabbages	Corn	Cauliflowers	Carrots
Carrots	Cucumbers	Celery	Cauliflowers
Cauliflowers	Eggplants	Chillies	Celeriac
Cucumbers	Green beans	Cucumbers	Celery
Globe artichokes	Leeks	Eggplants	Fennel
Green beans	Lettuces	Fennel	Globe artichokes
Leeks	Peas	Leeks	Jerusalem artichokes
Lettuces	Radishes	Lettuces	Kale
Peas	Red onions	Mushrooms	Leeks
Potatoes	Snow peas	Onions	Lettuces
Radishes	Spring onions	Parsnips	Mushrooms
Silverbeet	Squashes	Peas	Onions
Snow peas	Sugar-snap peas	Potatoes	Parsnips
Spinach	Tomatoes	Pumpkins	Peas
Spring onions	Zucchini	Radicchio	Potatoes
Sugar-snap peas		Red cabbages	Pumpkins
Zucchini		Silverbeet	Radicchio
		Spinach	Silverbeet
		Squashes	Snow peas
		Swedes	Spinach
		Sweet potatoes	Spring onions
		Tomatoes	Swedes
		Turnips	Turnips
		Zucchini	White cabbages

EGGPLANT & TOMATO CURRY

SERVES 4

2 large eggplants, cut into 5-cm (2-in) cubes
salt
½ cup (125 ml/4 fl oz) vegetable oil
2 medium-sized onions, halved and thinly sliced
2 cloves garlic, finely chopped
7 fresh curry leaves
1 teaspoon black mustard seeds
2 teaspoons ground cumin

2 teaspoons ground coriander
1 teaspoon ground chilli
1 teaspoon ground turmeric
1 tablespoon dried split black lentils (white lentils)
3 medium-sized tomatoes, coarsely chopped
1 cup coarsely chopped coriander
steamed basmati rice, natural yoghurt and pappadums, to serve

Place the eggplant in a colander set over a bowl and sprinkle with 1–2 tablespoons salt. Set aside to drain for 30 minutes. Rinse under cold running water and pat dry with paper towel.

Heat a little of the oil in a pressure cooker over medium–high heat. Cook the eggplant, in batches, for 3–4 minutes, adding more oil as required, until golden brown. Transfer to a plate lined with paper towel.

Add a little more oil to the pot, decrease the heat to low–medium and cook the onion and garlic until the onion is clear and softened. Add the curry leaves, spices and lentils, and cook until the mustard seeds begin to pop and the spices are fragrant. Add the tomato and ½ cup (125 ml/4 fl oz) water and stir to combine. Lock the lid in place and bring to high pressure over high heat. Cook for 5 minutes, adjusting the heat as necessary to maintain a high pressure.

Release the pressure using the quick-release method.

Return the eggplant to the pot, lock the lid in place and bring back up to high pressure over high heat. Cook for a further 2 minutes, adjusting the heat as necessary to maintain a high pressure.

Release the pressure using the quick-release method.

Cook the curry, uncovered, over medium heat for 2–3 minutes, until the sauce thickens. Stir through the coriander and season with salt. Serve with steamed rice, yoghurt and pappadums.

MOROCCAN BEETROOT SALAD

SERVES 4

4 medium-sized beetroots, unpeeled, washed and stems trimmed
½ teaspoon cumin seeds
½ teaspoon ground coriander
3 tablespoons (60 ml/2 fl oz) extra-virgin olive oil

2 tablespoons (40 ml/1½ fl oz) freshly squeezed lemon juice
½ small red onion, finely sliced
¼ cup coarsely chopped coriander
2 tablespoons coarsely chopped flat-leaf parsley
salt and freshly ground black pepper
ground cumin, for sprinkling

Place the beetroots in a pressure cooker and pour in enough water to just cover. Lock the lid in place and bring to high pressure over high heat. Cook for 20 minutes, adjusting the heat as necessary to maintain a high pressure.

Release the pressure using the quick-release method. Drain the beetroots and set aside to cool slightly.

Dry-fry the cumin seeds in a small frying pan over low–medium heat for 30 seconds or until fragrant. Transfer to a small bowl, add the ground coriander and oil, and stir to combine. Gradually whisk in the lemon juice.

Wearing food-handling gloves (to prevent staining), peel the beetroots, then dice them into bite-sized pieces.

Combine the beetroot with the onion, coriander and parsley in a medium-sized bowl. Pour the dressing over and toss to coat. Serve warm or cold, sprinkled with ground cumin.

SPICED CAULIFLOWER WITH LEMON & ALMONDS

SERVES 4–6

3 tablespoons (60 ml/2 fl oz) olive oil
2 medium-sized onions, halved and sliced
2 cloves garlic, finely chopped
2 teaspoons paprika
1 teaspoon ground cumin
1 teaspoon ground turmeric
½ teaspoon saffron threads
1 large cauliflower, cut into medium-sized florets
2 medium-sized tomatoes, coarsely chopped

1 preserved lemon, pulp discarded and skin finely sliced
⅓ cup (80 ml/3 fl oz) vegetable stock (page 30) or chicken stock (page 27)
1 tablespoon (20 ml/¾ fl oz) freshly squeezed lemon juice
80 g (3 oz) baby spinach
½ cup whole almonds, toasted and coarsely chopped
salt and freshly ground black pepper

Heat the oil in a pressure cooker over low–medium heat. Cook the onion and garlic until the onion is clear and softened. Add the spices and cook for 30 seconds or until fragrant. Add the cauliflower, tomato and preserved lemon, and stir to combine. Pour in the stock and lemon juice, then lock the lid in place and bring to high pressure over high heat. Cook for 1 minute.

Release the pressure using the quick-release method.

Simmer the sauce, uncovered, over medium heat for 1 minute or until the liquid reduces slightly. Add the spinach and almonds and stir until the spinach has wilted. Season with salt and pepper.

Serve warm or cold as an accompaniment for chicken or fish.

POTATO & CAULIFLOWER CURRY

SERVES 6

⅓ cup (80 ml/3 fl oz) melted ghee or vegetable oil

1 large onion, halved and thinly sliced

2 cloves garlic, finely chopped

2 teaspoons finely grated ginger

1 small green chilli, deseeded and finely sliced

1 teaspoon cumin seeds

1 teaspoon garam masala

½ teaspoon ground turmeric

½ teaspoon ground chilli

2 large potatoes, cut into 5-cm (2-in) cubes

1 medium-sized cauliflower, cut into large florets

4 tomatoes, quartered

salt

steamed basmati rice and natural yoghurt, to serve

coarsely chopped coriander, for garnish

Heat the ghee or oil in a pressure cooker over low–medium heat. Cook the onion, garlic and ginger until the onion is clear and softened. Add the chilli and spices, and cook for 30 seconds or until fragrant. Pour in ⅓ cup (80 ml/3 fl oz) water, then lock the lid in place and bring to high pressure over high heat. Cook for 2 minutes.

Release the pressure using the quick-release method.

Add the potato, cauliflower and tomato to the pot. Lock the lid in place and bring back up to high pressure over high heat. Cook for 2 minutes.

Release the pressure using the quick-release method.

Simmer the curry, uncovered, over medium heat for 2–3 minutes, until the sauce thickens. Season with salt.

Serve with steamed rice and yoghurt. Garnish with coriander.

SOUTH INDIAN PUMPKIN & SPINACH CURRY

SERVES 6

2 tablespoons (40 ml/1½ fl oz) vegetable oil

1 large onion, diced

2 cloves garlic, finely chopped

2 teaspoons finely grated ginger

2 green cayenne chillies, sliced lengthways

7 fresh curry leaves

½ teaspoon black mustard seeds

1 teaspoon ground cumin

½ teaspoon ground turmeric

½ cup (125 ml/4 fl oz) coconut milk

500 g (1 lb 2 oz) pumpkin, cut into 5-cm (2-in) cubes

3 medium-sized tomatoes, cut into wedges

1 tablespoon (20 ml/¾ fl oz) freshly squeezed lemon juice

120 g (4 oz) baby spinach

salt

tamarind rice (page 203), to serve

Heat the oil in a pressure cooker over low–medium heat. Cook the onion, garlic and ginger until the onion is clear and softened. Add the chillies, curry leaves, mustard seeds, cumin and turmeric, and cook for about 30 seconds, until the mustard seeds begin to pop and the spices are fragrant. Pour in the coconut milk, then lock the lid in place and bring to high pressure over high heat. Cook for 2 minutes, adjusting the heat as necessary to maintain a high pressure.

Release the pressure using the quick-release method.

Add the pumpkin and tomato to the pot, lock the lid in place and bring back up to high pressure over high heat. Cook for 2 minutes.

Release the pressure using the quick-release method.

Add the lemon juice to the curry and simmer, uncovered, over medium heat for a further 2–3 minutes, until the sauce thickens. Add the spinach and stir until wilted. Season with salt. Serve with tamarind rice.

Green cayenne chillies, also referred to as finger chillies, are often used in Indian and Cajun cooking. Find them at Indian grocers (or use green bird's eye chillies instead).

GREEN THAI VEGETABLE CURRY

SERVES 4

2 tablespoons (40 ml/1½ fl oz) vegetable oil
1 medium-sized onion, sliced
3 tablespoons Thai green curry paste
1 × 400-ml (13½-fl oz) can coconut milk
⅓ cup (80 ml/3 fl oz) vegetable stock (page 30)
2 tablespoons (40 ml/1½ fl oz) soy sauce
1 tablespoon (20 ml/¾ fl oz) fish sauce
1 tablespoon (15 g/½ oz) grated palm sugar
zest and juice of 1 lime
4 kaffir lime leaves

1 medium-sized potato, quartered
1 slender Japanese eggplant, coarsely chopped
1 small head broccoli, cut into florets
1 green capsicum, coarsely diced
150 g (5 oz) green beans, trimmed
1 bunch bok choy, trimmed and
   quartered lengthways
steamed jasmine rice, to serve
100 g (3½ oz) bean shoots
coriander leaves, for garnish

Heat the oil in a pressure cooker over low–medium heat and cook the onion until softened. Add the curry paste and cook for 30 seconds or until fragrant. Pour in the coconut milk and bring to the boil. Decrease the heat and simmer for 3–4 minutes, until the milk splits. Add the stock, soy sauce, fish sauce, palm sugar, lime zest and kaffir lime leaves, and stir to combine. Lock the lid in place and bring to high pressure over high heat. Cook for 5 minutes, adjusting the heat as necessary to maintain a high pressure.

Release the pressure using the quick-release method.

Add the potato, eggplant, broccoli, capsicum and beans to the pot. Lock the lid in place and bring back up to high pressure over high heat. Cook for 2 minutes, adjusting the heat as necessary to maintain a high pressure.

Release the pressure using the quick-release method.

Add the bok choy to the curry and cook, uncovered, for 2–3 minutes, until it has wilted and the sauce has thickened slightly.

Serve with steamed rice, scattered with the bean shoots and garnished with coriander.

PEPERONATA & MOZZARELLA BRUSCHETTA

SERVES 4–6

3 tablespoons (60 ml/2 fl oz) olive oil, plus extra for drizzling
1 medium-sized onion, halved and thickly sliced
2 cloves garlic, crushed
2 red capsicums, sliced lengthways
2 yellow capsicums, sliced lengthways

2 medium-sized tomatoes, coarsely chopped
½ cup coarsely chopped flat-leaf parsley
4 white anchovies, thinly sliced (optional)
1 tablespoon (20 ml/¾ fl oz) red-wine vinegar
salt and freshly ground black pepper
8 slices ciabatta bread
1 ball buffalo mozzarella, sliced

To make the peperonata, heat the oil in a pressure cooker over low–medium heat. Cook the onion and garlic until the onion is clear and softened. Add the capsicum and tomato, lock the lid in place and bring to low pressure over medium heat. Cook for 3 minutes, adjusting the heat as necessary to maintain a low pressure.

Release the pressure using the quick-release method.

Cook the peperonata, uncovered, over medium heat for 2–3 minutes, until thickened. Add the parsley, anchovies and vinegar, and stir to combine. Season with salt and pepper, and set aside to cool.

Preheat the griller to medium–high.

Drizzle the bread slices with a little olive oil and grill on each side until golden. Spoon the peperonata onto the bread and arrange slices of mozzarella on top. Grill for 2–3 minutes, until the cheese is melted.

Season with freshly ground black pepper and serve.

CAPONATA

SERVES 4

2 large eggplants, cut into 5-cm (2-in) cubes
salt
½ cup (125 ml/4 fl oz) olive oil
4 sticks celery, coarsely chopped
2 cloves garlic, finely chopped
6 medium-sized tomatoes, quartered

120 g (4 oz) pitted green olives
2 tablespoons tomato paste
2 tablespoons (40 ml/1½ fl oz) red-wine vinegar
¼ cup coarsely chopped oregano
1 tablespoon capers
freshly ground black pepper

Place the eggplant in a colander set over a bowl and sprinkle with 1–2 tablespoons salt. Set aside to drain for 30 minutes. Rinse under cold running water and pat dry with paper towel.

Heat half the oil in a pressure cooker over medium–high heat. Cook the eggplant, in batches, for 3–4 minutes, adding more oil as required, until golden brown. Transfer to a plate lined with paper towel.

Add the celery and garlic to the pot and cook over low–medium heat until softened. Return the eggplant to the pot and add the remaining ingredients. Lock the lid in place and bring to low pressure over medium heat. Cook for 7 minutes, adjusting the heat as necessary to maintain a low pressure.

Release the pressure using the natural-release method.

Cook the caponata, uncovered, over medium heat for 2–3 minutes, until thickened. Season with salt and freshly ground black pepper.

Serve warm or cold as an accompaniment for chicken or fish.

SPICED GREEN BEAN & TOMATO STEW

SERVES 4

3 tablespoons (60 ml/2 fl oz) olive oil
1 medium-sized onion, halved and sliced
2 cloves garlic, finely chopped
1 teaspoon ground cumin
1 teaspoon ground coriander
1 teaspoon paprika
½ teaspoon ground turmeric
⅓ cup (80 ml/3 fl oz) chicken stock
(page 27)

5 medium-sized vine-ripened tomatoes,
coarsely chopped
2 teaspoons harissa
600 g (1 lb 5 oz) green beans, trimmed
1 tablespoon (20 ml/¾ fl oz) freshly squeezed
lemon juice
½ cup coarsely chopped coriander, plus extra
for garnish
salt and freshly ground black pepper
couscous, to serve

Heat the oil in a pressure cooker over low–medium heat. Cook the onion and garlic until the onion is clear and softened. Add the spices and cook for 30 seconds or until fragrant. Add the chicken stock, tomato and harissa, and bring to the boil. Add the beans and stir to combine, then lock the lid in place and bring to low pressure over medium heat. Cook for 5 minutes, adjusting the heat as necessary to maintain a low pressure.

Release the pressure using the quick-release method.

Add the lemon juice to the stew and cook, uncovered, over medium heat for 2–3 minutes, until thickened. Stir in the coriander and season with salt and pepper.

Serve with couscous, garnished with coriander.

Harissa is a North African chilli paste. It is available from gourmet delicatessens and some supermarkets.

MUSHROOM & CHESTNUT RAGOUT

SERVES 4

2 tablespoons (40 ml/1½ fl oz) olive oil
1 tablespoon (20 g/¾ oz) butter
1 large onion, halved and sliced
2 cloves garlic, thinly sliced
500 g (1 lb 2 oz) Swiss brown mushrooms, sliced
500 g (1 lb 2 oz) oyster mushrooms
250 g (9 oz) peeled chestnuts, halved

3 tablespoons (60 ml/2 fl oz) dry white wine
½ cup (125 ml/4 fl oz) vegetable stock (page 30) or chicken stock (page 27)
3 tablespoons (60 ml/2 fl oz) cream
¼ cup chives cut into short lengths
salt and freshly ground black pepper
soft polenta and shaved parmesan cheese, to serve

Heat the oil and butter together in a pressure cooker over low–medium heat. Cook the onion and garlic until the onion is clear and softened. Add the mushrooms and chestnuts, and cook for 3–4 minutes, until golden brown. Pour in the wine and bring to the boil. Pour in the stock, then lock the lid in place and bring to high pressure over high heat. Cook for 8 minutes, adjusting the heat as necessary to maintain a high pressure.

Release the pressure using the natural or quick-release method.

Stir the cream into the ragout and simmer, uncovered, over medium heat for 2–3 minutes, or until thickened. Stir in the chives and season with salt and pepper.

Serve with soft polenta, scattered with parmesan cheese.

BRAISED BABY LEEKS

SERVES 4

2 tablespoons (40 g/1½ oz) butter
1 clove garlic, crushed
8 baby leeks (white parts only),
halved lengthways

4 sprigs thyme
1 bay leaf
½ cup (125 ml/4 fl oz) chicken stock (page 27)
salt and freshly ground black pepper

Melt the butter in a pressure cooker over low–medium heat. Cook the garlic until clear and softened. Add the leeks, thyme and bay leaf, and stir to coat. Pour in the stock, then lock the lid in place and bring to low pressure over medium heat. Cook for 4 minutes, adjusting the heat as necessary to maintain a low pressure.

Release the pressure using the quick-release method. Season with salt and pepper.

MASHED POTATO

SERVES 4–6

6 large floury potatoes (such as pontiac or
sebago), peeled and quartered
⅓ cup (80 ml/3 fl oz) chicken stock (page 27)
or water

1 clove garlic, peeled and bruised
⅓ cup (80 ml/3 fl oz) cream
2 tablespoons (40 g/1½ oz) butter
salt and freshly ground black pepper

Place the potato, stock and garlic in a pressure cooker. Lock the lid in place and bring to high pressure over high heat. Cook for 5 minutes, adjusting the heat as necessary to maintain a high pressure.

Release the pressure using the natural-release method.

Add the cream and butter to the potato and mash using a potato masher. Season with salt and pepper.

BRUSSELS SPROUTS WITH PANCETTA & WALNUTS

SERVES 4-6

2 tablespoons (40 ml/1½ fl oz) olive oil
1 medium-sized onion, halved and thinly sliced
2 cloves garlic, thinly sliced
125 g (4½ oz) pancetta, cut into thin strips
500 g (1 lb 2 oz) brussels sprouts, trimmed

½ teaspoon freshly grated nutmeg
1 bay leaf
⅓ cup (80 ml/3 fl oz) chicken stock (page 27)
100 g (3½ oz) walnut halves, roasted
salt and freshly ground black pepper

Heat the oil in a pressure cooker over low–medium heat. Cook the onion and garlic until the onion is clear and softened. Increase the heat to medium, add the pancetta and cook until golden brown. Add the brussels sprouts, nutmeg and bay leaf, and stir to combine. Pour in the stock, then lock the lid in place and bring to high pressure over high heat and cook for 1 minute.

Release the pressure using the quick-release method.

Add the walnuts to the sprouts and stir to combine. Season with salt and pepper.

Serve as an accompaniment for chicken, pork or fish.

APPLE & CELERIAC MASH

SERVES 4

1 celeriac (about 800 g/1 lb 12 oz), peeled and quartered
1 large potato, peeled and quartered
1 tart green cooking apple (such as Granny Smith), peeled, cored and quartered

3 tablespoons (60 ml/2 fl oz) chicken stock (page 27) or water
salt and freshly ground black pepper

Place the celeriac, potato, apple and stock in a pressure cooker. Lock the lid in place and bring to high pressure over high heat. Cook for 5 minutes, adjusting the heat as necessary to maintain a high pressure.

Release the pressure using the natural-release method.

Mash the cooked ingredients using a potato masher and season with salt and pepper.

Serve as an accompaniment for chicken, veal or pork.

BRAISED RED CABBAGE

SERVES 4–6

2 tablespoons (40 ml/1½ fl oz) olive oil
1 tablespoon (20 g/¾ oz) butter
1 medium-sized red onion, halved and sliced
2 cloves garlic, finely chopped
1 teaspoon caraway seeds
2 bay leaves
1 small red cabbage, shredded

¼ cup currants
½ cup (125 ml/4 fl oz) chicken stock (page 27)
2 tablespoons (40 ml/1½ fl oz) apple-cider vinegar
1 cup coarsely chopped flat-leaf parsley
salt and freshly ground black pepper

Heat the oil and butter in a pressure cooker over low–medium heat. Cook the onion and garlic until the onion is clear and softened. Add the caraway seeds and bay leaves, and cook for 30 seconds or until fragrant. Add the cabbage and currants, and stir to combine. Pour in the stock and vinegar, then lock the lid in place and bring to high pressure over high heat. Cook for 3 minutes, adjusting the heat as necessary to maintain a high pressure.

Release the pressure using the natural-release method.

Simmer the cabbage, uncovered, over medium heat for 2–3 minutes, or until the liquid reduces by half. Stir the parsley through and season with salt and pepper.

Serve as an accompaniment for chicken, pork or fish.

RATATOUILLE

SERVES 4

2 large eggplants, cut into 5-cm (2-in) cubes
salt
½ cup (125 ml/4 fl oz) olive oil
1 medium-sized red onion, thickly sliced
2 cloves garlic, thinly sliced
1 green capsicum, thickly sliced lengthways
2 medium-sized zucchini, halved crossways
then quartered lengthways

4 large tomatoes, quartered
½ cup coarsely chopped basil
1 tablespoon (20 ml/¾ fl oz) red-wine vinegar
freshly ground black pepper
freshly cooked pasta and grated pecorino
cheese, to serve

Place the eggplant in a colander set over a bowl and sprinkle with 1–2 tablespoons salt. Set aside to drain for 30 minutes. Rinse under cold running water and pat dry with paper towel.

Heat half the oil in a pressure cooker over medium–high heat. Cook the eggplant, in batches, for 3–4 minutes, adding more oil as required, until golden brown. Transfer to a plate lined with paper towel.

Add the onion and garlic to the pot and cook over low–medium heat until the onion is clear and softened. Add the capsicum, zucchini and tomato to the pot. Pour in ⅓ cup (80 ml/3 fl oz) water, then lock the lid in place and bring to low pressure over medium heat. Cook for 7 minutes, adjusting the heat as necessary to maintain a low pressure.

Release the pressure using the quick-release method.

Stir the basil and vinegar into the sauce and cook, uncovered, over medium heat for 2–3 minutes, until thickened. Season with salt and pepper.

Serve with freshly cooked pasta, scattered with pecorino cheese.

ITALIAN-STYLE STUFFED ARTICHOKES

SERVES 4

8 medium-sized globe artichokes
6 medium-sized vine-ripened tomatoes
3 tablespoons (60 ml/2 fl oz) olive oil
1 small onion, finely chopped
2 cloves garlic, finely chopped
⅓ cup (80 ml/3 fl oz) vegetable stock
(page 30) or chicken stock (page 27)

STUFFING
1 cup day-old breadcrumbs
½ cup pitted kalamata olives, coarsely chopped
½ cup grated parmesan cheese
¼ cup chopped flat-leaf parsley
2 tablespoons chopped basil
2 tablespoons chopped oregano
salt and freshly ground black pepper

To prepare the artichokes, remove the tough outer leaves and trim the stem. Trim off a third of the top, and scoop out and discard the choke. Submerge the artichokes in a large bowl of lemon water, to prevent discolouration, and set aside.

Score a cross in the base of each tomato, then blanch them in boiling water for 20 seconds. Drain and peel the tomatoes, then cut each in half horizontally and remove the seeds. Dice the flesh and set aside.

To make the stuffing, combine the breadcrumbs, olives, cheese and herbs in a medium-sized bowl. Season with salt and pepper.

Drain the artichokes and pat dry with paper towel. Stuff the breadcrumb mixture into the cavity of each artichoke and between the leaves.

Heat the oil in a pressure cooker over low–medium heat. Cook the onion and garlic until the onion is clear and softened. Add the tomato and stock, then arrange the artichokes on top. Lock the lid in place and bring to high pressure over high heat. Cook for 7 minutes, adjusting the heat as necessary to maintain a high pressure.

Release the pressure using the natural-release method.

Serve the artichokes with the tomato sauce.

NORTH AFRICAN ROOT-VEGETABLE STEW

SERVES 4-6

2 tablespoons (40 ml/1½ fl oz) olive oil

1 large onion, coarsely chopped

3 cloves garlic, finely chopped

2 teaspoons finely grated ginger

1 teaspoon ground cumin

1 teaspoon ground paprika

1 teaspoon ground coriander

½ teaspoon ground turmeric

2 bay leaves

2 parsnips, coarsely chopped

2 carrots, coarsely chopped

1 medium-sized sweet potato, coarsely chopped

1 turnip, coarsely chopped

2 medium-sized vine-ripened tomatoes, coarsely chopped

1 cup (250 ml/8½ fl oz) vegetable stock (page 30) or chicken stock (page 27)

1 cup coarsely chopped coriander

salt and freshly ground black pepper

couscous, to serve

Heat the oil in a pressure cooker over low–medium heat. Cook the onion, garlic and ginger until onion is clear and softened. Add the spices and bay leaves, and cook for 30 seconds or until fragrant. Add the vegetables and stir to combine. Pour in the stock, then lock the lid in place and bring to low pressure over medium heat. Cook for 7 minutes, adjusting the heat as necessary to maintain a low pressure.

Release the pressure using the natural-release method.

Simmer the stew, uncovered, for 2–3 minutes, until the liquid reduces.

Stir the coriander through and season with salt and pepper. Serve with couscous.

RICE & OTHER GRAINS

Rice and other grains can be transformed into myriad dishes with the pressure cooker, and all with minimal effort. Add just a few ingredients to make a delicious side dish, salad, light lunch or satisfying meal.

Grains make fantastic accompaniments to many of the meat and vegetable recipes featured in this book. They soak up the rich sauces of stews and curries, and make a lovely textural contrast. And best of all, they're incredibly quick to make in the pressure cooker – a rice pilaf is cooked to perfection in just 3 minutes! Pair the spiced Indian pilaf (page 197), lemon rice (page 202) or tamarind rice (page 203) with any of the Indian curries. Serve the Mexican red rice (page 210) or green rice (page 209) with chicken mole (page 67) or chilli con carne (page 88), or with a variety of dishes as part of a Mexican feast.

Delicious, protein-packed quinoa cooks in just 1 minute under pressure, and is perfect for making nutritious salads. For something a little exotic, try the Middle Eastern jewelled quinoa salad (page 205), or perhaps the quinoa tabbouleh (page 206) will take your fancy.

Wild rice has an unusual nutty flavour and slightly chewy texture that goes nicely with lamb or chicken. A moghrabieh salad, like the date, orange and walnut salad on page 207, teams well with a grilled chicken breast. And don't forget brown rice, which cooks in half the time when using a pressure cooker.

Winter warmers such as creamy risotto can be ready in less than 5 minutes, with no stirring required. For a variation, try a barley or farro 'risotto' – or perhaps a congee or spiced paella may be more to your liking?

MINTED PEA & SCALLOP RISOTTO

SERVES 4

2 tablespoons (40 g/1½ oz) butter
1 medium-sized onion, finely chopped
1 clove garlic, crushed
1½ cups arborio, carnaroli or vialone nano rice
½ cup (125 ml/4 fl oz) dry white wine
4½ cups (1.1 L/2 pt 6 fl oz) chicken stock (page 27)

1 cup fresh or frozen peas
½ cup coarsely chopped mint
2 teaspoons finely grated lemon zest
salt and freshly ground black pepper
2 tablespoons (40 ml/1½ fl oz) olive oil
16–20 scallops, cleaned and roe removed

Melt the butter in a pressure cooker over low–medium heat. Cook the onion and garlic until the onion is clear and softened. Add the rice and stir to coat in butter. Pour in the wine and bring to the boil. Pour in the stock, then lock the lid in place and bring to low pressure over medium heat. Cook for 4 minutes, adjusting the heat as necessary to maintain a low pressure.

Release the pressure using the quick-release method.

Add the peas, mint and lemon zest to the rice and cook, stirring continuously, over low–medium heat for 1–2 minutes, until the peas are tender. Season with salt and pepper.

Heat the oil in a large frying pan over medium–high heat. Fry the scallops for 1–2 minutes on each side, or until golden brown and just cooked through. Add the scallops to the risotto and stir to combine.

Serve immediately, seasoned with freshly ground black pepper.

ROAST PUMPKIN, CHICKEN & ROCKET RISOTTO

SERVES 4

500 g (1 lb 2 oz) butternut pumpkin, peeled and cut into 2.5-cm (1-in) cubes
2 tablespoons (40 ml/1½ fl oz) olive oil
salt and freshly ground black pepper
2 tablespoons (40 g/1½ oz) butter
1 medium-sized onion, finely chopped
2 cloves garlic, crushed
3 skinless chicken thigh fillets, cut into 2.5-cm (1-in) cubes

1½ cups arborio, carnaroli or vialone nano rice
½ cup (125 ml/4 fl oz) dry white wine
4½ cups (1.1 L/2 pt 6 fl oz) chicken stock (page 27)
120 g (4 oz) rocket
½ cup grated parmesan cheese
100 g (3½ oz) marinated goat's cheese, sliced

Preheat the oven to 200°C (390°F).

Spread the pumpkin on a baking tray, drizzle with the oil and toss to coat. Season with salt and pepper. Roast in the oven for 25–30 minutes, until tender and golden brown.

Melt the butter in a pressure cooker over low–medium heat. Cook the onion and garlic until the onion is clear and softened. Increase the heat to medium, then add the chicken and cook for 3–4 minutes, until golden brown. Add the rice and stir to coat in butter. Pour in the wine and bring to the boil. Pour in the stock, then lock the lid in place and bring to low pressure over medium heat. Cook for 5 minutes, adjusting the heat as necessary to maintain a low pressure.

Release the pressure using the quick-release method.

Add the pumpkin, rocket and parmesan to the rice and stir to combine. Season with salt and pepper.

Serve immediately, scattered with goat's cheese.

ROASTED PARSNIP, CHESTNUT & SPINACH RISOTTO

SERVES 4

4 medium-sized parsnips, cut in half crossways
then into 2-cm (¾-in) thick strips
200 g (7 oz) chestnuts
2 tablespoons (40 ml/1½ fl oz) olive oil
1 teaspoon freshly grated nutmeg
salt and freshly ground black pepper
2 tablespoons (40 g/1½ oz) butter
1 large red onion, halved and thickly sliced

1 clove garlic, crushed
1½ cups arborio, carnaroli or vialone nano rice
4½ cups (1.1 L/2 pt 6 fl oz) chicken stock
(page 27)
½ cup shaved parmesan cheese, plus extra
to serve
120 g (4 oz) baby spinach

Preheat the oven to 200°C (390°F).

Place the parsnip and chestnuts on a baking tray, drizzle with the oil and toss to coat. Season with the nutmeg and salt and pepper. Cook in the oven for 25–30 minutes, until tender and golden brown. Peel the chestnuts and chop the flesh coarsely.

Melt the butter in a pressure cooker over low–medium heat. Cook the onion and garlic until the onion is clear and softened. Add the rice and stir to coat. Pour in the stock, then lock the lid in place and bring to low pressure over medium heat. Cook for 5 minutes, adjusting the heat as necessary to maintain a low pressure.

Release the pressure using the quick-release method.

Add the parmesan, parsnip, chestnuts and spinach to the rice and stir to combine. Season with salt and pepper.

Serve immediately, scattered with shaved parmesan.

If fresh chestnuts are unavailable, use 120 g (4 oz) dried chestnuts: soak them in boiling water for 15 minutes before use.

SAFFRON & BLUE-EYE RISOTTO

SERVES 4

4 medium-sized tomatoes
2 tablespoons (40 g/1½ oz) butter
1 medium-sized onion, finely chopped
1 clove garlic, crushed
1½ cups arborio, carnaroli or vialone nano rice
½ cup (125 ml/4 fl oz) dry white wine
1 teaspoon saffron threads, soaked in
2 tablespoons (40 ml/1½ fl oz) water
4½ cups (1.1 L/2 pt 6 fl oz) fish stock (page 29)

150 g (5 oz) snow peas, trimmed and cut into
2.5-cm (1-in) pieces
500 g (1 lb 2 oz) blue-eye fillets, cut into
2.5-cm (1-in) cubes
2 tablespoons coarsely chopped basil
1 tablespoon (20 ml/¾ fl oz) freshly squeezed
lemon juice
salt and freshly ground black pepper

Score a cross in the base of each tomato, then blanch them in boiling water for 20 seconds. Drain, and refresh in cold water. Peel the tomatoes, then cut each in half horizontally and remove the seeds. Dice the flesh and set aside.

Melt the butter in a pressure cooker over low–medium heat. Cook the onion and garlic until the onion is clear and softened. Add the rice and stir to coat. Pour in the wine and saffron water, and bring to the boil. Pour in the stock, then lock the lid in place and bring to low pressure over medium heat. Cook for 5 minutes, adjusting the heat as necessary to maintain a low pressure.

Release the pressure using the quick-release method.

Add the snow peas and fish to the rice. Cover, but do not lock the lid in place, and cook for 2 minutes, or until the fish is just cooked through and the snow peas are tender. Stir in the tomato, basil and lemon juice, and season with salt and pepper.

Serve immediately.

PEARL BARLEY, KALE & WILD MUSHROOM 'RISOTTO'

SERVES 4

20 g (¾ oz) dried porcini mushrooms
2 tablespoons (40 g/1½ oz) butter
1 medium-sized onion, finely chopped
2 cloves garlic, crushed
500 g (1 lb 2 oz) mixed wild mushrooms, sliced
300 g (10½ oz) pearl barley
½ cup (125 ml/4 fl oz) red wine

5 cups (1.25 L/2 pt 10 fl oz) chicken stock
(page 27) or vegetable stock (page 30)
4 kale leaves (about 150 g/5 oz),
coarsely chopped
½ cup grated pecorino cheese, plus extra
(shaved) to serve
salt and freshly ground black pepper

Soak the porcini mushrooms in ½ cup (125 ml/4 fl oz) warm water for 15 minutes. Drain, reserving the liquid, and finely chop.

Melt the butter in a pressure cooker over low–medium heat. Cook the onion and garlic until the onion is clear and softened. Increase the heat to medium, add the wild mushrooms and cook for 3–5 minutes, until golden brown. Add the barley and stir to coat in butter. Pour in the wine and bring to the boil. Pour in the stock and reserved porcini liquid, then lock the lid in place and bring to high pressure over high heat. Cook for 20 minutes, adjusting the heat as necessary to maintain a high pressure.

Release the pressure using the quick-release method.

Add the kale to the pot and cook, stirring continuously, for 5 minutes, or until the kale is tender. Add the pecorino and stir to combine. Season with salt and pepper.

Serve scattered with shaved pecorino.

FARRO, PANCETTA & RADICCHIO 'RISOTTO'

SERVES 4

2 tablespoons (40 g/1½ oz) butter
1 large red onion, halved and
    thickly sliced
2 cloves garlic, crushed
150 g (5 oz) pancetta, diced
300 g (10½ oz) farro
½ cup (125 ml/4 fl oz) red wine
5 cups (1.25 L/2 pt 10 fl oz) chicken stock
    (page 27)

1 large head radicchio, leaves separated
    and coarsely chopped
100 g (3½ oz) walnut halves, lightly toasted
1 cup coarsely chopped flat-leaf parsley,
    plus extra for garnish
2 tablespoons (40 ml/1½ fl oz) freshly squeezed
    lemon juice
salt and freshly ground black pepper
125 g (4½ oz) taleggio cheese, thinly sliced

Melt the butter in a pressure cooker over low–medium heat. Cook the onion and garlic until the onion is clear and softened. Increase the heat to medium, add the pancetta and cook for 3–5 minutes, until golden brown. Add the farro and stir to coat in butter. Pour in the wine and bring to the boil. Pour in the stock, then lock the lid in place and bring to high pressure over high heat. Cook for 20 minutes, adjusting the heat as necessary to maintain a high pressure.

Release the pressure using the quick-release method.

Preheat the griller to high.

Add the radicchio to the rice and cook, stirring continuously, for 3–5 minutes, until the radicchio is tender. Stir in the walnuts, parsley and lemon juice. Season with salt and pepper.

Spoon the 'risotto' into heatproof serving dishes and scatter with slices of taleggio. Place under the grill for 1–2 minutes to melt the cheese.

Serve sprinkled with parsley.

Substitute pearl barley for the farro if desired.

SEAFOOD PAELLA

SERVES 4–6

2 tablespoons (40 ml/1½ fl oz) olive oil
1 large red onion, halved and thickly sliced
2 cloves garlic, finely chopped
1½ cups calasparra or other short-grain
white rice (such as arborio)
4 medium-sized tomatoes, cut into wedges
2 large red chillies, deseeded and finely sliced
1 teaspoon smoked paprika
½ cup (125 ml/4 fl oz) dry white wine
1 teaspoon saffron threads, soaked in
2 tablespoons (40 ml/1½ fl oz) water

1 L (34 fl oz) fish stock (page 29)
12 mussels, scrubbed and debearded
350 g (12 oz) firm white fish fillets,
cut into 2-cm (¾-in) cubes
250 g (9 oz) raw (green) prawns, shelled and
deveined but tails left on
½ cup fresh or frozen peas
1 cup coarsely chopped flat-leaf parsley
salt and freshly ground black pepper
lemon wedges, to serve

Heat the oil in a pressure cooker over low–medium heat. Cook the onion and garlic until the onion is clear and softened. Add the rice and stir to coat in oil. Add the tomato, chilli and paprika and stir to combine. Pour in the wine and saffron water and bring to the boil. Pour in the stock, then lock the lid in place and bring to low pressure over medium heat. Cook for 3 minutes, adjusting the heat as necessary to maintain a low pressure.

Release the pressure using the quick-release method.

Add the mussels to the pot, lock the lid in place and bring to high pressure over high heat. Immediately release the pressure using the quick-release method.

Scatter the fish, prawns and peas over the rice. Cover, but do not lock the lid in place, and cook over low heat for 3 minutes, or until the fish is just cooked through, the prawns are pink and the peas are tender. Stir the parsley through and season with salt and pepper.

Serve with lemon wedges.

JAMBALAYA

SERVES 6

2 tablespoons (40 ml/1½ fl oz) olive oil
1 large onion, halved and thinly sliced
2 sticks celery, finely sliced
3 cloves garlic, finely chopped
3 skinless chicken thigh fillets, quartered
1 andouille sausage, diced
2 cups long-grain white rice
1 × 400-g (14-oz) can chopped tomatoes
1 red capsicum, sliced
1 green capsicum, sliced

1 teaspoon dried thyme
1 teaspoon cayenne pepper
½ teaspoon dried chilli flakes
1 L (34 fl oz) chicken stock (page 27)
250 g (9 oz) raw (green) prawns, shelled and
   deveined but tails left on
4 spring onions, finely chopped
½ cup finely chopped flat-leaf parsley
salt and freshly ground black pepper

Heat the oil in a pressure cooker over low–medium heat. Cook the onion, celery and garlic until the onion is clear and softened. Increase the heat to medium, add the chicken and sausage, and cook for 3–4 minutes, until golden brown. Add the rice and stir to coat. Add the tomatoes, capsicum, thyme, cayenne pepper and chilli flakes, and stir to combine. Pour in the stock, then lock the lid in place and bring to high pressure over high heat. Cook for
3 minutes, adjusting the heat as necessary to maintain a high pressure.

Release the pressure using the natural-release method.

Add the prawns to the rice. Cover, but do not lock the lid in place, and cook over low heat for 1–2 minutes, until the prawns are pink and just cooked through. Stir in the spring onion and parsley, and season with salt and pepper.

Use chorizo or another spicy smoked sausage if andouille is unavailable.

CREOLE RICE & BEANS

SERVES 4–6

1 cup dried kidney beans
1 tablespoon (20 ml/¾ fl oz) vegetable oil
2 tablespoons (40 ml/1½ fl oz) olive oil
3 rashers bacon, sliced
1 medium-sized onion, halved and sliced
2 cloves garlic, finely chopped

1½ cups long-grain white rice
1 bay leaf
½ teaspoon dried thyme
1 cup (250 ml/8½ fl oz) coconut milk
salt and freshly ground black pepper

Soak the beans in a large bowl of cold water for at least 4 hours (or overnight). Drain and rinse.

Place the beans, 3 cups (750 ml/25 fl oz) water and the vegetable oil in a pressure cooker. Lock the lid in place and bring to high pressure over high heat. Cook for 4 minutes, adjusting the heat as necessary to maintain a high pressure.

Release the pressure using the natural-release method.

Drain the beans and transfer to a medium-sized bowl.

Heat the olive oil in the pressure cooker over low–medium heat. Sauté the bacon, onion and garlic until golden brown. Add the rice, beans, bay leaf and thyme, and stir to combine. Pour in 1½ cups (375 ml/12½ fl oz) water and the coconut milk. Lock the lid in place and bring to high pressure over high heat. Cook for 5 minutes, adjusting the heat as necessary to maintain a high pressure.

Release the pressure using the natural-release method.

Discard the bay leaf and season with salt and pepper to serve.

SPICED INDIAN PILAF WITH FRIED ONION

SERVES 4-6

2 cups basmati rice
2 tablespoons (40 ml/1½ fl oz) melted ghee or vegetable oil
1 small onion, finely chopped
2 cloves garlic, finely chopped
1 green cayenne chilli, deseeded and finely sliced
1 bay leaf
1 cinnamon stick

3 cardamom pods, bruised
1 teaspoon garam masala
½ teaspoon cumin seeds
¼ teaspoon ground turmeric
3 cups (750 ml/25 fl oz) chicken stock (page 27)

FRIED ONION
3 tablespoons (60 ml/2 fl oz) vegetable oil
1 large onion, thinly sliced into rounds

To prepare the fried onion, heat the oil in a frying pan over medium–high heat. Fry the onion, turning frequently, for 1–2 minutes, or until crisp and golden brown. Remove using a slotted spoon and set aside on paper towel.

Wash the rice in a fine mesh sieve under cold running water until the water runs clear. Set aside to drain.

Heat the ghee or oil in a pressure cooker over low–medium heat. Cook the onion, garlic, chilli, bay leaf and spices until the onion has softened and the spices are fragrant. Add the rice and stir to coat. Pour in the stock, then lock the lid in place and bring to high pressure over high heat. Cook for 3 minutes, adjusting the heat as necessary to maintain a high pressure.

Release the pressure using the natural-release method.

Fluff the rice with a fork. Serve scattered with fried onion.

CINNAMON RICE WITH CHICKEN, PISTACHIOS & BARBERRIES

SERVES 4–6

2 cups basmati rice
2 tablespoons (40 g/1½ oz) butter
1 tablespoon (20 ml/¾ fl oz) vegetable oil
1 small onion, finely chopped
2 cloves garlic, finely chopped
3 skinless chicken thigh fillets, cut into
2.5-cm (1-in) cubes
1 teaspoon ground cinnamon

½ teaspoon ground cardamom
½ teaspoon saffron threads
3 cups (750 ml/25 fl oz) chicken stock (page 27)
1 teaspoon caster sugar
½ cup pistachios, lightly toasted
¼ cup barberries
½ cup flat-leaf parsley leaves
salt and freshly ground black pepper

Wash the rice in a fine mesh sieve under cold running water until the water runs clear. Set aside to drain.

Heat the butter and oil in a pressure cooker over low–medium heat. Cook the onion and garlic until the onion is clear and softened. Increase the heat to medium, add the chicken and spices, and cook for 2–3 minutes, until the chicken is golden brown and the spices fragrant. Add the rice and stir to coat. Pour in the stock and add the sugar. Lock the lid in place and bring to high pressure over high heat. Cook for 3 minutes, adjusting the heat as necessary to maintain a high pressure.

Release the pressure using the natural-release method.

Fluff the rice with a fork. Stir in the pistachios, barberries and parsley. Season with salt and pepper, and serve.

Use dried cranberries if barberries are unavailable.

MALAYSIAN-STYLE COCONUT RICE WITH CRISP SALTY FISH, BOILED EGG & CHILLI

SERVES 4

2 cups basmati rice
2 tablespoons (40 ml/1½ fl oz) vegetable oil
1 cup (250 ml/8½ fl oz) coconut milk
½ teaspoon salt
ACCOMPANIMENTS
4 hard-boiled eggs, peeled and cut in half lengthways

½ cup ikan bilis (dried anchovies)
½ cup roasted peanuts
sambal ulek
½ Continental cucumber, halved lengthways then sliced on the diagonal
2 medium-sized tomatoes, cut into wedges

Wash the rice in a fine mesh sieve under cold running water until the water runs clear. Set aside to drain.

Heat the oil in a pressure cooker over low–medium heat. Add the rice and stir to coat. Pour in 1½ cups (375 ml/12½ fl oz) water and the coconut milk, add the salt and stir to combine. Lock the lid in place and bring to high pressure over high heat. Cook for 3 minutes, adjusting the heat as necessary to maintain a high pressure.

Release the pressure using the natural-release method.

Fluff the rice with a fork.

Serve the rice with the hard-boiled eggs, ikan bilis, peanuts and a dollop of sambal ulek. Garnish with the cucumber and tomato.

BROWN RICE WITH SPICED EGGPLANT & SPINACH

SERVES 4–6

1 large eggplant, cut into 2.5-cm (1-in) cubes
salt
3 tablespoons (60 ml/2 fl oz) olive oil
1 large onion, halved and thinly sliced
2 cloves garlic, thinly sliced
2 teaspoons finely grated ginger
1 large red chilli, deseeded and finely sliced
1 teaspoon yellow mustard seeds
1 teaspoon ground coriander

1 teaspoon ground turmeric
1 teaspoon ground cumin
½ teaspoon ground chilli
2 cups short-grain brown rice
2 medium-sized tomatoes, coarsely chopped
3 cups (750 ml/25 fl oz) boiling water
90 g (3 oz) baby spinach
natural yoghurt, to serve

Place the eggplant in a colander set over a bowl and sprinkle with 1 tablespoon salt. Set aside to drain for 30 minutes. Rinse under cold running water and pat dry with paper towel.

Heat a little of the oil in a pressure cooker over medium–high heat. Cook the eggplant, in batches, for 3–4 minutes, adding more oil as required, until golden brown. Transfer to a plate lined with paper towel.

Add the onion and garlic to the pot and cook over low–medium heat until the onion is clear and softened. Add the ginger, chilli and spices, and cook for 30 seconds or until the mustard seeds begin to pop and the spices are fragrant. Add the rice and stir to coat. Return the eggplant to the pot and add the tomato. Pour in the boiling water, then lock the lid in place and bring to high pressure over high heat. Cook for 15 minutes, adjusting the heat as necessary to maintain a high pressure.

Release the pressure using the natural-release method.

Add the spinach to the rice and stir until it has wilted. Season with salt.

Serve with natural yoghurt.

BROWN RICE WITH SHIITAKES, SEAWEED & TOASTED SEEDS

SERVES 4–6

50 g (1¾ oz) dried shiitake mushrooms
2 tablespoons (40 ml/1½ fl oz) vegetable oil
1 teaspoon sesame oil
1 small onion, finely chopped
1 clove garlic, finely chopped
2 cups short-grain brown rice
2½ cups (625 ml/21 fl oz) dashi stock, hot
3 tablespoons (60 ml/2 fl oz) soy sauce

4 × 15-cm (6-in) strips dried wakame
3 spring onions, finely sliced
⅓ cup pickled ginger, drained
¼ cup sunflower seeds, lightly toasted
2 tablespoons white sesame seeds, lightly toasted
2 teaspoons black sesame seeds

Place the shiitakes in a bowl and just cover with boiling water. Set aside to soak for 30 minutes, or until softened. Drain and slice thinly.

Heat the vegetable oil and sesame oil in a pressure cooker over low–medium heat. Cook the onion and garlic until clear and softened. Add the shiitakes and cook for a further 2–3 minutes, until golden brown. Add the rice and stir to coat in oil. Pour in the hot stock and soy sauce, and add the wakame. Lock the lid in place and bring to high pressure over high heat. Cook for 15 minutes, adjusting the heat as necessary to maintain a high pressure.

Release the pressure using the natural-release method.

Add the spring onion, ginger and seeds to the rice and stir to combine. Serve.

LEMON RICE

SERVES 4–6

2 cups basmati rice
2 tablespoons (40 ml/1½ fl oz) melted ghee or vegetable oil
1 small onion, finely chopped
1 teaspoon finely grated ginger
1 small dried red chilli

7 fresh curry leaves
1 teaspoon black mustard seeds
1 teaspoon ground turmeric
juice of 1 lemon
salt

Wash the rice in a fine mesh sieve under cold running water until the water runs clear. Set aside to drain.

Heat the ghee or oil in a pressure cooker over low–medium heat. Cook the onion and ginger until the onion is clear and softened. Add the chilli, curry leaves and spices, and cook for 30 seconds or until the mustard seeds begin to pop and the spices are fragrant. Add the rice and stir to coat. Pour in 2½ cups (625 ml/21 fl oz) water, then lock the lid in place and bring to high pressure over high heat. Cook for 3 minutes, adjusting the heat as necessary to maintain a high pressure.

Release the pressure using the natural-release method.

Fluff the rice with a fork. Stir in the lemon juice and season with salt to serve.

TAMARIND RICE

SERVES 4–6

4 tablespoons tamarind pulp
2 cups basmati rice
3 tablespoons (60 ml/2 fl oz) melted ghee or vegetable oil
¼ cup raw peanuts
2 green cayenne chillies

2 small dried red chillies
10 fresh curry leaves
1 teaspoon black mustard seeds
1 teaspoon cumin seeds
salt

Combine the tamarind with 1 cup (250 ml/8½ fl oz) water in a small bowl and set aside for 15 minutes, to soften. Stir to make a paste, then pass through a fine mesh sieve, discarding the solids.

Wash the rice in a fine mesh sieve under cold running water until the water runs clear. Set aside to drain.

Heat half the ghee or oil in a pressure cooker over low–medium heat. Add the rice and stir to coat. Pour in 2¼ cups (560 ml/19 fl oz) water, then lock the lid in place and bring to high pressure over high heat. Cook for 3 minutes, adjusting the heat as necessary to maintain a high pressure.

Release the pressure using the natural-release method.

Heat the remaining ghee or oil in a medium-sized frying pan. Fry the peanuts until golden brown, then transfer to paper towel to drain. To the frying pan, add the fresh and dried chillies (whole), curry leaves, and mustard and cumin seeds, and cook for 30 seconds, or until the mustard seeds begin to pop and the spices are fragrant.

Fluff the rice with a fork. Stir in the tamarind liquid, peanuts and fried spices. Season with salt.

CARROT & TOASTED ALMOND PILAF

SERVES 4–6

2 cups basmati rice
3 tablespoons (60 g/2 oz) butter
1 medium-sized onion, halved and thinly sliced
1 clove garlic, finely chopped
1 teaspoon ground turmeric
½ teaspoon ground coriander
3 cups (750 ml/25 fl oz) chicken stock (page 27)

2 medium-sized carrots, coarsely grated
½ cup (80 g/3 oz) flaked almonds, lightly toasted
2 tablespoons (40 ml/1½ fl oz) freshly squeezed lemon juice
salt
coriander leaves, for garnish

Wash the rice in a fine mesh sieve under cold running water until the water runs clear. Set aside to drain.

Melt the butter in a pressure cooker over low–medium heat. Cook the onion, garlic and spices until the onion has softened and the spices are fragrant. Add the rice and stir to coat. Pour in the stock, then lock the lid in place and bring to high pressure over high heat. Cook for 3 minutes, adjusting the heat as necessary to maintain a high pressure.

Release the pressure using the natural-release method.

Fluff the rice with a fork. Stir in the carrot, almonds and lemon juice, and season with salt.

Serve garnished with coriander leaves.

JEWELLED QUINOA SALAD

SERVES 4–6

200 g (7 oz) quinoa
3 tablespoons (60 ml/2 fl oz) extra-virgin olive oil
¼ cup pine nuts
¼ cup pistachios
¼ cup currants
½ teaspoon ground cinnamon

½ cup pomegranate seeds
¼ cup coarsely chopped mint
¼ cup coarsely chopped coriander
2 tablespoons (40 ml/1½ fl oz) white-wine vinegar
salt and freshly ground black pepper

Toast the quinoa in a pressure cooker over medium heat for 1 minute, or until it begins to pop. Pour in 2 cups (500 ml/17 fl oz) water, then lock the lid in place and bring to low pressure over high heat. Cook for 1 minute.

Release the pressure using the natural-release method.

Fluff the quinoa with a fork, then spread it out on a large tray to cool.

Heat 1 tablespoon (20 ml/¾ fl oz) of the oil in a medium-sized frying pan over low–medium heat. Fry the pine nuts and pistachios until golden brown. Add the currants and cinnamon, and toss to coat.

In a medium-sized bowl, combine the quinoa, nuts and currants, pomegranate seeds and herbs. Add the vinegar and remaining oil, and toss to combine. Season with salt and pepper.

QUINOA TABBOULEH

SERVES 4–6

2 cups quinoa
⅓ cup (80 ml/3 fl oz) freshly squeezed lemon juice
2 cloves garlic, crushed
1 teaspoon Dijon mustard
⅓ cup (80 ml/3 fl oz) extra-virgin olive oil

salt and freshly ground black pepper
250 g (9 oz) cherry tomatoes, halved
2 cups coarsely chopped flat-leaf parsley
½ cup coarsely chopped mint
½ small red onion, finely chopped

Toast the quinoa in a pressure cooker over medium heat for 1 minute, or until it begins to pop. Pour in 2½ cups (625 ml/21 fl oz) water, then lock the lid in place and bring to low pressure over high heat. Cook for 1 minute.

Release the pressure using the natural-release method.

Fluff the quinoa with a fork, then spread it out on a large tray to cool.

Combine the lemon juice, garlic and mustard in a small bowl. Gradually whisk in the oil, and season with salt and pepper.

Place the quinoa, tomato, herbs and red onion in a medium-sized bowl. Pour the dressing over and toss to coat.

MOGHRABIEH, DATE, ORANGE & WALNUT SALAD

SERVES 4

2 tablespoons (40 ml/1½ fl oz) olive oil
1 small onion, finely chopped
1 clove garlic, finely chopped
1 cinnamon stick
300 g (10½ oz) moghrabieh
grated zest of 1 orange
3 cups (750 ml/25 fl oz) chicken stock (page 27)
60 g (2 oz) baby spinach, coarsely chopped

1 tablespoon (20 ml/¾ fl oz) freshly squeezed
  lemon juice
1 orange, segmented
150 g (5 oz) pitted dried dates,
  coarsely chopped
150 g (5 oz) walnuts, lightly toasted and
  coarsely chopped
salt and freshly ground black pepper

Heat the oil in a pressure cooker over low–medium heat. Cook the onion and garlic until the onion is clear and softened. Add the cinnamon stick and cook for 30 seconds or until fragrant. Add the moghrabieh and orange zest, and stir to coat. Pour in the chicken stock, then lock the lid in place and bring to high pressure over high heat. Cook for 7 minutes, adjusting the heat as necessary to maintain a high pressure.

Release the pressure using the natural-release method.

Remove the cinnamon stick from the mixture. Stir the spinach and lemon juice through the moghrabieh. Add the orange, dates and walnuts and stir to combine. Season with salt and pepper.

Serve warm.

CHINESE SAUSAGE CONGEE

SERVES 4

1½ cups short-grain white rice
1 tablespoon (20 ml/¾ fl oz) vegetable oil
1 teaspoon sesame oil
2 Chinese sausages, thinly sliced
2-cm (¾-in) piece ginger, sliced
5 cups (1.25 L/2 pt 10 fl oz) chicken stock
(page 27)

1 large egg, lightly beaten
⅓ cup coarsely chopped roasted peanuts,
  for garnish
4 thinly sliced spring onions, for garnish
soy sauce, to serve (optional)

Place the rice in a fine mesh sieve and wash under cold running water until the water runs clear. Drain well.

Place the rice in a food processor and blend until finely chopped.

Heat the vegetable and sesame oils in a pressure cooker over low–medium heat. Add the ground rice, sausage and ginger, and stir to coat. Pour in the stock, then lock the lid in place and bring to low pressure over high heat. Cook for 5 minutes, adjusting the heat as necessary to maintain a high pressure.

Release the pressure using the natural-release method.

Cook the congee, uncovered, over medium heat for a further 3–5 minutes, until thickened to a thin porridge consistency. Pour in the egg in a thin steady stream while stirring, to create strands of cooked egg.

Serve scattered with peanuts and spring onion, with a splash of soy sauce if desired.

MEXICAN GREEN RICE

2 cups basmati rice

1 small onion, coarsely chopped

1 large green chilli, deseeded and coarsely chopped

2 cloves garlic, coarsely chopped

1 teaspoon sea salt

½ teaspoon freshly ground black pepper

3 cups coriander leaves

3 tablespoons (60 ml/2 fl oz) olive oil

2½ cups (625 ml/21 fl oz) chicken stock (page 27)

2 tablespoons (40 ml/1½ fl oz) lime juice

Wash the rice in a fine mesh sieve under cold running water until the water runs clear. Set aside to drain.

Place the onion, chilli, garlic, salt and pepper in a food processor and blend to a coarse paste. Add the coriander and blend while gradually pouring in 2 tablespoons (40 ml/1½ fl oz) of the oil, to make a smooth paste.

Heat the remaining oil in a pressure cooker over low–medium heat. Add the green paste and cook, stirring constantly, for 2–3 minutes, until the onion has softened. Add the rice and stir to coat. Pour in the stock, then lock the lid in place and bring to high pressure over high heat. Cook for 3 minutes, adjusting the heat as necessary to maintain a high pressure.

Release the pressure using the natural-release method.

Fluff the rice with a fork. Stir in the lime juice to serve.

MEXICAN RED RICE

SERVES 4–6

2 cups basmati rice
2 tablespoons (40 ml/1½ fl oz) olive oil
1 small onion, finely chopped
1 large red chilli, deseeded and finely chopped
1 clove garlic, crushed

1 × 400-g (14-oz) can chopped tomatoes
1 tablespoon tomato paste
2 cups (500 ml/17 fl oz) chicken stock
  (page 27)
salt and freshly ground black pepper

Wash the rice in a fine mesh sieve under cold running water until the water runs clear. Set aside to drain.

Heat the oil in a pressure cooker over low–medium heat. Cook the onion, chilli and garlic until softened. Add the rice and stir to coat. Add the tomatoes and tomato paste, and stir to combine. Pour in the stock, then lock the lid in place and bring to high pressure over high heat. Cook for 3 minutes, adjusting the heat as necessary to maintain a high pressure.

Release the pressure using the natural-release method.

Fluff the rice with a fork and season with salt and pepper to serve.

WILD RICE PILAF WITH MUSHROOMS & HAZELNUTS

SERVES 4

2 tablespoons (40 ml/1½ fl oz) olive oil
1 tablespoon (20 g/¾ oz) butter
6 shallots, halved lengthways
2 cloves garlic, finely chopped
250 g (9 oz) button mushrooms, sliced
1 cup wild rice
2 cups (500 ml/17 fl oz) chicken stock (page 27)

2 tablespoons (40 ml/1½ fl oz) white-wine
  vinegar
120 g (4 oz) hazelnuts, lightly toasted and skins
  removed, coarsely chopped
¼ cup chives cut into short lengths
salt and freshly ground black pepper

Heat the oil and butter in a pressure cooker over low–medium heat. Cook the shallots and garlic until softened. Add the mushrooms and cook for 2–3 minutes, until golden brown. Add the rice and stir to coat. Pour in the stock, then lock the lid in place and bring to high pressure over high heat. Cook for 20 minutes, adjusting the heat as necessary to maintain a high pressure.

Release the pressure using the quick-release method.

Fluff the rice with a fork. Stir in the vinegar, hazelnuts and chives. Season with salt and pepper to serve.

WILD RICE SALAD WITH PRUNES, APRICOTS & ALMONDS

SERVES 4

1 tablespoon (20 ml/¾ fl oz) olive oil
1 cup wild rice
100 g (3½ oz) pitted prunes, finely sliced
100 g (3½ oz) dried apricots, finely sliced
½ cup slivered almonds, lightly toasted
1 cup coarsely chopped coriander

DRESSING
2 tablespoons (40 ml/1½ fl oz) red-wine vinegar
2 teaspoons finely grated orange zest
1 teaspoon wholegrain mustard
3 tablespoons (60 ml/2 fl oz) extra-virgin olive oil
salt and freshly ground black pepper

Heat the oil in a pressure cooker over low–medium heat. Add the rice and stir to coat. Pour in 3 cups (750 ml/25 fl oz) water, then lock the lid in place and bring to high pressure over high heat. Cook for 20 minutes, adjusting the heat as necessary to maintain a high pressure.

Release the pressure using the quick-release method.

Drain the rice and rinse under cold water. Drain again, then spread the rice on a large tray to cool.

To make the dressing, combine the vinegar, zest and mustard in a small bowl. Gradually whisk in the oil, and season with salt and pepper.

Place the rice, prunes, apricots, almonds and coriander in a serving bowl. Pour the dressing over and toss to combine.

DOLMADES

30–35 vine leaves (fresh or in brine)
⅓ cup (80 ml/3 fl oz) olive oil
4 shallots, finely chopped
2 cloves garlic, finely chopped
200 g (7 oz) mushrooms, finely chopped
1 cup medium-grain white rice
½ cup finely chopped dill

¼ cup finely chopped flat-leaf parsley
salt and freshly ground black pepper
2 cups (500 ml/17 fl oz) chicken stock
  (page 27)
3 tablespoons (60 ml/2 fl oz) freshly squeezed
  lemon juice
natural yoghurt, to serve

If using fresh vine leaves, blanch them in boiling water for 30 seconds, then refresh in cold water. If using leaves preserved in brine, soak them in warm water for 10 minutes.

Drain and separate the vine leaves. Gently pat the leaves dry using paper towel, setting aside any torn ones.

Heat half the oil in a medium-sized saucepan over low–medium heat. Add the shallot and garlic, and cook until softened. Add the mushrooms and cook for 2–3 minutes, until golden brown. Add the rice, dill and parsley, and stir to coat. Remove the pan from the heat and season the rice with salt and pepper.

Spread the leaves out on a clean kitchen surface with the smooth side down and the stems facing towards you. (You may need to overlap two leaves if they are small.) Cut off the stems. Place a teaspoonful of rice mixture at the base of each leaf. Fold the sides in, then roll up to enclose the rice – don't roll too tightly, as the rice will swell during cooking.

Spread any torn leaves in the base of the pressure cooker, then arrange the dolmades on top, seam-side down – pack them in tightly, so they don't unravel. Pour the stock over, then drizzle in the remaining oil and the lemon juice. Lock the lid in place and bring to low pressure over medium heat. Cook for 10 minutes, adjusting the heat as necessary to maintain a low pressure.

Release the pressure using the natural-release method.

Leave the dolmades in the cooker for 30 minutes, to cool.

Serve at room temperature, with yoghurt.

ROASTED BUCKWHEAT WITH EGG

SERVES 4

300 g (10½ oz) whole roasted buckwheat (kasha)

2 large eggs, lightly beaten

3 tablespoons (60 ml/2 fl oz) olive oil

1 small onion, halved and thinly sliced

3 cups (750 ml/25 fl oz) chicken stock (page 27)

1 tablespoon (20 g/¾ oz) butter

salt and freshly ground black pepper

Combine the buckwheat and eggs in a medium-sized bowl.

Heat the oil in a pressure cooker over medium heat. Add the onion and cook until softened. Add the buckwheat and egg mixture, and cook, stirring continuously, for 3 minutes, or until the grains separate. Pour in the stock, then lock the lid in place and bring to high pressure over high heat. Cook for 3 minutes, adjusting the heat as necessary to maintain a high pressure.

Release the pressure using the natural-release method.

Cook the buckwheat, stirring continuously, for a further 2–3 minutes, until of a thick porridge consistency. Stir in the butter and season with salt and pepper to serve.

MIDDLE EASTERN SPICED MILLET PILAF

SERVES 4

270 g (9½ oz) white French millet, rinsed and drained
2 tablespoons (40 ml/1½ fl oz) olive oil
1 tablespoon (20 g/¾ oz) butter
1 small onion, finely chopped
2 cloves garlic, finely chopped
½ teaspoon ground cinnamon
½ teaspoon ground allspice
¼ teaspoon ground chilli

½ teaspoon caster sugar
2 bay leaves
3 cups (750 ml/25 fl oz) chicken stock (page 27)
½ cup currants
¼ cup pine nuts, lightly toasted
1 cup coarsely chopped flat-leaf parsley
salt and freshly ground black pepper
natural yoghurt, to serve (optional)

Toast the millet in a pressure cooker over medium–high heat, until it begins to pop and turn golden brown. Transfer to a bowl and set aside.

Add the oil and butter to the pot, decrease the heat to low–medium and cook the onion and garlic until the onion is clear and softened. Add the spices, sugar and bay leaves, and cook for 30 seconds or until fragrant. Add the millet and stir to coat. Pour in the stock, then lock the lid in place and bring to high pressure over high heat. Cook for 45 minutes, adjusting the heat as necessary to maintain a high pressure.

Release the pressure using the natural-release method.

Stir the currants, pine nuts and parsley through the millet, and season with salt and pepper.

Serve with natural yoghurt, if desired.

BEANS & PULSES

Beans and pulses are a fabulous source of protein and fibre. They are an essential part of a vegetarian diet and for the carnivores amongst us they make a substantial, affordable and cholesterol-free meat alternative.

Pressure cookers have revolutionised the cooking of beans and pulses, slashing cooking times to make them a convenient, nutritious everyday food. There's no longer any need to stock your pantry with canned beans, which can be expensive and are often high in salt. Dried beans are cheap, easy to store (keep them in a cool dark place and they'll last for years) and now, with the help of your pressure cooker, also quick to prepare. No more boiling beans on the stove top for 40 minutes or more – now you can have a creamy bean stew or nutritious salad in minutes! Buying dried beans and pulses saves you money and is an environmentally responsible choice due to the minimal processing and packaging they require. And what's more, they taste better!

The choices are endless when it comes to cooking beans and pulses. You can eat them cold or hot, mashed or whole. Purée them to create flavoursome dips such as hummus (page 220) or pinto bean dip (page 221) and serve with pre-dinner drinks or as an afternoon snack. Add them to soups to transform a broth into a hearty, satisfying meal. Toss them with just a few other ingredients and add a zesty dressing for a nutritious summer salad like the Puy lentil and green bean salad with spiced yoghurt dressing (page 227). Try whipping up a red bean chilli (page 232), spiced dal or comforting stew to warm your belly in the colder months. Don't forget 'baked' beans (page 223) – perfect for a lazy Sunday morning.

TIPS FOR PREPARING BEANS

SOAKING BEANS

Most dried beans require soaking prior to cooking. Soaking rehydrates and softens the beans, speeding up the cooking process and helping the beans cook more evenly. Soaking also plays another very important role: it removes some of the complex sugars, which are difficult to digest and often give beans a bad name. (Lentils usually don't require any soaking.)

Pre-soak Method

If you've planned ahead, soak your beans in four times their volume of water, overnight or for a minimum of 4 hours. Drain, discarding the soaking water, and rinse the beans thoroughly.

Quick-soak Method

If you're rushed for time or have a sudden craving for refried-bean burritos, use the quick-soak method. Place the dried beans and four times their volume of water in a saucepan and bring to the boil. Boil the beans, uncovered, for 2 minutes. Remove the pan from the heat, cover, and set aside to soak for 1 hour. Drain, discarding the soaking water, and rinse the beans thoroughly. Cook as specified in the recipe.

COOKING BEANS

Ensure beans have sufficient liquid when cooking in the pressure cooker. Use 2 cups (500ml/17 fl oz) liquid for every 1 cup (approximately 200 g/7 oz) soaked beans, adding 1 tablespoon (20 ml/¾ fl oz) oil to help prevent foaming.

When cooking beans, do not fill the pressure cooker past the halfway mark. Beans swell to double their size when cooked and have a tendency to foam. Overfilling your cooker can result in the steam valve becoming clogged. (Refer to the safety instructions in your cooker's manual as to what to do in the event of a clogged steam valve.)

Cooking times for beans vary according to the age and dryness of the bean. Use the timing chart on page 23 as a guide, and cook for the shortest suggested time first. Check for doneness and if the beans are undercooked, lock the lid in place and cook for an extra minute or two.

Beans that require the same cooking time can be cooked together, but be aware that their colours may run and flavours will mingle. I suggest, time permitting, you cook them separately and combine afterwards.

Salt and acids toughen the skin of beans. Always salt your beans after cooking or when they are almost cooked. If adding acidic ingredients such as tomatoes, lemon juice or vinegar, do this at the end too. That said, a few tomatoes added to a soup or stew will cause no harm.

Always release the pressure using the natural-release method when cooking beans. This helps to prevent the steam valve from becoming clogged, and allows any foam to subside. Releasing the pressure gently also helps to prevent the beans from splitting or bursting, and the additional time allows the beans to finish cooking to a creamy texture.

Beans can be cooked ahead of time and stored in the refrigerator for 3–4 days or frozen for 4–6 months.

HUMMUS

MAKES 3 CUPS

1 cup dried chickpeas
1 small onion, halved
1 bay leaf
100 ml (3½ fl oz) extra-virgin olive oil,
plus extra for drizzling
3 cloves garlic, coarsely chopped
3 tablespoons (60 ml/2 fl oz) tahini

3 tablespoons (60 ml/2 fl oz) freshly squeezed
lemon juice
2 teaspoons ground cumin, plus extra
for sprinkling
½ teaspoon ground sweet paprika,
plus extra for sprinkling
salt

Soak the chickpeas in cold water for at least 4 hours (or overnight). Use the quick-soak method (page 218) if you are short of time. Drain and rinse.

Transfer the chickpeas to a pressure cooker and add the onion, bay leaf and 1 tablespoon (20 ml/¾ fl oz) of the oil. Pour in 3 cups (750 ml/25 fl oz) water and stir. Lock the lid in place and bring to high pressure over high heat. Cook for 15 minutes, adjusting the heat as necessary to maintain a high pressure.

Release the pressure using the natural-release method.

Drain the chickpeas, reserving ½ cup (125 ml/4 fl oz) of the cooking liquid. Discard the onion and bay leaf. Transfer the chickpeas to a food processor, add the garlic, and blend to a coarse paste. Add the remaining oil, the tahini, lemon juice, cumin and paprika, and blend to combine. Gradually pour in the reserved cooking liquid, blending until mixture is thick and smooth. Season with salt.

Serve drizzled with oil and sprinkled with cumin and paprika.

Serve immediately or store in an airtight container in the refrigerator for 4–5 days.

MEXICAN PINTO-BEAN DIP

MAKES 3 CUPS

1 cup dried pinto beans
1 small onion, halved
1 bay leaf
2 tablespoons (40 ml/1½ fl oz) olive oil
1 clove garlic, finely chopped
1 chipotle chilli in adobo sauce, finely chopped
1 teaspoon ground cumin

1 teaspoon hot paprika
¼ teaspoon ground chilli
⅓ cup (80 ml/3 fl oz) sour cream
1 tablespoon (20 ml/¾ fl oz) lime juice
salt and freshly ground black pepper
corn chips, to serve

Soak the pinto beans in cold water for at least 4 hours (or overnight). Use the quick-soak method (page 218) if you are short of time. Drain and rinse.

Place the beans in a pressure cooker with 3 cups (750 ml/25 fl oz) water, the onion, the bay leaf and 1 tablespoon (20 ml/¾ fl oz) of the oil. Lock the lid in place and bring to high pressure over high heat. Cook for 6 minutes, adjusting the heat as necessary to maintain a high pressure.

Release the pressure using the natural-release method.

Drain the beans, reserving ½ cup (125 ml/4 fl oz) of the cooking liquid. Discard the onion and bay leaf.

Heat the remaining oil in a small frying pan over low–medium heat. Cook the garlic and chipotle chilli until softened. Add the ground spices and cook for 30 seconds or until fragrant.

Place the beans and spiced oil in a food processor and blend to a coarse paste. Add the sour cream and lime juice and blend to combine. Gradually pour in the reserved cooking liquid, blending until thick and smooth. Season with salt and pepper.

Serve with corn chips.

Serve immediately or store in an airtight container in the refrigerator for 4–5 days.

BLACK BEAN, CORN, AVOCADO & FETTA SALAD

SERVES 4

1 cup dried black turtle beans
1 tablespoon (20 ml/¾ fl oz) vegetable oil, plus extra for brushing
1 bay leaf
1 corn cob
1 avocado, diced
1 small red onion, finely sliced
1 cup coarsely chopped coriander
100 g (3½ oz) fetta, crumbled

DRESSING
3 tablespoons (60 ml/2 fl oz) lime juice
1 jalapeno chilli, finely chopped
1 clove garlic, crushed
½ teaspoon ground cumin
½ teaspoon hot paprika
3 tablespoons (60 ml/2 fl oz) extra-virgin olive oil
salt and freshly ground black pepper

Soak the beans in cold water for at least 4 hours (or overnight). Use the quick-soak method (page 218) if you are short of time. Drain and rinse.

Place the beans in a pressure cooker with 3 cups (750 ml/25 fl oz) water, the oil and the bay leaf. Lock the lid in place and bring to high pressure over high heat. Cook for 7 minutes, adjusting the heat as necessary to maintain a high pressure.

Release the pressure using the natural-release method.

Drain the beans, discarding the bay leaf. Rinse the beans under cold running water and spread out on a tray to cool.

Preheat a char grill or barbecue to medium–high.

Remove the husk from the corn and brush the cob with oil. Grill, turning occasionally, for 10 minutes, or until the corn is tender and slightly charred. Use a sharp knife to slice the kernels off the cob.

Combine the beans and corn with the remaining salad ingredients in a serving bowl.

To make the dressing, combine the lime juice, chilli, garlic and spices in a small bowl. Gradually whisk in the oil, and season with salt and pepper. Pour the dressing over the salad and toss to coat.

'BAKED' BEANS WITH SMOKY BACON

SERVES 4-6

1½ cups dried haricot beans
2 tablespoons (40 ml/1½ fl oz) olive oil
1 large onion, halved and thinly sliced
2 cloves garlic, finely chopped
200 g (7 oz) pancetta, diced
2 tablespoons (40 ml/1½ fl oz) maple syrup

1 teaspoon smoked paprika
1 bay leaf
1 × 400-g (14-oz) can chopped tomatoes
½ cup (125 ml/4 fl oz) chicken stock (page 27)
salt and freshly ground black pepper
crusty bread, to serve

Soak the beans in cold water for at least 4 hours (or overnight). Use the quick-soak method (page 218) if you are short of time. Drain and rinse.

Place the beans in a pressure cooker with 3 cups (750 ml/25 fl oz) water and 1 tablespoon (20 ml/¾ fl oz) of the oil. Lock the lid in place and bring to high pressure over high heat. Cook for 4 minutes, adjusting the heat as necessary to maintain a high pressure.

Release the pressure using the natural-release method.

Drain the beans and set aside.

Heat the remaining oil in the pressure cooker over low–medium heat. Cook the onion and garlic until the onion is clear and softened. Add the pancetta and cook for 3–4 minutes, until golden brown. Add the maple syrup, paprika and bay leaf, and stir to combine. Pour in the tomatoes and stock, then lock the lid in place and bring to high pressure over high heat. Cook for 5 minutes, adjusting the heat as necessary to maintain a high pressure.

Release the pressure using the quick-release method.

Return the beans to the pot and simmer, uncovered, for 5 minutes, or until the sauce has thickened and the beans are tender. Season with salt and pepper.

Serve with crusty bread.

REFRIED-BEAN BURRITOS

SERVES 4

8 flour tortillas
90 g (3 oz) cheddar cheese, coarsely grated
coriander leaves and sour cream, to serve
REFRIED BEANS
2 cups dried pinto beans
1 medium-sized onion, halved
1 bay leaf
⅓ cup (80 ml/3 fl oz) vegetable oil
1 rasher bacon, finely chopped
1 large onion, finely chopped
2 cloves garlic, finely chopped

1 teaspoon ground cumin
1 chipotle chilli in adobo sauce, finely chopped
GUACAMOLE
2 avocadoes, coarsely chopped
½ small red onion, finely chopped
1 clove garlic, finely chopped
½ green bird's eye chilli, deseeded and
  finely chopped
2 tablespoons (40 ml/1½ fl oz) lime juice
salt and freshly ground black pepper

Soak the beans in cold water for at least 4 hours (or overnight). Use the quick-soak method (page 218) if you are short of time. Drain and rinse.

Place the beans in a pressure cooker with 6 cups (1.5 L/3 pt 3 fl oz) water, the onion halves, the bay leaf and 2 tablespoons (40 ml/1½ fl oz) of the oil. Lock the lid in place and bring to high pressure over high heat. Cook for 6 minutes, adjusting the heat as necessary to maintain a high pressure.

Meanwhile, to make the guacamole, place the avocado, onion, garlic and chilli in a medium-sized bowl and mash roughly with a fork to combine. Stir in the lime juice and season with salt and pepper.

Release the cooker's pressure using the natural-release method.

Drain the beans, reserving ½ cup (125 ml/4 fl oz) of the cooking liquid. Discard the bay leaf.

Place the beans and cooked onion in a food processor, and blend while gradually adding enough of the reserved cooking liquid to make a thick paste.

Heat the remaining oil in a large heavy-based frying pan over low–medium heat. Cook the bacon for 2–3 minutes, until golden brown. Add the chopped onion and garlic, and cook until the onion has softened. Add the beans, cumin and chipotle chilli, and cook, stirring frequently, for 10–15 minutes, until thick and well fried. Add a little more of the cooking liquid to adjust the consistency to a thick, moist paste.

To serve, heat the tortillas in the microwave or oven (following the packet instructions). Spread each warmed tortilla with refried bean mixture, sprinkle with cheese and add some guacamole, sour cream and coriander. Wrap to enclose the filling, and serve.

WARM WHITE BEAN & ARTICHOKE SALAD

SERVES 4

1½ cups dried cannellini beans
2 tablespoons (40 ml/1½ fl oz) olive oil
1 medium-sized onion, halved and thickly sliced
3 cloves garlic, thinly sliced
8 marinated artichoke hearts, thickly sliced

2 tablespoons (40 ml/1½ fl oz) freshly squeezed lemon juice
2 tablespoons (40 ml/1½ fl oz) extra-virgin olive oil
1 cup coarsely chopped flat-leaf parsley
salt and freshly ground black pepper

Soak the beans in cold water for at least 4 hours (or overnight). Use the quick-soak method (page 218) if you are short of time. Drain and rinse.

Combine the beans with 4½ cups (1.1 L/2 pt 6 fl oz) water and 1 tablespoon (20 ml/¾ fl oz) of the olive oil in a pressure cooker. Lock the lid in place and bring to high pressure over high heat. Cook for 6 minutes, adjusting the heat as necessary to maintain a high pressure.

Release the pressure using the natural-release method.

Drain the beans, then place in a medium-sized bowl and set aside.

Heat the remaining olive oil in a medium-sized frying pan. Cook the onion and garlic until clear and softened. Add the artichoke, lemon juice and extra-virgin olive oil and toss to warm through. Pour the mixture over the beans, stir the parsley through, and season with salt and pepper.

Serve warm.

PUY LENTIL & GREEN BEAN SALAD WITH SPICED YOGHURT DRESSING

SERVES 6

2 cups dried Puy lentils, rinsed
2 tablespoons (40 ml/1½ fl oz) olive oil
2 bay leaves
150 g (5 oz) green beans, trimmed
3 medium-sized tomatoes, diced
60 g (2 oz) baby spinach
1 small red onion, halved and thinly sliced
½ preserved lemon, pulp discarded and skin thinly sliced lengthways
1 teaspoon Dijon mustard
2 tablespoons (40 ml/1½ fl oz) freshly squeezed lemon juice

3 tablespoons (60 ml/2 fl oz) extra-virgin olive oil
½ cup flaked almonds, lightly toasted

YOGHURT DRESSING
1 cup (250 ml/8½ fl oz) natural yoghurt
1 tablespoon (20 ml/¾ fl oz) lemon juice
1 clove garlic, crushed
1 teaspoon ground cumin, plus extra for sprinkling
½ teaspoon paprika, plus extra for sprinkling
salt and freshly ground black pepper

Place the lentils in a pressure cooker with 3½ cups (875 ml/30 fl oz) water and the olive oil. Lock the lid in place and bring to high pressure over high heat. Cook for 4 minutes, adjusting the heat as necessary to maintain a high pressure.

Meanwhile, to make the yoghurt dressing, place all the ingredients in a small bowl and stir to combine.

Release the cooker's pressure using the natural-release method. Drain the lentils and spread out on a large tray to cool. Discard the bay leaf.

Blanch the green beans in boiling water for 1–2 minutes, until just tender. Refresh under cold water.

In a serving bowl, combine the lentils with the beans, tomato, spinach, onion and preserved lemon.

Whisk together the mustard, lemon juice and extra-virgin olive oil in a small bowl. Pour over the salad and toss to combine.

Serve the salad drizzled with the yoghurt dressing and scattered with the flaked almonds.

BORLOTTI-BEAN SALAD WITH TUNA & GOAT'S CURD

SERVES 4

1 cup dried borlotti beans
1 tablespoon (20 ml/¾ fl oz) olive oil
1 bay leaf
1 × 425-g (15-oz) can tuna in olive oil, drained and oil reserved
1 head radicchio, torn
1 small red onion, halved and thinly sliced
1 tablespoon capers

120 g (4 oz) goat's curd

DRESSING

2 tablespoons (40 ml/1½ fl oz) white-wine vinegar
1 tablespoon rosemary leaves
2 teaspoons Dijon mustard
1 tablespoon (20 ml/¾ fl oz) olive oil
salt and freshly ground black pepper

Soak the beans in cold water for at least 4 hours (or overnight). Use the quick-soak method (page 218) if you are short of time. Drain and rinse.

Place the beans in a pressure cooker with 1 L (34 fl oz) water, the olive oil and the bay leaf. Lock the lid in place and bring to high pressure over high heat. Cook for 6 minutes, adjusting the heat as necessary to maintain a high pressure.

Release the pressure using the natural-release method.

Drain the beans, discarding the bay leaf. Rinse under cold running water and spread out on a large tray to cool.

Flake the tuna into a serving bowl. Add the beans, radicchio, onion and capers, and stir to combine.

To make the dressing, combine the vinegar, rosemary and mustard in a small bowl. Combine the olive oil with 2 tablespoons (40 ml/1½ fl oz) of the reserved tuna oil, and gradually whisk into the dressing. Season with salt and pepper.

Pour the dressing over the salad, crumble the goat's curd over the top and toss to combine.

LIMA BEANS WITH CHORIZO & LEEK

SERVES 4

1 cup dried lima beans
2 tablespoons (40 ml/1½ fl oz) olive oil
2 chorizo sausages, sliced
2 leeks (white parts only), coarsely chopped
2 cloves garlic, finely chopped
½ small white cabbage, shredded
1 teaspoon smoked paprika
1 bay leaf

¾ cup (180 ml/6 fl oz) chicken stock
  (page 27)
½ cup flat-leaf parsley leaves
1 tablespoon (20 ml/¾ fl oz) sherry vinegar
  (or red-wine vinegar)
salt and freshly ground black pepper
crusty bread, to serve

Soak the beans in cold water for at least 4 hours (or overnight). Use the quick-soak method (page 218) if you are short of time. Drain and rinse.

Place the beans in a pressure cooker with 3 cups (750 ml/25 fl oz) water and 1 tablespoon (20 ml/¾ fl oz) of the oil. Lock the lid in place and bring to low pressure over high heat. Cook for 4 minutes, adjusting the heat as necessary to maintain a low pressure.

Release the pressure using the natural-release method.

Drain the beans and set aside.

Heat the remaining oil in the pressure cooker over low–medium heat. Cook the chorizo until golden brown. Add the leek and garlic, and cook until softened. Add the cabbage, paprika and bay leaf, and stir to combine. Pour in the stock, then lock the lid in place and bring to high pressure over high heat. Cook for 4 minutes, adjusting the heat as necessary to maintain a high pressure.

Release the pressure using the quick-release method.

Return the beans to the pot and simmer, uncovered, over medium heat for 3–5 minutes, until the liquid reduces and the sauce thickens. Stir in the parsley and vinegar, and season with salt and pepper.

Serve with crusty bread.

MOROCCAN SPICED CHICKPEA & TOMATO TAGINE

SERVES 4

1 cup dried chickpeas
3 tablespoons (60 ml/2 fl oz) olive oil
1 large onion, coarsely chopped
3 cloves garlic, finely chopped
2 red bird's eye chillies, deseeded and finely chopped
2 teaspoons finely grated ginger
2 teaspoons paprika

1 teaspoon ground cumin
1 teaspoon ground turmeric
3 cups (750 ml/25 fl oz) vegetable stock (page 30) or chicken stock (page 27)
1 cup coarsely chopped coriander
1 × 400-g (14-oz) can chopped tomatoes
salt and freshly ground black pepper
couscous, to serve

Soak the chickpeas in cold water for at least 4 hours (or overnight). Use the quick-soak method (page 218) if you are short of time. Drain and rinse.

Heat the oil in a pressure cooker over low–medium heat. Cook the onion and garlic until the onion is clear and softened. Add the chilli, ginger and spices, and cook for 30 seconds or until fragrant. Add the stock, chickpeas and half the coriander, then lock the lid in place and bring to high pressure over high heat. Cook for 15 minutes, adjusting the heat as necessary to maintain a high pressure.

Release the pressure using the natural-release method.

Add the tomatoes to the pot and cook, uncovered, over medium heat for 5–10 minutes, or until the sauce has thickened. Stir in the remaining coriander and season with salt and pepper.

Serve with couscous.

LENTIL & VEGETABLE SHEPHERD'S PIE

SERVES 6–8

2 tablespoons (40 ml/1½ fl oz) olive oil

1 large onion, finely chopped

2 cloves garlic, finely chopped

2 teaspoons ground cumin

2 teaspoons ground coriander

1 teaspoon ground chilli

½ teaspoon ground turmeric

2 medium-sized zucchini, finely diced

1 medium-sized carrot, coarsely grated

150 g (5 oz) button mushrooms, finely sliced

1½ cups dried brown lentils, rinsed

2 cups (500 ml/17 fl oz) vegetable stock (page 30)

1 × 400-g (14-oz) can chopped tomatoes

1 tablespoon tomato paste

1 teaspoon sugar

1 cup coarsely chopped flat-leaf parsley

salt and freshly ground black pepper

1 quantity mashed potato (page 179)

½ cup grated tasty cheese

Preheat the oven to 200°C (390°F).

Heat the oil in a pressure cooker over low–medium heat. Sauté the onion and garlic until golden brown. Add the spices and cook for 30 seconds or until fragrant. Add the vegetables and lentils, and stir to combine. Pour in the stock, then lock the lid in place and bring to high pressure over high heat. Cook for 3 minutes, adjusting the heat as necessary to maintain a high pressure.

Release the pressure using the natural-release method.

Add the tomatoes, tomato paste and sugar to the pot, and cook, uncovered, over medium heat for 5–10 minutes, until thickened. Stir in the parsley and season with salt and pepper.

Spoon the lentil mixture into a large, deep ovenproof dish. Spread the mashed potato over the top, and sprinkle with the cheese.

Bake in the oven for 20–30 minutes, until the cheese is golden brown. Serve immediately.

RED-BEAN CHILLI

SERVES 4–6

1½ cups dried kidney beans
3 tablespoons (60 ml/2 fl oz) olive oil
1 large onion, diced
2 cloves garlic, finely chopped
2 teaspoons ground cumin
2 teaspoons hot paprika
1 teaspoon ground chilli
1 teaspoon dried oregano
2 bay leaves

2 red capsicums, diced
1 × 400-g (14-oz) can chopped tomatoes
2 tablespoons tomato paste
2 ancho chillies, finely chopped
1 tablespoon (20 ml/¾ fl oz) cider vinegar
1 tablespoon (15 g/½ oz) soft brown sugar
salt
steamed long-grain white rice and sour cream, to serve

Soak the beans in cold water for at least 4 hours (or overnight). Use the quick-soak method (page 218) if you are short of time. Drain and rinse.

Place the beans in a pressure cooker with 6 cups (1.5 L/3 pt 3 fl oz) water and 2 tablespoons (40 ml/1½ fl oz) of the oil. Lock the lid in place and bring to high pressure over high heat. Cook for 8 minutes, adjusting the heat as necessary to maintain a high pressure.

Release the pressure using the natural-release method.

Drain the beans and set aside.

Heat the remaining oil in the pressure cooker over low–medium heat. Cook the onion and garlic until the onion is clear and softened. Add the spices and herbs, and cook for 30 seconds or until fragrant. Add the beans, capsicum, tomatoes, tomato paste, chilli, vinegar and sugar. Pour in ⅓ cup (80 ml/3 fl oz) water, then lock the lid in place and bring to high pressure over high heat. Cook for 5 minutes, adjusting the heat as necessary to maintain a high pressure.

Release the pressure using the natural-release method.

Simmer the bean mixture, uncovered, over medium heat for 5–10 minutes, until thickened. Season with salt.

Serve with steamed rice and sour cream.

SPICED RED-LENTIL DAL

SERVES 4–6

⅓ cup (80 ml/3 fl oz) melted ghee or vegetable oil

1 medium-sized onion, halved and thinly sliced

2 cloves garlic, crushed

1 teaspoon ground cumin

1 teaspoon ground coriander

1 teaspoon ground turmeric

1 cup split red lentils, rinsed

3 medium-sized tomatoes, coarsely chopped

salt

2 green cayenne chillies, halved lengthways

10 fresh curry leaves

½ cinnamon stick, broken into pieces

1 teaspoon black mustard seeds

1 teaspoon cumin seeds

steamed basmati rice or roti bread, to serve

Heat half the ghee or oil in a pressure cooker over low–medium heat. Cook the onion and garlic until the onion is clear and softened. Add the ground spices and cook for 30 seconds or until fragrant. Add the lentils and tomatoes, and stir to coat. Pour in 2½ cups (625 ml/21 fl oz) water, lock the lid in place and bring to high pressure over high heat. Cook for 4 minutes, adjusting the heat as necessary to maintain a high pressure.

Reduce the pressure using the natural-release method.

Simmer the dal, uncovered, for 5 minutes, or until it has a thick soupy consistency. Season with salt.

Heat the remaining ghee or oil in a small frying pan. Fry the chilli, curry leaves, cinnamon stick, and mustard and cumin seeds until the spices are fragrant and the mustard seeds begin to pop.

Serve the dal drizzled with the spice oil and accompanied with steamed rice or roti bread.

MUNG BEAN & TAMARIND DAL

SERVES 4–6

2 tablespoons tamarind pulp
⅓ cup (80 ml/3 fl oz) melted ghee or vegetable oil
1 medium-sized onion, finely chopped
2 teaspoons finely grated ginger
2 tablespoons desiccated coconut
1 teaspoon garam masala
1 teaspoon ground cumin
1 teaspoon ground coriander
½ teaspoon ground chilli
1 cup dried mung beans, rinsed

2 medium-sized tomatoes, coarsely chopped
1 teaspoon caster sugar
1 cup coarsely chopped coriander
salt
7 fresh curry leaves
2 small dried red chillies
1 teaspoon black mustard seeds
1 teaspoon cumin seeds
steamed basmati rice and natural yoghurt, to serve

Combine the tamarind with ⅓ cup (80 ml/3 fl oz) water in a small bowl and set aside for 15 minutes, to soften. Stir to make a paste, then pass through a fine mesh sieve, discarding the solids.

Heat half the ghee or oil in a pressure cooker over low–medium heat. Cook the onion and ginger until the onion is clear and softened. Add the coconut and ground spices, and cook for 30 seconds or until fragrant. Add the mung beans, tomatoes and sugar, and stir to combine. Pour in 1 L (34 fl oz) water and the tamarind liquid, then lock the lid in place and bring to high pressure over high heat. Cook for 5 minutes, adjusting the heat as necessary to maintain a high pressure.

Release the pressure using the natural-release method.

Simmer the dal, uncovered, over medium heat for 2–3 minutes, until it thickens. Stir the coriander through and season with salt.

Heat the remaining ghee or oil in a small frying pan. Fry the curry leaves, chillies, and mustard and cumin seeds until the spices are fragrant and the mustard seeds begin to pop.

Serve the dal drizzled with the spice oil and accompanied with steamed rice and yoghurt.

PUY LENTIL & SAUSAGE STEW

SERVES 6

3 tablespoons (60 ml/2 fl oz) olive oil
1 large onion, coarsely chopped
2 cloves garlic, finely chopped
4 fennel and pork sausages, skin removed, coarsely chopped
60 g (2 oz) pancetta, finely diced
2 cups dried Puy lentils, rinsed
2 sticks celery, coarsely chopped

1 medium-sized carrot, diced
1 medium-sized parsnip, diced
6 sprigs thyme
2 bay leaves
3 cups (750 ml/25 fl oz) chicken stock (page 27)
1 tablespoon (20 ml/¾ fl oz) red-wine vinegar
salt and freshly ground black pepper
crusty bread, to serve

Heat the oil in a pressure cooker over low–medium heat. Cook the onion and garlic until the onion is clear and softened. Add the sausage and pancetta, and cook until golden brown. Add the lentils, celery, carrot, parsnip and herbs, and stir to combine. Pour in the stock, then lock the lid in place and bring to high pressure over high heat. Cook for 5 minutes, adjusting the heat as necessary to maintain a high pressure.

Release the pressure using the natural-release method.

Stir the vinegar into the stew, and season with salt and pepper.

Serve with crusty bread.

MIDDLE EASTERN CHICKPEA STEW

SERVES 4–6

2 cups dried chickpeas
2 tablespoons (40 ml/1½ fl oz) olive oil
2 medium-sized onions, halved and thinly sliced
2 cloves garlic, finely chopped
2 cinnamon sticks
1 teaspoon ground cumin
½ teaspoon ground turmeric

1 bay leaf
1 cup pitted prunes, coarsely chopped
6 cups (1.5 L/3 pt 3 fl oz) chicken stock (page 27)
120 g (4 oz) baby spinach
1 cup coarsely chopped coriander
salt and freshly ground black pepper
couscous, to serve

Soak the chickpeas in cold water for at least 4 hours (or overnight). Use the quick-soak method (page 218) if you are short of time. Drain and rinse.

Heat the oil in a pressure cooker over low–medium heat. Sauté the onion and garlic until golden brown. Add the spices and bay leaf, and cook for 30 seconds or until fragrant. Add the chickpeas and prunes, and stir to combine. Pour in the stock, then lock the lid in place and bring to high pressure over high heat. Cook for 12 minutes, adjusting the heat as necessary to maintain a high pressure.

Release the pressure using the natural-release method.

Simmer the stew, uncovered, for 5–10 minutes, until the sauce thickens. Add the spinach and coriander, and stir until wilted. Season with salt and pepper.

Serve with couscous.

BROAD BEAN, CAVOLO NERO & TOMATO STEW

SERVES 4-6

1½ cups peeled dried broad beans
2 tablespoons (40 ml/1½ fl oz) olive oil
1 medium-sized onion, diced
2 cloves garlic, finely chopped
2 tablespoons finely chopped oregano
1 large red chilli, deseeded and finely sliced
1 bay leaf
1 L (34 fl oz) chicken stock (page 27)

3 medium-sized vine-ripened tomatoes, quartered
1 bunch cavolo nero, coarsely chopped
1 tablespoon (20 ml/¾ fl oz) freshly squeezed lemon juice
salt and freshly ground black pepper
mashed potato (page 179), to serve

Soak the beans in cold water for at least 4 hours (or overnight). Use the quick-soak method (page 218) if you are short of time. Drain and rinse.

Heat the oil in a pressure cooker over low–medium heat. Cook the onion and garlic until the onion is clear and softened. Add the beans, oregano, chilli and bay leaf, and stir to combine. Pour in the stock, then lock the lid in place and bring to high pressure over high heat. Cook for 12 minutes, adjusting the heat as necessary to maintain a high pressure.

Release the pressure using the natural-release method.

Add the tomato, cavolo nero and lemon juice to the beans. Cook, uncovered, over medium heat for 5–10 minutes, or until the stew thickens. Season with salt and pepper.

Serve with mashed potato.

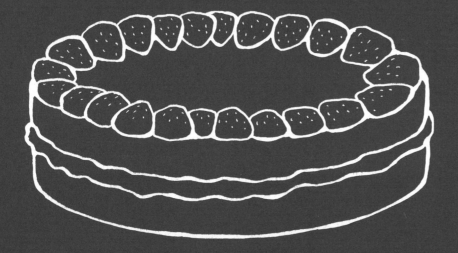

DESSERTS

Poached fruits will be a familiar favourite for seasoned pressure-cooker users. Poached quinces are one of my favourites. They take 6–8 hours to cook in the conventional manner, but can be ready in less than 2 hours when prepared with the help of a pressure cooker – just 45 minutes in the cooker, then an hour cooling in the poaching liquid to allow the flavours to develop. The sweet, dark-pink flesh is guaranteed to impress at any dinner party.

Delicate desserts, such as smooth custards and crème caramel, are quick and easy to make too. You can create the creamiest cheesecake ever in just 20 minutes! And steamed puddings can be whipped up in a fraction of the usual time, using mainly pantry staples. Preparing the traditional Christmas pudding (page 264) no longer has to be a time-consuming chore, with hours trimmed from the cooking time.

Afternoon and morning teas are covered too. Cakes and loaves made in a pressure cooker are moist and have a longer life as a result. The banana, date and walnut loaf on page 252 is delicious with a cup of tea. The orange and poppy-seed cake (page 256) or decadent cherry and chocolate brownie cake (page 246) are just right for special guests or celebrations.

STICKY BLACK RICE PUDDING WITH COCONUT SAUCE

SERVES 4

1 cup black glutinous rice
1 tablespoon (20 g/¾ oz) unsalted butter
½ cup (135 g/5 oz) coarsely grated palm sugar
½ cup (125 ml/4 fl oz) coconut milk
1 large mango, sliced

COCONUT SAUCE
½ cup (125 ml/4 fl oz) coconut cream
3 tablespoons (45 g/1½ oz) coarsely grated palm sugar
1 tablespoon (20 ml/¾ fl oz) lime juice

Soak the rice in cold water for at least 4 hours (or overnight). Drain and rinse.

To make the coconut sauce, combine the coconut cream and sugar in a small saucepan. Simmer over low heat for 3 minutes, or until the sugar dissolves and the sauce thickens slightly. Stir in the lime juice. Set aside to cool.

Melt the butter in a pressure cooker over low–medium heat. Add the rice and stir to coat. Pour in 2½ cups (625 ml/21 fl oz) water and bring to high pressure over high heat. Cook for 5 minutes, adjusting the heat as necessary to maintain a high pressure.

Release the pressure using the natural-release method.

Stir the sugar and coconut milk into the rice and cook, uncovered, for a further 3–5 minutes, until the sugar dissolves and the coconut milk is absorbed.

Serve warm or cold, garnished with the mango slices and drizzled with the coconut sauce.

VANILLA & ROSEWATER POACHED QUINCES

SERVES 4

1½ cups (330 g/11½ oz) caster sugar
2 tablespoons (40 ml/1½ fl oz) rosewater
1 vanilla bean, split in half lengthways
juice of 1 lemon
4 black peppercorns
4 quinces
mascarpone cheese, to serve

PISTACHIO DUKKAH
1 teaspoon coriander seeds
1 teaspoon cardamom seeds
½ teaspoon black peppercorns
½ cup pistachios, finely chopped
2 tablespoons white sesame seeds, lightly toasted

Combine the sugar, rosewater, vanilla bean, lemon juice and peppercorns with 1½ cups (375 ml/12½ fl oz) water in a pressure cooker. Bring to the boil over medium heat, stirring to dissolve the sugar. Remove from the heat.

Peel the quinces, then cut into quarters lengthways. Remove and discard the cores using a small sharp knife. Place the quinces in the poaching liquid. Lock the lid in place and bring to low pressure over high heat. Cook for 45 minutes, adjusting the heat as necessary to maintain a low pressure.

Meanwhile, to make the pistachio dukkah, dry-fry the spices in a small frying pan over medium heat for 30 seconds or until fragrant. Transfer to a mortar or spice grinder and blend to a coarse powder. Combine the spices with the pistachios and sesame seeds, and set aside.

Release the cooker's pressure using the natural-release method.

Leave the quinces to cool in the poaching liquid for at least 1 hour, to allow the flavours to fully develop.

Serve warm or cold, with a little of the poaching liquid and a dollop of mascarpone. Sprinkle with the dukkah.

The season for quinces is short, so be sure to keep an eye out for them in the winter months.

DRIED FRUIT COMPOTE

SERVES 4–6

1 cup (220 g/8 oz) caster sugar
grated zest and juice of 1 lemon
1 cinnamon stick
4 cardamom pods, bruised
5 black peppercorns

400 g (14 oz) dried figs
200 g (7 oz) dried apricots
200 g (7 oz) pitted prunes
natural yoghurt, to serve
coarsely chopped walnuts, to serve

Combine the sugar, lemon zest and juice, cinnamon stick, cardamom pods and peppercorns with 2 cups (500 ml/17 fl oz) water in a pressure cooker. Bring to the boil over medium heat, stirring to dissolve the sugar. Add the dried fruit, then lock the lid in place and bring to low pressure over medium heat. Cook for 10 minutes, adjusting the heat as necessary to maintain a low pressure.

Release the pressure using the natural-release method.

Leave the fruit in the poaching liquid to cool.

Serve warm or cold, with a little of the poaching liquid and a dollop of yoghurt. Sprinkle with walnuts.

PLUMS POACHED IN RED WINE

SERVES 4–6

1½ cups (375 ml/12½ fl oz) red wine
½ cup (125 ml/4 fl oz) port
1½ cups (330 g/11½ oz) caster sugar
juice of 1 orange
2 strips orange zest
1 cinnamon stick

2 star anise
6 cloves
12 firm blood plums
vanilla ice-cream, to serve
finely sliced mint, for garnish

Combine the wine, port, sugar, orange juice, zest and spices in a pressure cooker. Bring to the boil over medium heat, stirring to dissolve the sugar. Remove from the heat.

Place the plums in the poaching liquid. Lock the lid in place and bring to low pressure over medium heat. Cook for 5 minutes, adjusting the heat as necessary to maintain a low pressure.

Release the pressure using the natural-release method.

Leave the plums in the poaching liquid to cool.

Serve warm or cold, with a little of the poaching liquid and a scoop of vanilla ice-cream. Sprinkle with mint.

BANANA PUDDING WITH SALTY CARAMEL SAUCE

SERVES 6–8

1½ cups (225 g/8 oz) self-raising flour
1 teaspoon bicarbonate of soda
1 teaspoon ground cinnamon
150 g (5 oz) softened unsalted butter
½ cup (110 g/4 oz) firmly packed soft brown sugar
2 large eggs, lightly beaten
2 medium-sized ripe bananas, mashed

½ cup (125 ml/4 fl oz) milk
cream or ice-cream, to serve
icing sugar, for dusting (optional)

SALTY CARAMEL SAUCE
1 cup (220 g/8 oz) caster sugar
½ cup (125 ml/4 fl oz) cream
1 teaspoon sea salt

Lightly grease a 6-cup (1.5-L/3 pt 3-fl oz) capacity heatproof pudding basin.

To make the pudding, sift the flour, bicarbonate of soda and cinnamon together into a medium-sized bowl.

In a separate bowl, cream the butter and sugar until pale and creamy. Beat in the eggs one at a time. Stir in the mashed banana. Add the sifted dry ingredients and milk a little at a time, stirring to combine. Pour the mixture into the prepared pudding basin. Cover the basin with a piece of baking paper large enough to fold over the edges, and tie with kitchen string to secure.

Place the trivet in the base of the pressure cooker. Fold a tea towel into thirds lengthways to make a thick strip. Place the pudding basin in the centre of the strip and, using the ends of the towel as handles, lower the basin into the pressure cooker. Fold the ends of the towel over the top of the basin. Pour enough boiling water into the cooker to come halfway up the sides of the pudding basin. Lock the lid in place and bring to low pressure over high heat. Cook for 50 minutes, adjusting the heat as necessary to maintain a low pressure.

Meanwhile, to make the sauce, combine the sugar and 2 tablespoons (40 ml/1½ fl oz) water in a small saucepan over low–medium heat. Heat, without stirring, for 5–10 minutes, until the sugar has dissolved and begins to caramelise. Remove the pan from the heat and stir in the cream. Add the salt. Return the pan to the heat and bring to the boil, then immediately remove from the heat and set aside.

Release the cooker's pressure using the natural-release method.

Lift the basin out of the cooker using the tea towel. Remove the baking paper and test the pudding with a skewer; if the skewer comes out clean it is cooked. If the mixture is still sticky, return the basin to the cooker, lock the lid in place and cook on low pressure for a further 3–5 minutes.

Invert the pudding onto a serving plate. Serve the pudding hot, with the salty caramel sauce and cream or ice-cream. Dust with icing sugar if desired.

CHERRY & CHOCOLATE BROWNIE CAKE

SERVES 8–10

250 g (9 oz) good-quality dark chocolate, coarsely chopped
3 tablespoons (60 g/2 oz) unsalted butter
4 eggs, separated
¼ cup (55 g/2 oz) caster sugar
½ cup (125 g/4½ oz) canned pitted cherries, drained and coarsely chopped, plus extra whole cherries to decorate

¼ cup desiccated coconut
¼ cup (35 g/1¼ oz) plain flour
cocoa, for dusting
whipped cream and shaved dark chocolate, to decorate

Lightly grease a 20-cm (8-in) round cake tin and line with baking paper.

Place the chocolate and butter in a medium-sized heatproof bowl. Place the bowl over a saucepan of barely simmering water and stir until the chocolate is melted and smooth. Set aside to cool slightly.

Whip the egg whites until soft peaks begin to form. Gradually add half the sugar, continuing to whip until firm peaks form.

In a separate bowl, whisk together the egg yolks and remaining sugar. Add the melted chocolate mixture, chopped cherries, coconut and sifted flour, and stir to combine. Add one large spoonful of the whites and stir to combine. Gently fold in the remaining whites. Pour the mixture into the prepared tin. Cover the tin with a piece of baking paper large enough to fold over the edges, and tie with kitchen string to secure.

Place the trivet in the base of the pressure cooker. Fold a tea towel into thirds lengthways to make a thick strip. Place the cake tin in the centre of the strip and, using the ends of the towel as handles, lower the tin into the pressure cooker. Fold the ends of the towel over the top of the tin. Pour enough boiling water into the cooker to come halfway up the sides of the cake tin. Lock the lid in place and bring to low pressure over high heat. Cook for 20 minutes, adjusting the heat as necessary to maintain a low pressure.

Release the pressure using the natural-release method.

Lift the tin out of the cooker using the tea towel. Remove the baking paper and test the cake with a skewer; if the skewer comes out clean it is cooked. If the mixture is still sticky, return the tin to the cooker, lock the lid in place and cook on low pressure for a further 3–5 minutes.

Set the cake aside for 10 minutes to cool slightly.

To serve, dust the cake with cocoa and decorate with whipped cream, cherries and chocolate shavings.

STICKY DATE & WHISKY PUDDING

SERVES 8

225 g (8 oz) pitted dried dates, coarsely chopped
½ cup (125 ml/4 fl oz) whisky
50 g (1¾ oz) dark chocolate, coarsely chopped
1 cup (150 g/5 oz) self-raising flour
½ teaspoon bicarbonate of soda
¼ cup (55 g/2 oz) firmly packed soft brown sugar
3 tablespoons (60 g/2 oz) unsalted butter, melted and cooled

3 tablespoons (60 ml/2 fl oz) milk
1 large egg, lightly beaten
cream or ice-cream, to serve

WHISKY SAUCE

3 tablespoons (60 g/2 oz) unsalted butter
¾ cup (170 g/6 oz) firmly packed soft brown sugar
3 tablespoons (60 ml/2 fl oz) whisky
1 cup (250 ml/8½ fl oz) cream

Lightly grease a 5-cup (1.25-L/2 pt 10-fl oz) capacity heatproof pudding basin.

To make the pudding, combine the dates, whisky and 3 tablespoons (60 ml/2 fl oz) water in a small saucepan. Bring to the boil, then remove from the heat and add the chocolate, stirring until melted. Set aside for 5 minutes to cool.

Sift the flour and bicarbonate of soda into a medium-sized bowl. Stir in the sugar. Combine the butter, milk and egg in a small bowl. Add the wet ingredients to the dry ingredients and mix to combine. Stir in the date and chocolate mixture. Pour the batter into the prepared pudding basin. Cover the basin with a piece of baking paper large enough to fold over the edges, and tie with kitchen string to secure.

Place the trivet in the base of the pressure cooker. Fold a tea towel into thirds lengthways to make a thick strip. Place the pudding basin in the centre of the strip and, using the ends of the towel as handles, lower the basin into the pressure cooker. Fold the ends of the towel over the top of the basin. Pour enough boiling water into the cooker to come halfway up the sides of the pudding basin. Lock the lid in place and bring to low pressure over high heat. Cook for 50 minutes, adjusting the heat as necessary to maintain a low pressure.

Meanwhile, to make the sauce, heat the butter and sugar in a frying pan over medium heat until melted. Add the whisky and bring to the boil. Pour in the cream, stir to combine, and gently simmer over low–medium heat for 5 minutes, or until thickened to a sauce consistency.

Release the cooker's pressure using the natural-release method.

Lift the basin out of the cooker using the tea towel. Remove the baking paper and test the pudding with a skewer; if the skewer comes out clean it is cooked. If the mixture is still sticky, return the basin to the cooker, lock the lid in place and cook on low pressure for a further 3–5 minutes.

Invert the pudding onto a serving plate. Serve hot, with the whisky sauce and cream or ice-cream.

GINGER & PEAR PUDDING

SERVES 8

½ cup (110 g/4 oz) caster sugar
⅓ cup (80 ml/3 fl oz) ginger wine
60 g (2 oz) glacé ginger, finely chopped
½ cup (125 ml/4 fl oz) golden syrup
2 small pears
3 tablespoons (60 g/2 oz) unsalted butter
¼ cup (55 g/2 oz) firmly packed soft
brown sugar

½ teaspoon bicarbonate of soda
1 cup (150 g/5 oz) self-raising flour
1 teaspoon ground ginger
1 teaspoon mixed spice
pinch of salt
½ cup (125 ml/4 fl oz) milk
1 large egg
double cream, to serve

Lightly grease a 5-cup (1.25-L/2 pt 10-fl oz) capacity heatproof pudding basin.

Combine the caster sugar, ginger wine, half the glacé ginger and half the golden syrup in a medium-sized saucepan. Gently simmer over low–medium heat, stirring occasionally, until the sugar has dissolved.

Peel, quarter and core the pears, then slice thickly lengthways. Add the pear slices to the hot syrup and set aside.

Heat the remaining golden syrup with the butter and brown sugar in a small saucepan over low–medium heat, until melted. Remove the pan from the heat, stir in the bicarbonate of soda and set aside.

Sift the flour, ground ginger, mixed spice and salt into a medium-sized bowl. Add the melted-butter mixture, milk, egg and remaining glacé ginger, and stir to combine.

Arrange the pear slices decoratively in the base of the prepared pudding basin and pour in three-quarters of the syrup. Spoon the pudding batter over the top, then pour over the remaining syrup. Cover the basin with a piece of baking paper large enough to fold over the edges, and tie with kitchen string to secure.

Place the trivet in the base of the pressure cooker. Fold a tea towel into thirds lengthways to make a thick strip. Place the pudding basin in the centre of the strip and, using the ends of the towel as handles, lower the basin into the pressure cooker. Fold the ends of the towel over the top of the basin. Pour enough boiling water into the cooker to come halfway up the sides of the pudding basin. Lock the lid in place and bring to low pressure over high heat. Cook for 40 minutes, adjusting the heat as necessary to maintain a low pressure.

Release the pressure using the natural-release method.

Lift the basin out of the cooker using the tea towel. Remove the baking paper and test the pudding with a skewer; if the skewer comes out clean it is cooked. If the mixture is still sticky, return the basin to the cooker, lock the lid in place and cook on low pressure for a further 3–5 minutes.

Invert the pudding onto a serving plate. Serve hot with double cream.

BANANA, DATE & WALNUT LOAF

MAKES 2 LOAVES (EACH SERVES 4–6)

1 cup (250 ml/8½ fl oz) milk
1 tablespoon (20 g/¾ oz) butter
1 cup pitted dried dates, coarsely chopped
2 cups (300 g/10½ oz) self-raising flour
1 teaspoon bicarbonate of soda
1 teaspoon ground cinnamon
½ teaspoon ground nutmeg

pinch of salt
1 cup (220 g/8 oz) firmly packed soft brown sugar
2 medium-sized bananas, mashed
2 large eggs, lightly beaten
½ cup walnuts, coarsely chopped

Lightly grease two nut-loaf tins with lids, then dust with flour, tapping out any excess.

Combine the milk and butter in a small saucepan and bring to a simmer. Remove from the heat, add the dates and set aside.

Sift the flour, bicarbonate of soda, cinnamon, nutmeg and salt into a medium-sized bowl. Add the sugar and stir to combine. Pour in the milk and date mixture, then add the mashed banana, eggs and walnuts, and stir to combine. Spoon the mixture into the prepared loaf tins, filling each three-quarters full. Seal with the lid. Wrap the lid end of each tin with aluminium foil, to prevent steam from seeping in.

Place the trivet in the base of the pressure cooker and stand the loaf tins on top. Pour enough boiling water into the cooker to come a third of the way up the sides of the tins. Lock the lid in place and bring to high pressure over high heat. Cook for 30 minutes, adjusting the heat as necessary to maintain a high pressure.

Release the pressure using the natural-release method.

Lift the tins out of the cooker using a tea towel or oven mitts. Test the loaves with a skewer; if the skewer comes out clean they are cooked. If the mixture is still sticky, lock the lid in place, bring back up to high pressure and cook for a further 2–3 minutes.

Set the loaves aside for 10 minutes to cool slightly. Remove the loaves from the tins and transfer to a wire rack to cool.

Serve warm or cold, sliced into rounds and spread with butter.

GOLDEN-SYRUP DUMPLINGS

MAKES 12 (SERVES 4)

1 cup (150 g/5 oz) self-raising flour
2 tablespoons (40 g/1½ oz) unsalted butter
1 large egg
3 tablespoons (60 ml/2 fl oz) milk
cream or ice-cream, to serve

SYRUP

1 cup (220 g/8 oz) firmly packed soft
  brown sugar
⅓ cup (80 ml/3 fl oz) golden syrup
2 tablespoons (40 g/1½ oz) unsalted butter

To make the dumplings, place the flour and butter in a medium-sized bowl. Rub the butter into the flour using your fingertips, until the mixture resembles breadcrumbs. Lightly beat the egg and milk in a small bowl, then add to the flour, stirring to make a sticky dough.

To make the syrup, combine all the ingredients in a pressure cooker with 1½ cups (375 ml/12½ fl oz) water. Bring to the boil over medium heat, stirring to dissolve the sugar.

Drop spoonfuls of the dough into the syrup. Lock the lid in place and bring to low pressure over medium heat. Cook for 5 minutes, adjusting the heat as necessary to maintain a low pressure.

Release the pressure using the natural-release method.

Serve the dumplings with the syrup and a dollop of cream or scoop of ice-cream.

SPICED RICE PUDDING

SERVES 4

2 tablespoons (40 g/1½ oz) unsalted butter
1 cup long-grain white rice
3 cardamom pods, bruised
½ cinnamon stick
1 strip lemon zest
2 cups (500 ml/17 fl oz) milk

½ cup (110 g/4 oz) caster sugar
¼ cup sultanas
¼ cup flaked almonds
3 tablespoons (60 ml/2 fl oz) cream
honey and ground cinnamon,
   to serve

Melt 1 tablespoon (20 g/¾ oz) of the butter in a pressure cooker over low–medium heat. Add the rice, spices and lemon zest, and stir to coat the grains in butter. Pour in the milk and 2 cups (500 ml/17 fl oz) water. Add the sugar and sultanas, and stir to combine. Lock the lid in place and bring to high pressure over high heat. Cook for 5 minutes, adjusting the heat as necessary to maintain a high pressure.

Meanwhile, melt the remaining butter in a small frying pan over medium heat. Cook the almonds until golden brown. Set aside.

Release the cooker's pressure using the natural-release method.

Add the cream to the rice and cook over medium heat, stirring frequently, for 3–5 minutes, until the rice is tender and creamy.

Serve warm or cold, topped with honey, cinnamon and the almonds.

LEMON CURD PUDDING

SERVES 8

1 cup lemon curd (page 280)
180 g (6½ oz) softened unsalted butter
1 cup (220 g/8 oz) caster sugar
zest and juice of 1 lemon

3 large eggs
1¼ cups (185 g/6½ oz) self-raising flour
2 tablespoons (40 ml/1½ fl oz) milk
cream or ice-cream, to serve

Lightly grease a 5-cup (1.25-L/2 pt 10-fl oz) heatproof pudding basin.

Spoon the lemon curd into the pudding basin.

In a medium-sized mixing bowl, cream the butter, sugar and lemon zest, until pale and creamy. Beat in the eggs one at a time, then stir in the lemon juice. Add the sifted flour and the milk, a little at a time, to make a smooth batter. Spoon the batter on top of the lemon curd. Cover the basin with a piece of baking paper large enough to fold over the edges, and tie with kitchen string to secure.

Place the trivet in the base of the pressure cooker. Fold a tea towel into thirds lengthways to make a thick strip. Place the pudding basin in the centre of the strip and, using the ends of the towel as handles, lower the basin into the pressure cooker. Fold the ends of the towel over the top of the basin.

Pour enough boiling water into the cooker to come halfway up the sides of the pudding basin. Lock the lid in place and bring to low pressure over high heat. Cook for 30 minutes, adjusting the heat as necessary to maintain a low pressure.

Release the pressure using the natural-release method.

Lift the basin out of the cooker using the tea towel. Remove the baking paper and test the pudding with a skewer; if the skewer comes out clean it is cooked. If the mixture is still sticky, return the basin to the cooker, lock the lid in place and cook on low pressure for a further 3–5 minutes.

Serve hot with cream or ice-cream.

Substitute store-bought lemon curd for the homemade curd if desired.

ORANGE & POPPY-SEED CAKE

SERVES 10–12

1¼ cups (185 g/6½ oz) self-raising flour
½ teaspoon bicarbonate of soda
⅓ cup poppy seeds
1 cup (220 g/8 oz) caster sugar
125 g (4½ oz) softened unsalted butter
2 large eggs, separated
¾ cup (180 ml/6 fl oz) sour cream
zest and juice of 2 oranges

⅓ cup orange marmalade
glacé orange slices, to decorate
CREAM CHEESE FROSTING
125 g (4½ oz) cream cheese, softened
3 tablespoons (60 g/2 oz) softened
   unsalted butter
1 teaspoon vanilla extract
1 cup (160 g/5½ oz) icing sugar

Lightly grease a 20-cm (8-in) round cake tin and line with baking paper.

Sift the flour and bicarbonate of soda into a medium-sized bowl. Add the poppy seeds and stir to combine.

In a separate bowl, cream the sugar and butter until pale and creamy. Beat in the egg yolks, sour cream and orange zest. Add the dry ingredients and orange juice a little at a time, stirring to combine.

In a clean bowl, whip the egg whites until firm peaks form. Add one large spoonful of the whites to the orange mixture and stir to combine. Fold in the remaining whites. Pour the batter into the prepared tin. Cover the tin with a piece of baking paper large enough to fold over the edges, and tie with kitchen string to secure.

Place the trivet in the base of the pressure cooker. Fold a tea towel into thirds lengthways to make a thick strip. Place the cake tin in the centre of the strip and, using the ends of the towel as handles, lower the tin into the pressure cooker. Fold the ends of the towel over the top of the tin. Pour enough boiling water into the cooker to come halfway up the sides of the cake tin. Lock the lid in place and bring to low pressure over medium heat. Cook for 40 minutes, adjusting the heat as necessary to maintain a low pressure.

Meanwhile, combine the marmalade with 2 tablespoons (40 ml/1½ fl oz) water in a small saucepan over low–medium heat and stir until runny. Set aside.

Release the cooker's pressure using the natural-release method.

Lift the tin out of the cooker using the tea towel. Remove the baking paper and test the pudding with a skewer; if the skewer comes out clean it is cooked. If the mixture is still sticky, return the tin to the cooker, lock the lid in place and cook on low pressure for a further 3–5 minutes.

Set the cake aside for 10 minutes to cool slightly. Invert onto a wire tray and use a skewer to pierce holes over the top of the cake. Pour the marmalade glaze over, then set the cake aside to cool completely.

To make the cream cheese frosting, beat the cream cheese, butter and vanilla until pale and creamy. Gradually stir in the sifted icing sugar until combined.

Spread the frosting over the cake, and decorate with glacé orange slices.

SAFFRON POACHED PEARS

SERVES 6

1 cup (220 g/8 oz) caster sugar
½ teaspoon saffron threads
juice of 1 lemon

2 strips lemon zest
6 firm pears
crème fraîche, to serve

Combine the sugar, saffron, lemon juice and zest with 1½ cups (375 ml/12½ fl oz) water in a pressure cooker. Bring to the boil over medium heat, stirring to dissolve the sugar. Remove from the heat.

Peel the pears, leaving the stems intact. Use a melon baller or apple corer to scoop the core out from the base.

Place the pears in the poaching liquid. Lock the lid in place and bring to low pressure over medium heat. Cook for 15 minutes, adjusting the heat as necessary to maintain a low pressure.

Release the pressure using the natural-release method.

Leave the pears in the poaching liquid to cool.

Serve warm or cold, with a little of the poaching liquid and a dollop of crème fraîche.

RHUBARB & VANILLA CUSTARDS

SERVES 4

4 stalks rhubarb, coarsely chopped
2 tablespoons (30 g/1 oz) caster sugar
1 teaspoon finely grated ginger
1 teaspoon finely grated orange zest
1 vanilla bean, halved lengthways and
seeds scraped

2 large eggs plus 2 large egg yolks
½ cup (110 g/4 oz) caster sugar
1¼ cups (310 ml/10½ fl oz) cream
1 cup (250 ml/8½ fl oz) milk
double cream and thin wafer biscuits,
to serve (optional)

Cut four pieces of aluminium foil, each large enough to cover a 1-cup (250-ml/8½-fl oz) capacity ramekin.

Combine the rhubarb, sugar, ginger, orange zest, vanilla bean (but not the seeds) and 3 tablespoons (60 ml/2 fl oz) water in a pressure cooker. Lock the lid in place and bring to low pressure over medium heat. Cook for 2 minutes.

Release the pressure using the quick-release method.

Cook the mixture, uncovered, over low–medium heat for 2–3 minutes, until it reduces. Transfer to a small bowl and set aside to cool slightly.

To make the custard, beat the whole eggs, egg yolks, sugar and vanilla seeds until pale and fluffy. Gradually add the cream and milk, stirring to combine.

Divide the rhubarb mixture evenly between four ramekins. Pour the prepared custard over the top. Cover each dish with foil, pinching around the edges to seal. Place the trivet in the base of the pressure cooker and set the ramekins on top. Pour enough boiling water into the cooker to come halfway up the sides of the ramekins. Lock the lid in place and bring to low pressure over medium heat. Cook for 7 minutes, adjusting the heat as necessary to maintain a low pressure.

Release the pressure using the cold-water release method (or quick-release method for an electric cooker).

Check the custards; if they are still a little wobbly, cover the pot, but do not lock the lid in place, and cook for a further 3–10 minutes. Carefully lift the ramekins out of the cooker and set aside to cool.

Serve warm or chilled, with cream and wafer biscuits if desired.

PUMPKIN & COCONUT PUDDING

SERVES 8–10

1 cup (150 g/5 oz) self-raising flour
1 teaspoon bicarbonate of soda
1 teaspoon ground cardamom
pinch of salt
½ cup desiccated coconut
150 g (5 oz) softened unsalted butter
¾ cup (170 g/6 oz) caster sugar
1 teaspoon finely grated lime zest

2 large eggs, lightly beaten
1 cup mashed steamed pumpkin
½ cup (125 ml/4 fl oz) coconut milk
cream or ice-cream, to serve
COCONUT AND LIME SYRUP
½ cup (125 ml/4 fl oz) coconut milk
½ cup (110 g/4 oz) caster sugar
zest and juice of 2 limes

Lightly grease a 6-cup (1.5-L/3 pt 3-fl oz) capacity heatproof pudding basin.

To make the coconut and lime syrup, place all the ingredients in a small saucepan. Gently simmer over low–medium heat until the sugar dissolves and the sauce thickens slightly. Remove from the heat and set aside to cool a little.

To make the pudding, sift the flour, bicarbonate of soda, cardamom and salt into a medium-sized bowl. Add the coconut and stir to combine.

In a separate bowl, cream the butter, sugar and lime zest until pale and creamy. Beat in the eggs one at a time, then stir in the pumpkin. Add the dry ingredients and coconut milk a little at a time, stirring to combine.

Pour the lime syrup into the prepared pudding basin, then spoon in the batter. Cover the basin with a piece of baking paper large enough to fold over the edges, and tie with kitchen string to secure.

Place the trivet in the base of the pressure cooker. Fold a tea towel into thirds lengthways to make a thick strip. Place the pudding basin in the centre of the strip and, using the ends of the towel as handles, lower the basin into the pressure cooker. Fold the ends of the towel over the top of the basin. Pour enough boiling water into the cooker to come halfway up the sides of the pudding basin. Lock the lid in place and bring to low pressure over high heat. Cook for 50 minutes, adjusting the heat as necessary to maintain a low pressure.

Release the pressure using the natural-release method.

Lift the basin out of the cooker using the tea towel. Remove the baking paper and test the pudding with a skewer; if the skewer comes out clean it is cooked. If the mixture is still sticky, return the basin to the cooker, lock the lid in place and cook on low pressure for a further 3–5 minutes.

Invert the pudding onto a serving plate. Serve hot with cream or ice-cream.

SPIKED FIG, PRUNE & CHOCOLATE PUDDING

SERVES 8

250 g (9 oz) dried figs, coarsely chopped
150 g (5 oz) pitted dried prunes, coarsely chopped
2 teaspoons finely chopped mixed peel
½ cup (125 ml/4 fl oz) brandy
150 g (5 oz) dark chocolate, coarsely chopped
3 tablespoons (60 g/2 oz) unsalted butter
¼ cup (55 g/2 oz) firmly packed soft brown sugar
2 large eggs, lightly beaten
120 g (4 oz) soft breadcrumbs

½ cup walnuts, coarsely chopped
2 tablespoons (30 g/1 oz) plain flour
1 teaspoon mixed spice
1 teaspoon ground ginger
pinch of salt

CRÈME ANGLAISE
½ cup (125 ml/4 fl oz) milk
1¼ cups (310 ml/10½ fl oz) cream
3 large egg yolks
⅓ cup (75 g/2½ oz) caster sugar
1 teaspoon vanilla extract

Combine the figs, prunes, mixed peel and brandy in a medium-sized bowl. Cover and set aside overnight to macerate.

Lightly grease a 5-cup (1.25-L/2 pt 10-fl oz) capacity heatproof pudding basin.

Melt the chocolate, butter and sugar together in a heatproof bowl set over a saucepan of barely simmering water. Remove the bowl from the heat and whisk in the eggs.

Add the breadcrumbs and walnuts to the macerated fruit, and mix to combine. Stir in the chocolate mixture. Sift in the flour, mixed spice, ginger and salt, and mix well. Spoon the mixture into the prepared pudding basin. Cover the basin with a piece of baking paper large enough to fold over the edges, and tie with kitchen string to secure.

Place the trivet in the base of the pressure cooker. Fold a tea towel into thirds lengthways to make a thick strip. Place the pudding basin in the centre of the strip and, using the ends of the towel as handles, lower the basin into the pressure cooker. Fold the ends of the towel over the top of the basin.

Pour enough boiling water into the cooker to come halfway up the sides of the pudding basin. Lock the lid in place and bring to low pressure over high heat. Cook for 1 hour, adjusting the heat as necessary to maintain a low pressure.

Meanwhile, to make the crème anglaise, heat the milk and cream in a medium-sized saucepan over medium heat to scalding point. Beat the egg yolks, sugar and vanilla in a medium-sized bowl, until pale and creamy. Gradually add the hot cream mixture to the egg mixture, stirring to combine. Return the mixture to the saucepan and cook over low–medium heat, stirring constantly, until thickened to a sauce consistency. Do not boil. Strain the sauce through a fine mesh sieve and transfer to a serving jug. Cover with a piece of baking paper to prevent a skin from forming, and keep warm until required.

Release the cooker's pressure using the natural-release method.

Lift the basin out of the cooker using the tea towel. Remove the baking paper and test the pudding with a skewer; if the skewer comes out clean it is cooked. If the mixture is still sticky, return the basin to the cooker, lock the lid in place and cook on low pressure for a further 3–5 minutes.

Invert the pudding onto a serving plate. Serve hot with the crème anglaise.

CHRISTMAS PUDDING WITH BRANDY BUTTER

MAKES 2 PUDDINGS (EACH SERVES 10–12)

360 g (12½ oz) raisins
320 g (11¼ oz) currants
200 g (7 oz) pitted prunes, finely chopped
140 g (5 oz) dried cranberries
¾ cup slivered almonds
½ cup candied citrus peel
zest of 1 orange
1 cup (250 ml/8½ fl oz) brandy
1½ cups (225 g/8 oz) plain flour
1 teaspoon bicarbonate of soda
1 teaspoon ground cinnamon
1 teaspoon mixed spice
½ teaspoon ground nutmeg

pinch of salt
250 g (9 oz) softened unsalted butter
1 cup (220 g/8 oz) firmly packed soft
   brown sugar
4 large eggs
1 cup soft breadcrumbs
½ cup (125 ml/4 fl oz) milk
BRANDY BUTTER
500 g (1 lb 2 oz) softened unsalted butter
5 cups (800 g/1 lb 12 oz) icing sugar
2 teaspoons ground cinnamon
1 teaspoon ground nutmeg
⅓ cup (80 ml/3 fl oz) brandy

Combine the dried fruit, almonds, citrus peel and orange zest in a medium-sized bowl. Pour in the brandy and stir to combine. Cover and set aside for 1–2 days to macerate.

Lightly grease two 5-cup (1.25-L/2 pt 10-fl oz) capacity heatproof pudding basins.

To make the brandy butter, cream the butter until pale and creamy. Gradually sift in the icing sugar, cinnamon and nutmeg, beating until incorporated. Mix in the brandy. Transfer the butter to a serving bowl and refrigerate for 2 hours, or until firm. Keep refrigerated until required.

Sift the flour, bicarbonate of soda, spices and salt into a medium-sized bowl.

In a separate bowl, cream the butter and sugar until pale and creamy. Beat in the eggs, one at a time.

Mix the breadcrumbs into the soaked fruit, then stir in one large spoonful of the sifted flour mix. Add the fruit mixture to the creamed butter and stir to combine. Add the remaining flour and the milk, a little at a time, mixing until incorporated.

Spoon the batter into the prepared pudding basins. Cover each basin with a piece of baking paper large enough to fold over the edges, and tie with kitchen string to secure.

Cook each pudding separately, as follows. Place the trivet in the base of the pressure cooker. Fold a tea towel into thirds lengthways to make a thick strip. Place one of the pudding basins in the centre of the strip and, using the ends of the towel as handles, lower the basin into the pressure cooker. Fold the ends of the towel over the top of the basin. Pour enough boiling water into the cooker to come halfway up the sides of the pudding basin. Lock the lid in place and bring to low pressure over high heat. Cook for 1 hour, adjusting the heat as necessary to maintain a low pressure.

Release the pressure using the natural-release method.

Lift the basin out of the cooker using the tea towel and remove the baking paper. Set aside for 10 minutes, to cool slightly.

Invert the pudding onto a serving plate and serve immediately, with the brandy butter. Alternatively, allow to cool completely, then wrap in brandy-soaked muslin and store in the refrigerator for up to 4 weeks.

To reheat, place the pudding on a steamer tray in the pressure cooker, pour in about a cup of water, and cook on low pressure for 10 minutes.

To make one large pudding, spoon the batter into a 12-cup (3 L/6 pt 6-fl oz) capacity pudding basin and cook for 2 hours.

APRICOT BREAD & BUTTER PUDDING

SERVES 4–6

4 large eggs
¼ cup (55 g/2 oz) caster sugar
1 teaspoon ground cinnamon, plus extra for sprinkling
½ teaspoon ground nutmeg
1 cup (250 ml/8½ fl oz) cream
1 cup (250 ml/8½ fl oz) milk
8 × 1.5-cm (⅝-in) thick slices day-old ciabatta bread

3 tablespoons (60 g/2 oz) softened unsalted butter
¼ cup orange marmalade
200 g (7 oz) dried apricots, thickly sliced
¼ cup sultanas
¼ cup pecans, coarsely chopped
1 tablespoon (15 g/½ oz) raw sugar
cream or ice-cream, to serve

Lightly grease a 20-cm (8-in) round heatproof dish or cake tin.

Beat together the eggs, caster sugar, cinnamon and nutmeg until pale and creamy. Gradually add the cream and milk, stirring to combine.

Spread the bread slices with the butter and marmalade. Arrange half the bread slices in a layer, overlapping slightly, in the prepared dish. Scatter with half of the apricots, sultanas and pecans. Create another layer with the remaining bread slices, and scatter with the remaining fruit and pecans.

Pour the prepared custard over the top, pressing the bread down to soak up the custard. Sprinkle with the raw sugar and some extra cinnamon. Cover the dish with a piece of baking paper large enough to fold over the edges, and tie with kitchen string to secure.

Place the trivet in the base of the pressure cooker. Fold a tea towel into thirds lengthways to make a thick strip. Place the dish in the centre of the strip and, using the ends of the towel as handles, lower the dish into the pressure cooker. Fold the ends of the towel over the top of the dish. Pour enough boiling water into the cooker to come halfway up the sides of the dish. Lock the lid in place and bring to low pressure over medium heat. Cook for 15 minutes, adjusting the heat as necessary to maintain a low pressure.

Release the pressure using the natural-release method.

Lift the dish out of the cooker using the tea towel and remove the baking paper. Set aside for 5 minutes, to cool slightly. Serve warm with cream or ice-cream.

PASSIONFRUIT & ORANGE CHEESECAKE

SERVES 8

200 g (7 oz) Marie biscuits, finely crushed
80 g (3 oz) unsalted butter, melted
350 g (12 oz) cream cheese, softened
¾ cup (170 g/6 oz) caster sugar
½ cup (125 ml/4 fl oz) sour cream
4 large eggs
1 tablespoon (15 g/½ oz) cornflour

⅓ cup (80 ml/3 fl oz) passionfruit pulp, strained
finely grated zest of 1 orange
PASSIONFRUIT AND ORANGE SYRUP
¾ cup (180 ml/6 fl oz) passionfruit pulp
¼ cup (55 g/2 oz) caster sugar
juice of 1 orange, strained

Lightly grease an 18-cm (7-in) springform cake tin. Wrap the outside of the tin with a large piece of aluminium foil, to prevent water from seeping through.

Combine the crushed biscuits and butter, and press into the base of the prepared tin.

Beat together the cream cheese and sugar, until smooth. Add the sour cream, eggs, cornflour and passionfruit, and beat to combine. Pour the mixture over the prepared biscuit base. Cover the tin with a piece of baking paper large enough to fold over the edges, and tie with kitchen string to secure.

Place the trivet in the base of the pressure cooker. Fold a tea towel into thirds lengthways to make a thick strip. Place the tin in the centre of the strip and, using the ends of the towel as handles, lower the tin into the pressure cooker. Fold the ends of the towel over the top of the tin. Pour enough boiling water into the cooker to come halfway up the sides of the tin. Lock the lid in place and bring to low pressure over medium heat. Cook for 30 minutes, adjusting the heat as necessary to maintain a low pressure.

Meanwhile, to make the syrup, combine all the ingredients in a small saucepan. Simmer gently over low–medium heat, until the sugar has dissolved and the syrup has thickened slightly. Set aside to cool.

Release the cooker's pressure using the natural-release method. Lift the tin out of the cooker using the tea towel and remove the baking paper. Set aside to cool to room temperature.

Once the cake is cool, pour the passionfruit and orange syrup over the top. Cover the tin with cling wrap and refrigerate the cake for at least 4 hours (or overnight), until chilled.

To serve, release and remove the sides of the tin.

STRAWBERRY & RICOTTA CHEESECAKE

SERVES 8

250 g (9 oz) strawberries, hulled and coarsely chopped, plus extra (sliced) for decorating
½ cup (110 g/4 oz) caster sugar
¾ cup strawberry jam
200 g (7 oz) Scotch Finger biscuits, finely crushed
3 tablespoons (60 g/2 oz) butter, melted

½ teaspoon ground cinnamon
250 g (9 oz) smooth ricotta cheese
125 g (4½ oz) cream cheese, softened
½ cup (125 ml/4 fl oz) sour cream
3 large eggs
1 tablespoon (15 g/½ oz) cornflour
1 teaspoon vanilla extract

Lightly grease an 18-cm (7-in) springform cake tin. Wrap the outside of the tin with a large piece of aluminium foil, to prevent water from seeping through.

Place the strawberries, half of the sugar and ¼ cup of the strawberry jam in a small saucepan. Cook over low heat for 3–5 minutes, until the strawberries are soft and the mixture is syrupy. Pass through a fine mesh sieve and set aside to cool slightly.

Combine the crushed biscuits, butter and cinnamon in a medium-sized bowl. Press the biscuit mixture into the base of the prepared tin, smoothing it with the back of a spoon.

Beat together the ricotta, cream cheese and remaining sugar, until smooth. Add the sour cream and eggs, and beat to combine. Stir in the strawberry syrup, cornflour and vanilla extract. Pour the mixture over the prepared biscuit base. Cover the tin with a piece of baking paper large enough to fold over the edges, and tie with kitchen string to secure.

Place the trivet in the base of the pressure cooker. Fold a tea towel into thirds lengthways to make a thick strip. Place the cake tin in the centre of the strip and, using the ends of the towel as handles, lower the tin into the pressure cooker. Fold the ends of the towel over the top of the tin. Pour enough boiling water into the cooker to come halfway up the sides of the tin. Lock the lid in place and bring to low pressure over medium heat. Cook for 30 minutes, adjusting the heat as necessary to maintain a low pressure.

Release the pressure using the natural-release method.

Lift the tin out of the cooker using the tea towel and remove the baking paper. Set aside to cool to room temperature.

Heat the remaining strawberry jam and 2 tablespoons (40 ml/1½ fl oz) water in a small saucepan, to make a glaze. Set aside to cool slightly.

Decorate the top of the cheesecake with strawberry slices, then pour the prepared glaze over. Cover the tin with cling wrap and refrigerate the cake for at least 4 hours (or overnight), until chilled.

To serve, release and remove the sides of the tin.

SPANISH-STYLE CRÈME CARAMEL

SERVES 10

almond oil, for greasing
1½ cups (330 g/11½ oz) caster sugar
3 large eggs plus 2 large egg yolks

1 teaspoon vanilla extract
½ teaspoon ground cinnamon
3½ cups (875 ml/30 fl oz) milk

Lightly grease a 20-cm (8-in) round cake tin with almond oil.

Combine half the sugar with 3 tablespoons (60 ml/2 fl oz) water in a small saucepan. Simmer over low–medium heat until the syrup begins to turn a golden-caramel colour. Remove the pan from the heat immediately and swirl to create an even colour (do not stir). Pour the caramel into the prepared tin to cover the base. Set aside to cool.

Beat the remaining sugar with the whole eggs, egg yolks, vanilla and cinnamon, until pale and creamy. Gradually stir in the milk. Strain the mixture through a fine mesh sieve. Skim and discard the frothy top layer, then pour the custard over the caramel in the cake tin. Cover the tin with a piece of baking paper large enough to fold over the edges, and tie with kitchen string to secure.

Place the trivet in the base of the pressure cooker. Fold a tea towel into thirds lengthways to make a thick strip. Place the cake tin in the centre of the strip and, using the ends of the towel as handles, lower the tin into the pressure cooker. Fold the ends of the towel over the top of the tin. Pour enough boiling water into the cooker to come halfway up the sides of the tin. Lock the lid in place and bring to low pressure over medium heat. Cook for 15 minutes, adjusting the heat as necessary to maintain a low pressure.

Release the pressure using the quick-release method.

Lift the tin out of the cooker using the tea towel and remove the baking paper. If the custard is still a little wobbly, return the tin to the cooker, cover the pot but do not lock the lid in place, and cook for 3–5 minutes.

Set the crème caramel aside to cool to room temperature. Then cover the tin with cling wrap and refrigerate for at least 4 hours (or overnight), until chilled. To serve, carefully loosen the crème caramel from the tin by running a small knife around the edge, then invert it onto a serving plate.

CHOCOLATE & HAZELNUT PUDDING

SERVES 8

180 g (6½ oz) softened unsalted butter
1 cup (220 g/8 oz) caster sugar
3 large eggs
1 cup (150 g/5 oz) self-raising flour
3 tablespoons cocoa
½ teaspoon bicarbonate of soda
¼ cup (40 g/1½ oz) ground hazelnuts
3 tablespoons (60 ml/2 fl oz) milk

2 tablespoons (40 ml/1½ fl oz) Frangelico
cream or ice-cream, to serve
coarsely chopped roasted hazelnuts,
   for garnish
CHOCOLATE AND HAZELNUT SAUCE
250 g (9 oz) dark chocolate, coarsely chopped
1 cup (250 ml/8½ fl oz) cream
2 tablespoons (40 ml/1½ fl oz) Frangelico

Lightly grease a 5-cup (1.25-L/2 pt 10-fl oz) heatproof pudding basin.

In a medium-sized bowl, cream the butter and sugar until pale and creamy. Beat in the eggs one at a time. Sift in the flour, cocoa and bicarbonate of soda. Mix in the hazelnuts, milk and liqueur to make a smooth batter. Spoon the batter into the prepared pudding basin. Cover the basin with a piece of baking paper large enough to fold over the edges, and tie with kitchen string to secure.

Place the trivet in the base of the pressure cooker. Fold a tea towel into thirds lengthways to make a thick strip. Place the pudding basin in the centre of the strip and, using the ends of the towel as handles, lower the basin into the pressure cooker. Fold the ends of the towel over the top of the basin. Pour enough boiling water into the cooker to come halfway up the sides of the pudding basin. Lock the lid in place and bring to low pressure over high heat. Cook for 30 minutes, adjusting the heat as necessary to maintain a low pressure.

Meanwhile, to make the chocolate and hazelnut sauce, heat all the ingredients in a heatproof bowl set over a saucepan of barely simmering water. Stir to make a smooth sauce.

Release the cooker's pressure using the natural-release method.

Lift the basin out of the cooker using the tea towel. Remove the baking paper and test the pudding with a skewer; if the skewer comes out clean it is cooked. If the mixture is still sticky, return the basin to the cooker, lock the lid in place and cook on low pressure for a further 3–5 minutes.

Serve with the chocolate sauce and cream or ice-cream. Sprinkle with chopped hazelnuts.

PRESERVES & SAUCES

Jams, marmalades, fruit pastes, sauces and chutneys are all excellent ways to make use of plentiful seasonal produce. If you have a neighbour with a fruit-laden tree, why not ask if they have surplus fruit? If that's not possible, visit your local farmer's market or fresh produce market.

Ensure you buy quality fruit, and lean towards slightly underripe rather than overripe fruit – this is important to ensure the fruit has a sufficiently high level of pectin, which is needed for jams and marmalades to set. Refer to the hints and tips on page 274 for more advice on making jams and marmalades.

Using the pressure cooker makes it quick and easy to prepare traditional preserves and sauces, akin to those Grandma used to make. Although they can't be made entirely in the pressure cooker, the first stage – involving the cooking and softening of the fruit – can be performed effectively and in a fraction of the time.

The strawberry jam on page 279 is perfect with scones and cream for a Devonshire tea. Thick, spiced chutneys like the green tomato chutney (page 287) and beetroot and apple chutney (page 288) are delicious served with cheese or can transform a simple sandwich into one that's gourmet. Barbecue sauce (page 283) and red onion marmalade (page 282) complement grilled meats wonderfully, while mango chutney (page 289) pairs beautifully with chicken and fish.

With a little extra love, such as a decorative label or lid cover for the jar, preserves and sauces can also make excellent gifts.

TIPS FOR MAKING PRESERVES & SAUCES

Selecting Fruit

When making jams or marmalades, choose fruit that is in good condition, with no blemishes or bruises. It is best to use fruit that has been freshly picked and is just ripe or slightly underripe, as the pectin levels will be higher. Pectin is contained in the skin, pips and membranes of fruit and is needed for the jam or marmalade to reach setting point. Higher pectin levels decrease the boiling time required to reach setting point, saving you time and resulting in a better-quality product.

When making chutneys or sauces, the fruit can be ripe, but it is still important that it be in good condition. The higher the quality of the ingredients used, the better the result.

Setting Point

After your jam or marmalade has been boiling for 10–20 minutes, it will begin to thicken. At setting point, the mixture will fall off the spoon in a thin sheet rather than in drops. To double check that setting point has been reached, spoon a small amount of the jam or marmalade onto a chilled plate (you can chill it by putting it in the freezer for 15 minutes) and refrigerating it for 10 minutes. Press your finger into the jam or marmalade after this time – if it wrinkles, setting point has been reached. If not, return the pan to the heat and simmer gently for a further 2–5 minutes, then test again on another chilled plate.

The time it takes to reach setting point varies depending on the amount of pectin in the fruit. Powdered pectin is readily available from supermarkets and can be added to jams made with fruits low in pectin to aid setting. However, adding a muslin bag with some citrus pips or pith, or some citrus juice, to the jam can be just as effective and produces a better outcome.

Glass Jars & Bottles

Old jam jars and sauce bottles can be used for homemade preserves time and time again. Ask your family and friends to save jars for you so you have plenty when you need them. A jar filled with the fruits of your labour is always a welcome thank-you gift. Check to make sure lids are in good condition and that the seal is airtight. Alternatively, you can find jam-making jars at kitchen supply stores; however, if you need to buy a lot they can prove expensive.

Sterilising

All jars and bottles must be sterilised immediately before the preserve is added. Here are instructions for sterilising.

Preheat the oven to 120°C (250°F).

Wash the glass jars or bottles and their lids thoroughly in hot soapy water or in the dishwasher. Rinse well under hot water.

Put the jars or bottles and their lids on a tray and place in the oven for 15 minutes, or until completely dry. If the lids are not oven-safe, simmer them in boiling water for 2 minutes, then drain and dry using a clean tea towel.

Remove the jars or bottles from the oven and, while they are still warm, fill with your hot jam, marmalade, sauce or chutney. You can use a metal jam funnel to fill your jars or bottles – it decreases the risk of burning yourself and saves you cleaning up a sticky mess. (Remember that you will also need to sterilise the funnel before use.) Seal the jars or bottles and leave to cool.

LEMON MARMALADE

MAKES 12 CUPS (3 L /6 PT 6 FL OZ)

750 g (1 lb 10 oz) lemons, washed and scrubbed
8 cups (1.8 kg/4 lb) caster sugar

Day one: Cut the lemons in half lengthways. Remove and reserve the centre pith. Cut the lemons into 5-mm (¼-in) thick slices, reserving the pips.

Wrap the reserved pith and pips in a piece of clean muslin and tie to make a bag. Place in a medium-sized bowl, cover with 2 cups (500 ml/17 fl oz) water and set aside to soak overnight.

Place the sliced lemons in a pressure cooker and cover with 1 l (34 fl oz) water. Leave to soak overnight.

Day two: Strain the water containing the muslin bag into a bowl, squeezing out all the liquid from the bag. Add the liquid to the sliced lemon in the pressure cooker, lock the lid in place and bring to low pressure over medium heat. Cook for 8 minutes, adjusting the heat as necessary to maintain a low pressure.

Release the pressure using the natural-release method.

Add the sugar to the lemon mixture, stirring until it has dissolved. Boil rapidly over medium–high heat, uncovered, stirring occasionally, for 20–30 minutes, until the marmalade reaches setting point (see page 274).

Stir the marmalade to distribute the peel evenly, then pour into sterilised glass jars. Seal.

Store in a cool dark place for up to 6 months. Refrigerate after opening.

DRIED FIG & GINGER JAM

MAKES 8 CUPS (2 L/4 PT 4 FL OZ)

500 g (1 lb 2 oz) dried figs, stems trimmed
zest and juice of 2 lemons

4 cups (880 g/1 lb 15 oz) caster sugar
100 g (3½ oz) crystallised ginger, sliced

Day one: Place the figs in a medium-sized bowl and cover with boiling water. Stir well to wash. Drain and rinse. Finely slice the figs.

Combine the figs with the lemon zest and juice in a pressure cooker. Pour in 3 cups (750 ml/25 fl oz) water and set aside overnight to soften.

Day two: Lock the pressure cooker's lid in place and bring to low pressure over medium heat. Cook for 10 minutes, adjusting the heat as necessary to maintain a low pressure.

Release the pressure using the natural-release method.

Add the sugar and ginger to the figs, stirring until the sugar has dissolved. Boil rapidly over medium–high heat, uncovered, stirring occasionally, for 15–25 minutes, until the jam reaches setting point (see page 274). Skim any scum from the surface and discard.

Stir the jam to distribute the fruit evenly, then pour it into sterilised glass jars. Seal.

Store in a cool dark place for up to 6 months. Refrigerate after opening and use within 3 months.

DRIED APRICOT JAM

MAKES 8 CUPS (2 L/4 PT 4 FL OZ)

500 g (1 lb 2 oz) dried apricots
1 teaspoon bicarbonate of soda
½ cinnamon stick, broken into pieces
2 cardamom pods, bruised

2 cloves
zest and juice of 1 orange
4 cups (880 g/1 lb 15 oz) caster sugar

Day one: Place the apricots in a medium-sized bowl and cover with boiling water. Sprinkle with the bicarbonate of soda and stir well to wash. Drain and rinse.

Wrap the spices in a piece of clean muslin and tie to make a bag.

Place the spice bag, apricots, orange zest and juice in a pressure cooker. Pour in 3 cups (750 ml/25 fl oz) water and set aside overnight to soften.

Day two: Lock the pressure cooker's lid in place and bring to low pressure over medium heat. Cook for 10 minutes, adjusting the heat as necessary to maintain a low pressure.

Release the pressure using the natural-release method.

Add the sugar to the apricot mixture, stirring until it has dissolved. Boil rapidly over medium–high heat, uncovered, stirring frequently, for 5–10 minutes, until the jam reaches setting point (see page 274).

Remove the spice bag. Stir the jam to distribute the fruit evenly, then pour into sterilised glass jars. Seal.

Store in a cool dark place for up to 6 months. Refrigerate after opening and use within 3 months.

STRAWBERRY JAM

MAKES 8 CUPS (2 L/4 PT 4 FL OZ)

1 kg (2 lb 3 oz) strawberries, washed and hulled
juice of 2 lemons
4 cups (880 g/1 lb 15 oz) caster sugar

Combine the strawberries and lemon juice in a pressure cooker. Set aside for 1 hour to soften.

Lock the lid in place and bring to low pressure over medium heat. Cook for 5 minutes, adjusting the heat as necessary to maintain a low pressure.

Release the heat using the natural-release method.

Add the sugar to the strawberries, stirring until dissolved. Boil rapidly over medium–high heat, uncovered, stirring occasionally, for 10–20 minutes, until the jam reaches setting point (see page 274). Skim any scum from the surface and discard.

Stir the jam to distribute the fruit evenly, then pour into sterilised glass jars. Seal.

Store in a cool dark place for up to 6 months. Refrigerate after opening and use within 3 months.

LEMON CURD

MAKES 3 CUPS (750 ML/25 FL OZ)

4 large eggs, lightly beaten
finely grated zest and juice of 4 lemons

1½ cups (330 g/11½ oz) caster sugar
200 g (7 oz) unsalted butter, diced

In a 6-cup (1.5-L/3 pt 3-fl oz) capacity pudding basin, whisk together the eggs, lemon juice and zest, and sugar. Add the butter and stir to combine (the butter will still be in chunks). Cover the basin with a piece of baking paper large enough to fold over the edges, and tie with kitchen string to secure.

Place the trivet in the base of the pressure cooker. Fold a tea towel into thirds lengthways to make a thick strip. Place the pudding basin in the centre of the strip and, using the ends of the towel as handles, lower the basin into the pressure cooker. Fold the ends of the towel over the top of the basin. Pour enough boiling water into the cooker to come halfway up the sides of the pudding basin. Lock the lid in place and bring to low pressure over medium heat. Cook for 10 minutes, adjusting the heat as necessary to maintain a low pressure.

Release the pressure using the natural-release method.

Lift the basin out of the cooker using the tea towel and remove the baking paper. Whisk the lemon curd with a fork to combine, then strain through a fine mesh sieve into sterilised glass jars. Seal.

Store in the refrigerator for up to 2 weeks.

Use lemon curd as a spread on toast or fresh bread, as a filling for tarts, or to make steamed lemon curd pudding (page 255).

QUINCE PASTE

MAKES 8–12 PORTIONS (EACH SERVES 4)

1.8 kg (4 lb) quinces
about 4 cups (880 g/1 lb 15 oz) caster sugar
juice of 1 lemon

Line a 30-cm × 20-cm (12-in × 8-in) slice tin with baking paper.

Peel the quinces and cut them into quarters. Remove and discard the cores using a small sharp knife. Coarsely chop the flesh and place in a pressure cooker. Add 1 cup (250 ml/8½ fl oz) water, then lock the lid in place and bring to high pressure over high heat. Cook for 15 minutes, adjusting the heat as necessary to maintain a high pressure.

Release the pressure using the natural-release method.

Strain the quinces, discarding the liquid. Mash the fruit, then pass through a fine mesh sieve to make a smooth purée. Measure how many cups of purée you have, then measure out an equal quantity of sugar (i.e. 1 cup of sugar for every cup of pulp).

Return the quince purée to the pressure cooker. Add the sugar and lemon juice, and stir over low heat until the sugar dissolves. Continue to cook, uncovered, stirring frequently, for 15–25 minutes, until dark and very thick.

Spread the quince paste onto the prepared tray and set aside to cool slightly. Cover the paste with another piece of baking paper and smooth the top to create a flat, even surface. Refrigerate overnight to set.

Cut the paste into portions and wrap each in baking paper. Store in an airtight container in the refrigerator for up to 6 months.

Serve quince paste as part of a cheese platter. Alternatively, cut the paste into smaller portions, roll each in caster sugar, and serve as a sweet with coffee.

RED ONION MARMALADE

MAKES 4 CUPS (1 L/34 FL OZ)

1 tablespoon (20 g/¾ oz) butter
1 tablespoon (20 ml/¾ fl oz) olive oil
8 large red onions, halved and thinly sliced
2½ cups (550 g/1 lb 3 oz) firmly packed soft brown sugar

1 cup (250 ml/8½ fl oz) red-wine vinegar
1 teaspoon finely grated orange zest
3 sprigs thyme
2 bay leaves

Heat the butter and oil in a pressure cooker over low–medium heat. Cook the onion until clear and softened. Add the remaining ingredients and stir until the sugar has dissolved. Lock the lid in place and bring to high pressure over high heat. Cook for 5 minutes, adjusting the heat as necessary to maintain a high pressure. Reduce the heat to maintain a low pressure and cook for a further 10 minutes.

Release the pressure using the natural-release method.

Simmer, uncovered, over medium heat for 10–15 minutes, or until the marmalade is thick and syrupy.

Spoon the marmalade into sterilised glass jars. Seal.

Store in the refrigerator for up to 1 month.

BARBECUE SAUCE

MAKES 4 CUPS (1 L/34 FL OZ)

2 tablespoons (40 ml/1½ fl oz) olive oil

1 medium-sized onion, finely chopped

2 cloves garlic, crushed

2 × 400-g (14-oz) cans chopped tomatoes

⅓ cup (80 ml/3 fl oz) malt vinegar

⅓ cup (75 g/2½ oz) firmly packed soft brown sugar

2 tablespoons (40 ml/1½ fl oz) Worcestershire sauce

1 tablespoon (20 ml/¾ fl oz) freshly squeezed lemon juice

1 tablespoon Dijon mustard

1 chipotle chilli in adobo sauce, finely chopped

1 teaspoon ground cumin

salt

Heat the oil in a pressure cooker over low–medium heat. Sauté the onion and garlic until golden brown. Add the remaining ingredients (except the salt) and simmer, stirring occasionally, until the sugar dissolves. Lock the lid in place and bring to high pressure over high heat. Cook for 10 minutes, adjusting the heat as necessary to maintain a high pressure.

Release the pressure using the natural-release method.

Simmer, uncovered, over medium heat for 10–20 minutes, until the sauce is thick. Season with salt.

Pour the sauce into sterilised glass jars or bottles. Seal.

Store in a cool dark place for up to 6 months. Refrigerate after opening and use within 1 month.

PLUM SAUCE

MAKES 5 CUPS (1.25 L/2 PT 10 FL OZ)

1.5 kg (3 lb 5 oz) plums, halved and stoned (reserve the stones)
1 cinnamon stick, broken into pieces
2 star anise
4 cloves
2 cups (500 ml/17 fl oz) cider vinegar
2 medium-sized red onions, finely chopped
1 large red chilli, deseeded and finely chopped
2 cloves garlic, crushed
3-cm (1¼-in) piece ginger, finely grated
1 teaspoon salt
3 cups (660 g/1 lb 7 oz) firmly packed soft brown sugar

Crack the plum stones using a meat mallet or hammer. Wrap the cracked stones and spices in a piece of clean muslin and tie to make a bag.

Place the muslin bag and all other ingredients (except the sugar), in a pressure cooker. Lock the lid in place and bring to high pressure over high heat. Cook for 10 minutes, adjusting the heat as necessary to maintain a high pressure.

Release the pressure using the natural-release method.

Add the sugar to the plum mixture and stir until it has dissolved. Remove the muslin bag, squeezing any liquid back into the pot. Pass the mixture through a fine mesh sieve, discarding the solids.

Return the plum purée to the cooker and simmer over medium heat, uncovered, for 10–20 minutes, until the sauce is thick. Skim any scum from the surface and discard.

Pour the sauce into sterilised glass jars or bottles. Seal.

Store in a cool dark place for up to 6 months. Refrigerate after opening and use within 1 month.

MINCEMEAT

MAKES 6 CUPS (1.5 L/3 PT 3 FL OZ)

500 g (1 lb 2 oz) tart green apples (such as
Granny Smith), peeled, cored and finely diced
1 cup (220 g/8 oz) firmly packed soft
brown sugar
160 g (5½ oz) sultanas
160 g (5½ oz) currants
140 g (5 oz) dried cranberries
150 g (5 oz) beef or vegetarian suet,
coarsely grated
90 g (3 oz) mixed peel, finely chopped

½ cup (125 ml/4 fl oz) apple juice
zest and juice of 2 lemons
zest and juice of 1 orange
1 tablespoon finely grated ginger
2 teaspoons mixed spice
1 teaspoon ground cinnamon
1 teaspoon ground nutmeg
¼ teaspoon ground cloves
⅔ cup (160 ml/5½ fl oz) brandy
60 g (2 oz) slivered almonds, chopped

Combine all the ingredients (except the brandy and almonds) in a pressure cooker. Lock the lid in place and bring to low pressure over medium heat. Cook for 10 minutes, adjusting the heat as necessary to maintain a low pressure.

Release the pressure using the natural-release method.

Add the brandy and almonds to the fruit mixture and simmer, uncovered, over medium heat for 5–10 minutes, until all the liquid is absorbed.

Spoon the mincemeat into sterilised glass jars. Seal.

Store in a cool dark place for up to 4 months. Refrigerate after opening and use within 1 month.

Use mincemeat to make Christmas mince pies, or serve as a condiment with aged tasty cheese.

TOMATO PASTA SAUCE

MAKES 5 CUPS (1.25 L/2 PT 10 FL OZ)

1.5 kg (3 lb 5 oz) vine-ripened tomatoes
2 tablespoons (40 ml/1½ fl oz) olive oil
1 small onion, finely chopped
2 cloves garlic, finely chopped
2 tablespoons finely chopped oregano

4 sprigs thyme
2 bay leaves
2 tablespoons (40 ml/1½ fl oz) balsamic vinegar
1 teaspoon caster sugar
salt and freshly ground black pepper

Score a cross in the base of each tomato, then blanch them in boiling water for 20 seconds. Drain, and refresh in cold water. Peel the tomatoes, then cut each in half horizontally and remove the seeds. Dice the flesh and set aside.

Heat the oil in a pressure cooker over low–medium heat. Cook the onion and garlic until the onion is clear and softened. Add the tomato and herbs, and stir to combine. Lock the lid in place and bring to high pressure over high heat. Cook for 10 minutes, adjusting the heat as necessary to maintain a high pressure.

Release the pressure using the natural-release method.

Add the vinegar and sugar to the sauce, and simmer, uncovered, over medium heat for 10–20 minutes, until thick.

Remove the bay leaves and thyme stems, and season with salt and pepper. Pour the sauce into sterilised glass jars or bottles. Seal.

Store in a cool dark place for up to 4 months. Refrigerate after opening and use within 1 month.

GREEN TOMATO CHUTNEY

MAKES 6 CUPS (1.5 L/3 PT 3 FL OZ)

1.5 kg (3 lb 5 oz) green tomatoes, diced
2 medium-sized white onions, finely diced
2 large tart green apples (such as Granny Smith), peeled, cored and finely diced
1 cup (220 g/8 oz) caster sugar
¾ cup (180 ml/6 fl oz) cider vinegar
80 g (3 oz) sultanas
2 tablespoons finely grated ginger
1 teaspoon salt
2 bay leaves

Combine all the ingredients in a pressure cooker. Lock the lid in place and bring to high pressure over high heat. Cook for 10 minutes, adjusting the heat as necessary to maintain a high pressure.

Release the pressure using the natural-release method.

Simmer, uncovered, over medium heat for 10–15 minutes, until the chutney is thick.

Spoon the chutney into sterilised glass jars. Seal.

Store in a cool dark place for up to 6 months. Refrigerate after opening and use within 1 month.

BEETROOT & APPLE CHUTNEY

MAKES 4 CUPS (1 L/34 FL OZ)

1 cinnamon stick, broken into pieces
1 star anise
1 teaspoon black peppercorns
1 teaspoon cloves
2 large beetroots
2 medium-sized red onions, halved and thinly sliced

2 tart green apples (such as Granny Smith), peeled and coarsely grated
1 cup (220 g/8 oz) firmly packed soft brown sugar
1 cup (250 ml/8½ fl oz) white-wine vinegar
zest and juice of 1 orange

Wrap the spices in a clean piece of muslin and tie to make a bag.

Wearing food-handling gloves (to prevent staining), peel and coarsely grate the beetroots.

Place the beetroot, spice bag and remaining ingredients in a pressure cooker and stir to combine. Lock the lid in place and bring to high pressure over high heat. Cook for 10 minutes, adjusting the heat as necessary to maintain a high pressure.

Release the pressure using the natural-release method.

Simmer the chutney, uncovered, over medium heat for 10–15 minutes, or until thick. Remove the spice bag.

Spoon the chutney into sterilised glass jars. Seal.

Store in the refrigerator for up to 1 month.

MANGO & RED CAPSICUM CHUTNEY

MAKES 3 CUPS (750 ML/25 FL OZ)

4 medium-sized firm green mangoes, flesh finely chopped
¾ cup (180 ml/6 fl oz) white vinegar
½ cup (110 g/4 oz) firmly packed soft brown sugar
1 red capsicum, diced

2 tablespoons coarsely grated ginger
1 large red chilli, deseeded and finely sliced
1 teaspoon ground cumin
½ teaspoon ground coriander
½ teaspoon ground turmeric

Combine all the ingredients in a pressure cooker. Lock the lid in place and bring to high pressure over high heat. Cook for 5 minutes, adjusting the heat as necessary to maintain a high pressure.

Release the pressure using the natural-release method.

Simmer the chutney, uncovered, over medium heat for 10–15 minutes, until thick.

Spoon the chutney into sterilised glass jars. Seal.

Store in a cool dark place for up to 6 months. Refrigerate after opening and use within 1 month.

GLOSSARY

ANCHO CHILLIES Dried, heart-shaped chillies often used in Mexican cooking. They have a mild heat and sweet, rich flavour and are used in sauces, marinades and salsas. They can be sourced from South American grocers or gourmet food stockists.

ANDOUILLE SAUSAGE A spicy, smoked pork sausage used in Cajun cooking. It can be sourced from select delicatessens. Substitute chorizo if unavailable.

BARBERRIES Small, dried sour berries used in Middle Eastern cooking. They can be sourced from Middle Eastern stores or select delicatessens. Substitute dried cranberries or currants if unavailable.

BLACK GLUTINOUS RICE A dense, sticky black rice grain commonly used in South-East Asian cooking. It can be sourced from Asian grocers.

CANDLENUTS Round, hard, cream-coloured nuts most commonly used in Malaysian cooking. They may be roasted and ground, then used as a thickener in curries and sauces. They are readily available from Asian grocers, or from select supermarkets. Substitute macadamias or Brazil nuts if unavailable.

CAPERBERRIES Oblong, grape-sized berries from the caper plant. They are milder in flavour than caper buds and can be found, preserved in brine, at supermarkets and delicatessens.

CHINESE SAUSAGE A hard dried sausage made predominantly of pork. It is readily available, vacuum packed, at Asian food stores and some supermarkets.

CHIPOTLE CHILLIES Jalapeno chillies that have been dried and smoked. Used in Mexican cooking, they are quite hot and have a strong, smoky flavour. They can be found in their dried form or, more readily, canned in a sweet, spiced adobo sauce. Available from South American grocers or gourmet food stockists. They have a unique flavour, but if you can't find them you can use red bird's eye chillies instead.

DASHI STOCK A Japanese stock made from kombu (seaweed), fish, or shiitake mushrooms. It can be found in its dry form in small packets at health food stores, Asian grocers and select supermarkets. To reconstitute, just add boiling water as per the packet instructions.

FARRO A type of wheat used particularly in Italian cooking. It is very similar to spelt, another whole grain. It can be sourced from speciality grocers or health food stores. Substitute spelt or pearl barley if unavailable.

IKAN BILIS Dried salted anchovies used in South-East Asian cooking as a salty flavouring for soups and rice dishes. They can be readily sourced from Asian grocers, and from some supermarkets.

JERUSALEM ARTICHOKE A white-fleshed tuber resembling a ginger root. Sometimes known as sunchokes, they are a member of the sunflower family. With a sweet, nutty flavour like that of the water chestnut, they can be prepared in a similar way to potatoes or eaten raw in salads. They can be found at seasonal markets between autumn and winter.

KABANA A thin, smoked Polish sausage flavoured with garlic and spices. It is readily available at delicatessens and supermarkets.

KALE A member of the cabbage family. It comes in many varieties, including curly and flat-leaf, and cavolo nero. It is used in salads, soups and stews. It can be found at seasonal markets in the winter months.

MOGHRABIEH Also known as pearl couscous, this 'jumbo' couscous (with balls similar in size to tapioca) is made from rolled semolina. It has a chewy, starchy consistency and is used in Middle Eastern cooking. It can be sourced from Middle Eastern grocers and select health food stores and supermarkets.

PICKLED GINGER Thinly sliced young ginger marinated in a vinegar and sugar solution. It is yellow or light pink in colour and is commonly used in Japanese cuisine as a palate cleanser. It is readily available from supermarkets and Asian grocers.

POMEGRANATE JUICE The juice of the pomegranate fruit. It can be sourced from health food stores and some supermarkets.

POMEGRANATE MOLASSES A thick, tart syrup made from the juice of pomegranates. It is used in Iranian cooking and can be sourced from Middle Eastern grocers and select supermarkets.

PRESERVED LEMONS Lemons pickled in a brine made of water, lemon juice and salt. They are used in North African and Middle Eastern cooking to flavour stews, sauces and salads. They can be sourced from Middle Eastern grocers and select delicatessens and supermarkets.

QUINOA A South American seed with a mild, slightly nutty flavour. It is gluten free and highly nutritious, being high in protein and containing essential amino acids. Quinoa comes in three colours: red, black and, most commonly, yellow. It is readily available at health food stores and select supermarkets.

RED BEAN PASTE A sweet, thick dark-red paste made from the adzuki bean. It is used in Chinese, Japanese and Korean cooking, most often for making sweets. It can be sourced from Asian supermarkets.

SAMBAL ULEK A chilli sauce made from red chillies, white rice vinegar, salt and sugar. It is used as a condiment in Indonesian cooking. It is readily available from supermarkets and Asian grocers.

SAUERKRAUT Sour fermented cabbage used in Asian and Eastern European cooking. It can be found in cans or jars at most supermarkets and some delicatessens.

SHAOXING RICE WINE Named after the region in which it originated, this is a good-quality Chinese fermented rice wine. Dry sherry can be substituted if necessary.

SHIITAKE MUSHROOMS Small, dark-coloured, full-flavoured Asian mushrooms. Readily available dried from supermarkets, Asian grocers and health food stores, they require soaking in hot water to rehydrate before use. When in season, substitute double the quantity of fresh shiitakes for dried.

TAMARIND PULP A dark, sticky pulp made from the pods of the tamarind tree. It has a tangy, slightly sweet flavour and is used in South-East Asian cooking to flavour sauces, curries and chutneys. It can be sourced from Asian grocers and some supermarkets. Substitute lemon or lime juice mixed with a little brown sugar if unavailable.

VINE LEAVES Dark-green leaves from the grapevine. In Eastern European and Middle Eastern cooking they are often stuffed with meat or rice fillings. They can be used fresh, or purchased, preserved in brine, from delicatessens and some supermarkets.

WAKAME A type of seaweed used in Japanese and Korean cooking to flavour soups and salads. It is sold dried, in sheets or strips, at Asian grocers, some supermarkets and health food stores. It can be added to soups as is, or rehydrated as per the packet instructions and stirred through salads.

WHITE FRENCH MILLET A small, round, gluten-free grain. It is mild in flavour and takes well to spices and herbs. It can be toasted, ground or cooked whole and is often added to stews or used for making porridge. It can be sourced from health food stores and select supermarkets.

WHOLE BUCKWHEAT A three-sided seed from a member of the rhubarb family. It is also known as buckwheat groats or, when roasted, kasha. Buckwheat has a mild, nutty flavour and is often ground into a flour and used to make cakes, breads and noodles. It can also be cooked whole, as in Eastern European cuisine, to make a porridge. It can be found at health food stores.

WILD RICE A long black grass grain (not actually a rice at all) native to North America. It is slightly chewy and nutty in flavour. It can be quite expensive, as it is harvested by hand. However, it combines well with brown rice (both have a long cooking time), which can be used to bulk up small quantities of wild rice. It can be sourced from gourmet delicatessens, select supermarkets and health food stores.

CONVERSIONS

IMPORTANT NOTE: All cup and spoon measures given in this book are based on Australian standards. The most important thing to remember is that an Australian cup = 250 ml, while an American cup = 237 ml and a British cup = 284 ml. Also, an Australian tablespoon is equivalent to 4 teaspoons, not 3 teaspoons as in the United States and Britain. US equivalents have been provided throughout for all liquid cup/spoon measures. Equivalents for dry ingredients measured in cups/spoons have been included for flour, sugar and rising agents such as baking powder. For other dry ingredients (chopped vegetables, nuts, etc.), American cooks should be generous with their cup measures – slight variations in quantities of such ingredients are unlikely to affect results.

VOLUME

Australian cups/spoons	Millilitres	US fluid ounces
*1 teaspoon	5 ml	
1 tablespoon (4 teaspoons)	20 ml	¾ fl oz
1½ tablespoons	30 ml	1 fl oz
2 tablespoons	40 ml	1½ fl oz
¼ cup	60 ml	2 fl oz
⅓ cup	80 ml	3 fl oz
½ cup	125 ml	4 fl oz
¾ cup	180 ml	6 fl oz
1 cup	250 ml	8½ fl oz
4 cups	1 L	34 fl oz

*the volume of a teaspoon is the same around the world.

WEIGHT

Grams	Ounces
15 g	½ oz
30 g	1 oz
60 g	2 oz
85 g	3 oz
110 g	4 oz
140 g	5 oz
170 g	6 oz
200 g	7 oz
225 g	8 oz (½ lb)
450 g	16 oz (1 lb)
500 g	1 lb 2 oz
900 g	2 lb
1 kg	2 lb 3 oz

TEMPERATURE

Celcius	Fahrenheit
150°C	300°F
160°C	320°F
170°C	340°F
180°C	355°F
190°C	375°F
200°C	390°F
210°C	410°F
220°C	430°F

SIZE

Centimetres	Inches
1 cm	⅜ in
2 cm	¾ in
2.5 cm	1 in
5 cm	2 in
10 cm	4 in
15 cm	6 in
20 cm	8 in
30 cm	12 in

INDEX

PENGUIN BOOKS

Published by the Penguin Group
Penguin Group (Australia)
250 Camberwell Road, Camberwell, Victoria 3124, Australia
(a division of Pearson Australia Group Pty Ltd)
Penguin Group (USA) Inc.
375 Hudson Street, New York, New York 10014, USA
Penguin Group (Canada)
90 Eglinton Avenue East, Suite 700, Toronto, Canada ON M4P 2Y3
(a division of Pearson Penguin Canada Inc.)
Penguin Books Ltd
80 Strand, London WC2R 0RL England
Penguin Ireland
25 St Stephen's Green, Dublin 2, Ireland
(a division of Penguin Books Ltd)
Penguin Books India Pvt Ltd
11 Community Centre, Panchsheel Park, New Delhi – 110 017, India
Penguin Group (NZ)
67 Apollo Drive, Rosedale, Auckland 0632, New Zealand
(a division of Pearson New Zealand Ltd)
Penguin Books (South Africa) (Pty) Ltd
24 Sturdee Avenue, Rosebank, Johannesburg 2196, South Africa

Penguin Books Ltd, Registered Offices: 80 Strand, London, WC2R 0RL, England

First published by Penguin Group (Australia), 2011

10 9 8 7 6 5 4 3 2 1

Text, design and photographs copyright © Penguin Group (Australia), 2011
Illustrations copyright © Tamsin Ainslie

The moral right of the author has been asserted

Cover and text design by Claire Tice © Penguin Group (Australia)
Photographs by Paul Nelson
Illustrations by Tamsin Ainslie
Food styling by Lee Blaylock
Typeset in Gotham Narrow by Post Pre-Press Group, Brisbane, Queensland
Scanning and separations by Splitting Image P/L, Clayton, Victoria
Printed and bound in China by 1010 Printing International Limited

National Library of Australia
Cataloguing-in-Publication data:

Lane, Rachael.
Pressure cooker / Rachael Lane.
ISBN: 978 0 14 320624 8 (pbk.)
Includes index.
1. Pressure cooking.

641.587

penguin.com.au